Family and Contexts of Development

CHILD DEVELOPMENT IN CULTURAL CONTEXT

Series Editors
Cynthia Garcia Coll
Peggy Miller

Advisory Board
Jerome Kagan
Carol Worthman
Barrie Thorne

BOOKS IN THE SERIES:

Perfectly Prep: Gender Extremes at a New England Prep School
Sarah A. Chase

Academic Motivation and the Culture of Schooling
Cynthia Hudley and Adele E. Gottfried

Immigrant Stories: Ethnicity and Academics in Middle Childhood
Cynthia Garcia Coll and Amy Kerivan Marks

In a Younger Voice: Doing Child-Centered Qualitative Research
Cindy Dell Clark

Developing Destinies: A Mayan Midwife and Town
Barbara Rogoff

Bridging Multiple Worlds: Cultures, Identities, and Pathways to College
Catherine R. Cooper

Literacy and Mothering: How Women's Schooling Changes the Lives of the World's Children
Robert A. LeVine, Sarah E. LeVine, Beatrice Schnell-Anzola, Meredith L. Rowe, and Emily Dexter

The Culture of Child Care: Attachment, Peers, and Quality in Diverse Communities
Edited by Kay E. Sanders and Alison Wishard Guerra

Self-Esteem in Time and Place: How American Families Imagine, Enact, and Personalize a Cultural Ideal
Peggy J. Miller and Grace E. Cho

Disability, Stigma, and Children's Developing Selves: Insights from Educators in Japan, South Korea, Taiwan, and the U.S.
Wendy Haight, Misa Kayama, Mary May-Lee Ku, Minhae Cho, and Hee Yun Lee

Roma Minority Youth across Cultural Contexts: Taking a Positive Approach to Research, Policy, and Practice
Edited by Radosveta Dimitrova, David L. Sam, and Laura Ferrer Wreder

Learning without Lessons: Pedagogy in Indigenous Communities
David F. Lancy

FORTHCOMING BOOKS IN THE SERIES

Family and Contexts of Development: Challenges in Latin America
Edited by Mariano Rosabal-Coto and Javier Tapia-Balladares

Acquiring Culture: An Integrated Paradigm for Children's Development
Suzanne Gaskins

Growing up Latino/a/x in the Land of Lib: Drawing on Community and Culture to Face Contextual Challenges
Edited by Rosario Ceballo and Deborah Rivas-Drake

Family and Contexts of Development

Challenges in Latin America

Edited by
MARIANO ROSABAL-COTO
AND
JAVIER TAPIA-BALLADARES

OXFORD
UNIVERSITY PRESS

Oxford University Press is a department of the University of Oxford.
It furthers the University's objective of excellence in research, scholarship,
and education by publishing worldwide. Oxford is a registered trade mark of
Oxford University Press in the UK and in certain other countries.

Published in the United States of America by Oxford University Press
198 Madison Avenue, New York, NY 10016, United States of America.

© Oxford University Press 2025

All rights reserved. No part of this publication may be reproduced, stored in a retrieval system, transmitted, used for text and data mining, or used for training artificial intelligence, in any form or by any means, without the prior permission in writing of Oxford University Press, or as expressly permitted by law, by license or under terms agreed with the appropriate reprographics rights organization. Inquiries concerning reproduction outside the scope of the above should be sent to the Rights Department, Oxford University Press, at the address above.

You must not circulate this work in any other form
and you must impose this same condition on any acquirer.

CIP data is on file at the Library of Congress

ISBN 9780197675144

DOI: 10.1093/oso/9780197675144.001.0001

Printed by Marquis Book Printing, Canada

The manufacturer's authorized representative in the EU for product safety is
Oxford University Press España S.A., Parque Empresarial San Fernando de Henares,
Avenida de Castilla, 2 – 28830 Madrid (www.oup.es/en).

Acknowledgments

The editors would like to thank the following people and entities for their support throughout the various phases and who facilitated the successful completion of this project:

Judith Gibbons for giving us the initial impetus.

Heidi Keller for her inspiration and dialogue.

Jorge Sanabria-León for his constant and unconditional support and dialogue.

Cynthia García-Coll, Peggy Miller, and Abby Gross for their trust in undertaking this issue with Child Development in Cultural Context Series of Oxford University Press.

Harley Singer and Emily Mackenzie Benítez for their invaluable guidance and editorial support.

Raja Dharmaraj for Project Management.

ALAPSIDE (Latin American Network of Developmental Psychology), Escuela de Psicología and Instituto de Investigaciones Psicológicas from the Universidad de Costa Rica.

Oxford University Press for believing in this project.

Finally, to the fellow co-authors of this book, thank you for believing and remaining steadfast until the end.

San José, 2025

Foreword
Heidi Keller

Family matters. Families are important for providing individuals with a sense of belonging and feelings of security. And families are the primary institutions for children's development. Families evolved as the ultimate protection systems for children. Yet, what is understood as family and how family is defined differ widely across cultures. Family may be conceived of as the place where the fire is, as in some sub-Saharan cultures, family may represent a set of substructures in larger households like the group who shares a kitchen or the group who sleeps together as in the Northwest Cameroonian Nseh or a small group of biologically related individuals as the nuclear family prevalent in the Western urban world. Families may be two generations or extended with biologically related and non-related members. Family relationships may be egalitarian among its members or hierarchically organized. Families may be characterized by generational harmony or intergenerational tension. Families represent a cosmos of variation in multiple domains.

Nevertheless, research in the social sciences in mostly oriented toward the Western middle-class family model, that is, the two generation nuclear family, consisting of a mother, a father, and one or two children. Relationships between family members are mainly dyadically organized and studied: the mother-child relationship, the father-child relationship, the spousal relationship. Multiple relational networks may exist but are neglected in this family model. However, family relationships may also be based on a group level, like the older and younger siblings or the boys and girls in a family as in ultra-orthodox families in Israel or conceptualized from a communal identity where ego boundaries are permeable as described for Southeast Asian cultures and many other contexts. Yet, the structure and definition of relationships of the nuclear family are regarded as universally valid with a normative stance. It represents the moral standard against which also intervention programs are evaluated. The Western middle class, however, represents only a small minority of the world's population which is not at all representative of the large majority. The world's majority is underrepresented in terms of scientists/researchers, research participants, and research findings.

This book represents a notable correction to the Western middle-class bias. It adds a wealth of perspectives and research results to the dominant discourse about families from a particular geographical area with distinct cultural identities: Central and South America. In this part of the world, families are defined by close-knit social structures with particular norms, values, and behavioral regulations that are based on communality and cohesion. Families represent a deeply rooted societal value, which is often expressed in the conception of familism. The book includes chapters from Mexico, Costa Rica, Colombia, Brazil, and Argentina. Each of these countries represents multiple social realities. The chapters can thus be understood as case studies of particular family realities within these different countries. These family realities are bound moreover to particular contextual conditions, mainly addressed as challenges to family functioning and the psychological functioning of its members. Particularly low income and poverty in different countries are discussed in several chapters.

The eco-cultural, contextual approach, to which the book is devoted necessitates broadening the view to the social dimensions or layers in which families are embedded. Consequently, the importance of the wider community is stressed in several chapters. Several of the chapters focus on children's development within the particular family system and social context. These chapters cover a wide range of content from language to social development, from basic research to intervention. The chapters focus on different life stages of family members from pre- and perinatal life, to childhood, adolescence, and adulthood in various age ranges.

The chapters use multiple methodological approaches. In line with the commitment of the book, community-based development of methods and assessment tools are pivotal.

The chapters succeed in linking the cultural, societal, and psychological realities within the author's particular countries to the state of the art of the international scientific discourse.

The book has therefore an important mission: facilitate the establishment of a global science, which is based on different and differing cultural perspectives. Latin America's scientists have a lot to offer to the rest of the world. This book is making a powerful statement in this respect.

Osnabrück
Heidi Keller

Contents

List of Contributors — xi

Introduction — 1
Mariano Rosabal-Coto and Javier Tapia-Balladares

1. Social Development of Children Living in Poverty in Colombia: An Analysis from an Integrative Perspective — 18
Sonia Carrillo and Karen Ripoll-Núñez

2. Family-Based Developmental Intervention: Community-Based Participatory Research in a Brazilian Low-Income Neighborhood — 36
Bruna Larissa Seibel, Paul Springer, Cody Hollist, Lisiane Rech, Luiza Piccoli, Carmen Luiza C. Fernandes, Olga Falceto, and Silvia Koller

3. Motherhood in Poverty, a Perinatal Intervention Device to Detect Psychosocial Risk — 57
Alicia Oiberman, Manoel S. Santos, and Cynthia I. Paolini

4. Colombian Mothers' Intuitive Theories Regarding Their Children's Self-Regulation — 75
Jorge Mario Jaramillo, Mirjam Weis, and María Isabel Rendón

5. Multigenerational Cohabitation and Relationships in the Family: Losses and Gains for Children in the Interaction with Grandparents in Latin America — 97
Mónica Salazar-Villanea, Delia Tamara Fuster-Baraona, and Mauricio Blanco-Molina

6. Family Mechanisms Underlying Adolescent Development in Facing Changes and Adversities — 111
Blanca E. Barcelata Eguiarte

7. Emotion Talk during Reminiscing: A Comparative Study between Mother-Son and Mother-Daughter Dyads from Two Different Educational Backgrounds in Costa Rica 127
Nayuribe Sáenz, Marcela Ríos, Krissia Salazar, and Ana M. Carmiol

Conclusions and Future Orientations 154
Mariano Rosabal-Coto and Javier Tapia-Balladares

References 159
Index 192

List of Contributors

Blanca E. Barcelata Eguiarte, Psychologist, Universidad Nacional Autónoma de México

Mauricio Blanco-Molina, Psychologist, Universidad de Costa Rica, Universidad Nacional de Costa Rica, National University of Costa Rica

Ana M. Carmiol, Psychologist, Universidad de Costa Rica

Sonia Carrillo, Psychologist, Psychology Department, Universidad de los Andes, Bogotá, Colombia

Olga Falceto, Physician, Federal University of Rio Grande do Sul, Faculty of Medicine, Department of Psychiatry and Legal Medicine

Carmen Luiza C. Fernandes, Physician and Coordinator of Residency Program in Family and Community Medicine of the Hospitalar Conceição Group, Brazil

Cody Hollist, Marriage and Familiy Therapist, Child, Youth and Family Studies, University of Nebraska-Lincoln

Jorge Mario Jaramillo, Psychologist, Universidad Santo Tomás, Bogotá, Colombia

Silvia Koller, Psychologist, retired Full Professor and Chair of the Center for Psychological Studies of At Risk Youth and Families in the Department of Psychology at the Universidade Federal do Rio Grande do Sul, Porto Alegre, Brazil.

Alicia Oiberman, Centro Interdisciplinario de Investigaciones en Psicología Matemática y Experimental "Dr. HORACIO J. A. RIMOLDI"—Consejo Nacional de Investigaciones Científicas y Técnicas (CIIPME-CONICET), Facultad de Psicología, Universidad de Buenos Aires

Cynthia I. Paolini, Centro Interdisciplinario de Investigaciones en Psicología Matemática y Experimental "Dr. HORACIO J. A. RIMOLDI"—Consejo Nacional de Investigaciones Científicas y Técnicas (CIIPME-CONICET), Facultad de Ciencias Sociales, Carrera de Psicología, Universidad de Palermo

Luiza Piccoli, Independent Psychologist, Instituto da Família (INFAPA), Brazil

Lisiane Rech, Independent Psychologist, Ser Psicologia, Brazil

María Isabel Rendón, Psychologist, Universidad Santo Tomás, Bogotá, Colombia

Marcela Ríos, Psychologist, Universidad de Costa Rica

Karen Ripoll-Núñez, Psychologist, Psychology Department, Universidad de los Andes, Bogotá, Colombia

Mariano Rosabal-Coto, Psychologist, Instituto de Investigaciones Psicológicas y Escuela de Psicología, Universidad de Costa Rica, retired

Nayuribe Sáenz, Psychologist, Universidad de Costa Rica

Krissia Salazar, Psychologist, Universidad de Costa Rica

Mónica Salazar-Villanea, Psychologist, Universidad de Costa Rica

Manoel S. Santos, Psychologist, University College Roosevelt (UCR), The Netherlands

Bruna Larissa Seibel, Psychologist, Universidad Federal de Rio Grande do Sul (UFRGS) and Researcher at the CNPq en Startup Inceniv, Brazil

Paul Springer, Marriage and Family Therapist, College of Education and Human Sciences and Family Resource Center, University of Nebraska-Lincoln

Delia Tamara Fuster-Baraona, Universidad de Costa Rica, Universidad Nacional de Costa Rica

Javier Tapia-Balladares, Psychologist, Instituto de Investigaciones Psicológicas y Escuela de Psicología, Universidad de Costa Rica

Mirjam Weis, Psychologist, Technical University of Munich, TUM School of Education, Centre for International Student Assessment (ZIB), Germany

Introduction

Mariano Rosabal-Coto and Javier Tapia-Balladares

The scholastic and the professional Latin American psychologies are facing the challenge of covering the study of contexts, especially if they aspire to carry out interventions in accordance with factual conditions.[1] Latin American psychology should concern actual and current problems of social life in a very specific way. This commitment demands from its research strategies both to attend the international agenda and simultaneously to think over the real problems of real people, organizations, and institutions. If the question is about subjects that point toward adversity of variable origins, it is inevitable and rather of rigor to confront science to a large extent with experiences of human suffering.

Predominant mainstream psychological theory primes itself with a Western-oriented perspective of what development and its components should be, where 12% of the world's population composes more than the 96% of psychological samples (Heinrich et al., 2010) hence the majority of the world tends to be underrepresented in predominant theoretical models (Kağitçibaşi, 2007). Rather, it has been noted that current family research does not represent "family forms and family practices to be found around the world," failing to take in world diversity (Weisner et al., 2013, p. 174).

Hence, this book addresses the fundamental experience of family as a specific developmental niche (Super & Harkness, 1986), inasmuch as specific familial contexts surround the psychological development in different Latin American cultural contexts. In our continent, family represents a context for substantial and decisive practices of daily life, since essential psychological processes up to date occur in its bosom. Diverse as it is in the Latin American region, family still seems to concentrate dynamics associated with the life cycle, from toddlerhood to childhood, through adolescence and youth, up to adulthood and old age.

Cross-cultural and cultural approaches have significantly enriched theoretical approaches to universality and particularity with regard to human

---

[1] We want to acknowledge the invaluable support and theoretical resources that Dr Jorge Sanabria-León offered to the writing of this and the final section of the book.

Mariano Rosabal-Coto and Javier Tapia-Balladares, *Introduction*. In: *Family and Contexts of Development*. Edited by: Mariano Rosabal-Coto and Javier Tapia-Balladares, Oxford University Press. © Oxford University Press (2025). DOI: 10.1093/oso/9780197675144.003.0001 development. This compels us to identify parallels and distinctions in the development of children in specific contexts as contrasted to mainstream developmental psychology.

Main contributions offer wide evidence of the notion of family as a core structure, contextualized as an interface between culture and biology (Keller, 2002), shaped by culture but also transmitting culture. We assume that families are the privileged scenario, where diverse socialization domains converge and interact.

From an evolutionary perspective, families offer an optimal scenario for the learning and guidance of all the competences that the environment demands of every human. Bock proposes that "the acquisition of these abilities is result of natural selection on the patterning of developmental trajectories" (2010, p. 19).

Hence, culture and cultural transmission are structured by family, the family acquiring also its shape and dynamics from the particular culture itself. Culturally relevant knowledge is taught with regard to basic interactive, communicative, and social skills. Family conveys cultural scripts (Gaskins & Paradise, 2010) relevant to human development.

On the other hand, qualitative and ethnographic research methods approach first hand what troubles family and therefore which contextually meaningful aspects should be scientifically apprehended. As Weisner (2014) pointed out, each theoretical account rests on evidence that has qualitative nuances. Most theoretical frameworks in family research are suitable for qualitative evidence. With regard to beliefs and ecological settings, these frames have driven psychology to heuristically understand individual and familial experiences throughout the developmental cycle, which hints at a comprehension of "meaning systems and normative scripts" that comprise behavior within cultural contexts. Since inquiring into developmental settings requires fieldwork encounters, interpretation of the data gathered from robust theoretical perspectives is in place. Of especial consideration is, for instance, to examining in depth how participants talk and refer to their own familial world as well as the explanations they can offer as to their motives for facing developmental tasks the way they do. Furthermore, since observing, engaging, and dialoguing with participants within their everyday familial lives in any sense is essential for ethnographic fieldwork, narratives about theoretically differential settings are often its raw material which gains in heuristic potentiality as long as rapport and trust strengthen the ensuing relationship between researcher and participants, therefore allowing them to unpack commonsense categories into analytical ones in a contextualizing manner. Interpretation of robust data about pluralistic socialization endeavors in many dissimilar contexts around the world highlights the differential pathways families follow to address childhood in such important subjects as gender identity, raising practices, and intergenerational relationships systems whose variability and emotional meaning become cross-culturally traceable through understanding the specific contexts.

Developmental singularities and patterns in child development stem from a *developmental niche* (Molitor & Hsu, 2019 Super & Harkness, 1986) that covers normative and individual child-rearing practices, that is, the pragmatics of the culturally regulated symbolic endeavor which happens to occur in socially ecologically relevant settings. An important theoretical support relating to culture and individual development has been developed from Whiting & Whiting's (1975) mode and Berry's (1979) definition of the "ecocultural framework."

The psychology of caregiving goes beyond caretaker's individual psychological characteristics to include predominantly shared conceptions about how to normatively rear a child as well as the expectations and competencies to be individually achieved along a lifespan (goals for development). The process of socialization is hence attached to this ecological system of interrelated beliefs and practices; everything takes place within a cultural milieu (Keller & Kärtner, 2013). According to Molitor and Hsu (2019), even autobiographical memory diverges culturally into forms of what is particularly relevant to a "self-view," namely, what individually accounts for a cultural identity, for instance, whether an independence- or interdependence-based familial relationships system or how a developmentally determined crisis is to be dealt with.

Barely 20 years ago, Igor Bronfenbrenner (2002) wrote about the challenges of twenty-first-century childhood. He suggested an active loving care and, from child and parent, enduring reciprocity in the acknowledgment of each other. The main key for a progressively increasing and successful interaction appeared to him to be involvement in a familial third-party environment, no matter which constitution it may start from. Essential is adult partners who share an all-encompassing emotional entanglement. As psychological scaffold, continuity and regularity foster fundamental developmental conditions since they will maintain a harmonious pace for the child's growing potentiality to fully unfold. He added: "It's never too late to do that."

According to Abels and König (2016), to subjectively embody the cultural guidance which the social environment provides requires a cultural mediation to individually evolve an inner sense of belonging to a collective praxis. Hence socialization and embodiment are not separated but twofold processes in a continuing comprehension of the surrounding reality, with the family household being the primary context for the significant others to assemble such cultural mediation. To embody the emotionally mediated way of thinking and handling of significant others requires access to a self-identify within the world the individual is living in and to learn about their self-resources, also as part of a larger social arrangement.

This concern is also reflected on by Kağıtçıbaşi, where "family is the central component of the self-family-society interface" (2007, p. 125). Her theory of family and social change weaves the self within the family and family within cultural and socioeconomic environment (p. 133).

In technologically hectic, overwhelming everyday life nowadays, the central target of primary bonds in children still consists in the promotion of exploration, manipulation, elaboration, and imagination on the part of the child toward the extended social world. This clue should lead parents toward reflexive thinking about the availability they provide of suitable objects and settings for developmental tasks inside the familial framework. New developments stress a wider concept, talking about attachments and, moreover, about alloparenting when complex familial systems offer what mainstream attachment theory ascribes to the mother-child bond (Keller & Chaudhary, 2017). Families are settings that turn into developmental contexts with particularities in the Latin American cultural context.

Back in 2002, Bronfenbrenner expressed doubts about the current technically globalizing society. He wondered whether it was providing something other than rigid structures of communication. Perhaps, he thought, contrary to the commonsense belief that due to increasing technology children would acquire knowledge beyond their close context by experiencing relatedness to a broader human contact, outside family and community, the new generations are rather plunging into a societal settlement which is lacking both the needed interpersonal interactions and the emotional relationships an individual is supposed to rely on in order to withstand the pressures of the social world. Hence, Bronfenbrenner stressed the role of the family not just as an ephemeral period the subject has to go through either way, but as essential for school performance and further still as a basis—even though not a certainty—for successive social skills to act responsively and creatively as a growing person in every social field.

To these theoretical main subjects, Bronfenbrenner subjoined practical worries about the surrounding disadvantageous developmental conditions children have to cope with all over the world that are associated with critical risk factors. It means disrupting breakdown in developmental paths that strongly subdue supporting social webs. Poverty, single parenthood (lacking "the third party"), absent parents, divorces, remarriages and redivorces, and hectic familial styles exemplify merely some of his concerns.

A strategic axis to confronting these challenges postulated by Bronfenbrenner remains undeniably the child-rearing system within the family. On the other hand, we should not overlook the relevance of public policies and practices underlying social settings, which must provide favorable conditions in support of the former in micro- as well as in macrosystems of the whole society.

Furthermore, Brazelton (2002) argued for an agenda for stabilizing family life, in which the communal commitment to childhood's priorities plays a central role. To encourage empowerment of parenthood and a sense of collective pride in children's developmental success were not novel ideas at all, but they fitted in a scientific psychological perspective that would optimize collective resources to highlight prevention of risk factors. Today's adults would pass on this sense of security to the new generation and so on. Several critical "touch points," according to Brazelton, should be taken into special consideration along the developmental path. This point of view underscores opportunities for supporting strategies attuned to children's breakthroughs.

Barely 20 years after Bronfenbrenner's debate, Shelton (2019) has emphasized the individual's partaking in different social settings throughout the developmental paths children may engage in. Levels of congruence and integration of microsystems increase into constantly more complex mesosystems as children grow up. Consequently, attention to the settings should be paid in which a wide repertoire of children's endeavors takes place. Sets of activities conform children's experience over time, and the chain of events defines the developmental outcome, then actual behaviors in differential contexts might interfere or cooperate with each other. The characteristics of settings children participate in call attention to decisive activities, roles, and relationships in their developmental trajectories, favorable or unfavorable as they may be. Therefore, meso- and exosystems also stand out and draw significant influences. In this sense, culture acquires a determining significance.

Foremost, as Weisner (2013) poses it, the representativeness of the samples upon which contemporary knowledge regarding developmental conditions is based is still lacking at covering the wide diversity to be recognized as a potentially explicative account of the reasons that underlie the variations family forms and family practices around the world acquire. Since the variability of the Latin American developmental contexts represents an exceptional opportunity to expand the scope of these theoretical premises and to confirm (or not) their explicative power and range, perhaps the most fundamental challenge to developmental psychology in Latin America lies in critically incorporating the theoretical foundations of mainstream models by reflecting on their applicability and restrictions in the local contexts and fill the impending voids and gaps that are a result of an unreflective knowledge transfer. In this sense, the models of a "developmental niche" (Gallimore et al., 1989; Worthman, 2010) provide a theoretically insightful devise in looking into the interaction mechanisms that microsystems put in motion (settings, customs, and actors) in culturally different profiles evolving through time and adaptation that children confront in everyday familial practices while growing up and creating microsystems as individually shaped experiences. A central component of the niche approach consists in the socialization of emotions and particularly of emotion regulation instantiated in daily routines which heighten the belief systems in relation to daily developmental endeavors that depict both individual distinctions and possibly shared cultural styles (Tonyan, 2015). Hence, an eco-cultural approach leads to specific niches in which children and families live as pathways to communalities among contextually particular constructions that engulf developmental processes and outcomes (Vélez-Agosto et al., 2017), in the way Kağitçibaşi (2007) considers the "contextual-developmental-functional" approach, namely, contextual culture as organizer of meaning, development as a process that comprises the lifespan, and functions covering adaptive mechanisms so that family arises as a major mediating agency within culture and vice versa. Thus the concept of a niche of development is robust and versatile enough to study several developmental processes from different perspectives.

Of course, some other eco-cultural guidelines should be taken into consideration if the research in developmental psychology in Latin America is to pursue a deeper understanding of the surrounding conditions children are facing. For instance, Keller and Kärtner (2013) and Keller and Chaudhary (2017) also posit an eco-cultural model that highlights how hierarchical relationships within community and family meet the evolutionary needs of children to consolidate enough skills to survive in adverse environments. Georgas et al. (2006) talk about structural and functional dimensions of family by relating psychological relationships: the eco-cultural context and social change that explain individualization under the expansion of urbanization (modernization, globalization), alongside some other elements like allomothering or "cooperative breeding" and environments of evolutionary relevance (Hrdy, 2009) that refer to basal structures underlining psychological development in a diversity of contexts.

However, in spite of historical and cultural change, family remains the nuclear niche that intertwines different ecological levels in varied forms, as studies might show about socioemotional development and ethno-theories about self-regulation in Colombia or the community research-intervention in Brazil, the concerns about maternity and poverty in Argentina, adolescence in Mexico, or the multigenerational families and the emotionality in reminiscence in Costa Rica, along with the subjects pending further research into psychological development in Latin America.

Focus on family dynamics and their networks linked to developmental pathways, seen from an integrative ecological point of view, enables a deeper understanding of developmental processes, and for that reason an unavoidable scientific route becomes crucial hereafter.

Bearing in mind a "develecological" perspective (Shelton, 2019), this book seeks to fill a gap in psychological research in Latin America by introducing studies conducted by scholars of several countries on the subject of twenty-first-century children's micro- and mesosystems. A sequence of research about family life or familial subtleties under different social circumstances reports recent empirical findings that endorse the comparative discussion about ecological and contextual determinants of the developmental trajectories of children in Latin America.

Therefore, a model or, better still, a metamodel that emphasizes context and the interindividual developmental trajectory within the family strings together the chapters of this book. From a systematic ecological perspective, subjectivity is not seen in isolation, but embedded in social relationships. Such a model consists of describing or even explaining: a) familial development comprising specific psychological processes; b) these processes bonding with levels of variable complexity in the context; c) specificity of context meaning a cultural dynamic that encompasses universal as well as particular characteristics.

Hence, in this book family/families represents an axis on which different processes converge to offer an account of psychological development. It articulates the emotional bonding between child and primary caregiver and leading to a sense of self, the comprehension of the surrounding social environment, and the closeness to meaningful others. The differential attachment bonds that characterize the familial relationship system tend to remain stable as a substantial basis for future and further relationships, and such psychological structures emerge from the intrafamilial styles, intergenerationally transmitting safety and relatedness (Jiménez et al., 2017). In other words, socioaffective encouragement paves the way to activate the synaptic cerebral connections responsible for self-regulation of emotions, which is a basal biological process that puts in motion the entailment toward familial and social settings, crowning the circle that begins with an immature social interaction in the mother- (i.e., primary caregiver) baby dyad and ends up with a socially open-ended psychological capability for social relatedness.

A brief description of the linking elements should underscore or highlight theoretical or empirical keys for recognizing the point of convergence in each chapter.

Specificity and Sensibility of Familial Functioning

Beyond any doubt, familial functioning in Latin America embodies a trait very sensitive to cultural processes. This landscape is thrown into relief in the chapters of this book. Coherence is attained by considering family as an essential context for psychological development.

Familial functioning as the main subject of this book implies studying family as background as well as determinant influence for some of the most important processes of psychological development. The familial dynamic engulfs each developmental process to be analyzed, but it is also a psychological system on its own and with its own course. Seeing family not just as an outsider but also as an insider of the developmental scaffold is of great relevance for the analysis.

On the other hand, looking at the influence of cultural processes on the familial dynamic ensures its symbolic character. This symbolic dimension depicts the cultural reproduction of the dialectical constant between universalism and particularism. The cultural reproduction within family refers to beliefs, practices, world views, traditions, and values whose specific configuration of the psychological processes in different degrees forestalls the forms of psychosocial expression and regulation. These particular forms may or may not be shared with other cultural environments.

Levels of Context of Variable Complexity

The levels of context are of variable complexity. The proposal of the ecology of human development considers the levels of context as mutually interacting systems. Even if it could be mistrusted as a likely threat to internal validity, due to the impossibility to fully control all the participating variables, it is clear enough that psychological processes are by no means independent of their specific contexts. Therefore, a context-process model shall prevail.

An ecological perspective of human development is both a methodological and an analytical requisite: methodological insofar as scientific thinking in the categories of micro, meso-, exo-, and macrosystems would turn out to be relevant for sampling or participant selection; analytical insofar as explanations should be in agreement with descriptions of the contextual conditions surrounding the subject under study.

In a context-process model, the dynamic universal components covary, while the psychological processes depend substantially on the level of context to be worked out. Although roles, relationships, and activities are part of the same microsystem, namely family, under the perspective of this book the processes within the family reach also the levels of macro-, chrono-, and biosystems.

Familismo as a Culturally Specific Dimension

The dimension of familism (familismo) is portrayed as a main trait mostly shown in Latin American contexts. This dimension has been identified in various levels: attitudinal (Steidel & Contreras, 2003; Lay et al., 1998), living arrangements (Baca Zinn & Wells, 2000), among relational and support networks (Calzada et al., 2012), but nevertheless, as an embodiment of the self. Much emotion-based closeness, in hierarchical relational cultures (Keller

& Chaudhary, 2017), where kinship supports a strong sense of belongingness to the immediate group (the family), is embodied in values such *respeto*, obedience, support, and family obligation. It stresses the orientation to meet familial emotional bonds and social obligations.

Much evidence supports that familism plays relevant roles, such as being a protective factor for Latino youth in the USA, and promotes the positive role of parent-child closeness on Latino children (Calzada et al., 2012; Mahrer et al., 2019; Umaña-Taylor et al., 2011).

Evidence from Central American contexts shows the important role of extended family, where grandparents and other kin are part of children's lives. Rogoff (2003) describes these child-care networks as "funds of knowledge" (p. 120), which support learning skills in school, as companions in socialization, and as child-rearing support. Even more, Latin American cultures support the experience of community as caregivers (Chavajay et al., 1999).

For instance, it is possible for familism to cover systemic contexts, among which micro- and macrosystems tower over any other. But as part of the latter, familism is a specific cultural characteristic with its multiple regional variants. The impact of familism falls upon the family as a whole, but also upon the individual members. Thus, familism belongs to the cultural values which could become a factor either in risks to or opportunities for psychological development. According to Rogoff (2003, p. 51) development "is inherently involved with historical developments of both the species and cultural communities, development occurs in every-day moment-by-moment learning opportunities ... such contexts entangle four time frames: species change, community historical change, individual lifetimes, individual learning moments."

Hence, there must be a specification of the contextual or systemic level the psychological process is evolving in, which foreordains the explicative discussion; then the latter depends on the former. This is not just about a methodological artifact, but about an analytical foundation to prove a hypothesis or conduce scientific debate.

Covariation of Specific Psychological Processes

The chapters in this book pursue three prime psychological processes, none of which happen in isolation. In a model like this, the level of the processes hitches to the level of the contexts. The level of the processes depends upon the coordination of each single aspect with other subordinated processes in order to single out the one to be analyzed.

For instance, emotional distance (subprocess) covaries with closeness in order to produce a certain relational atmosphere (subprocess) between grandparents and grandchildren or even grandparents and their own progeny. In other words, the dynamic and ensuing covariation of processes are not necessarily predetermined but could be qualitatively transformed by the very coordination or interaction between the processes themselves. The simple covariation of psychological processes would make easier the description and explanation of cognitive functions, emotions, and actions within the family.

And then again, such a variation is linked to and influenced by a reality beyond household. Therefore, the covariation also occurs between the psychological processes and the differential levels of the context. This is what is meant by a process-context model. For the Latin American psychology this would be a subject of greater relevance in research.

Infancy and Toddlerhood as Developmentally Fundamental Stages

As patterns of developmental tasks and achievements, these two subsequent periods represent protruding phases that culminate in specific psychological traits such as socioemotional and sociocognitive skills that contribute essentially to further development. The uniqueness of the psychological characteristics that imprint these developmental transitions stands out also in its relevance to parental styles. Individually distinctive capabilities that ensue parenting practices depict a medullary issue granting the culturally defined processes of socialization that mostly encompass growth.

Regarding This Book

This book comprises seven chapters, each representing a sample of the psychological scientific production in some Latin American countries about child developmental contexts where families play a central role.

In the first chapter, Sonia Carrillo and Karen Ripoll-Núñez analyze issues among families in Colombia based on local field research. The authors display evidence and theory, while studying the socioemotional development of children in the frame of parent-offspring relationships within extreme poverty contexts. Further, theoretical perspectives about research on childhood living in familial contexts of poverty are linked with concern about likely factors of risk and protection for children's development in this population. Resilience hinges with development as a most important issue, when such unfavorable stressors as poverty are to the fore. The authors perceive children's socioemotional development as determined by parent-child relationships. The influence of diverse microsystems surrounding the familial niche is identified as leading individual trajectories. This ecological-systemic perspective is analyzed through a transactional model that highlights resilience to visualize familial trajectories under socioeconomically vulnerable conditions.

Carrillo and Ripoll-Núñez, who belong to one of the leading research groups in their homeland, offer a descriptive and analytical point of view, discussing from an interesting perspective data about Colombian public politics programs. Introducing scientific debate with the dominant theory about family in local context, international data are contrasted with local Colombian experiences. Risks and protective factors are identified and local policies on child development research are discussed. Methodological challenges and the formulation of new research programs are also the target of controversy.

A critical question is raised by the research of Bruna Larissa Seibel, Paul Springer, Cody Hollist, Lisiane Rech, Luiza Piccoli, Carmen Luiza C. Fernandes, Olga Falceto, and Sylvia Koller. On the subject of defining successful psychological interventions in Latin American contexts, authors, supported in a cultural perspective, drive an interesting debate. Cultural characteristics within family and community are viewed by the authors as of central meaning for a full comprehension of the relationship networks that underlie developmental processes. Individual traits and outcomes would be outlined step by step by familial dynamics surrounding the evolving young person; the same will protect or threaten his or her developmental path. From the perspective of the socioecological environment, community plays a central role when it comes to identifying disadvantageous conditions; family and individuals are threatened by a significant amount of risk factors that weaken or obtrude on the immediate resources of the microsystem. Instead mesosystems interfere with microsystems, challenging families and individuals, and overwhelming the capacities of the close relationship system as well as the individual's transit to a wider social commitment.

Therefore, the authors consider of decisive importance research into the concrete developmental conditions in concrete developmental contexts that might show which cultural factors, such as norms, values, and beliefs that affect familial dynamics, would play a significant role in confronting and overcoming problems. With this aim in mind, they discuss community-based participatory research (CBPR), which they thought of as "especially sensitive to culture and family developmental issues; as they engage families, communities, and key stakeholders, in not only understanding the problem, but in building community capacity in developing solutions." Their shared field experience is called the "Flourishing through Education Program," working with low-income youth and families in Southern Brazil's and placing the emphasis on school dropout prevention. Poverty, the highest rates of violence, and drug trafficking are just some of the main social problems people in that part of the country have to deal with in everyday life. School and public health systems among others would be confronted by this socially disruptive environment in as much as family and social resources had lost the reciprocal webbing connections needed to support the developmental path of younger generations. The acknowledgment of vulnerabilities as well as of strengths deriving from the community stakeholders' expertise, amidst the most important issues, led to a wider understanding of the communal social mesosystems. Hence the team could "harness the protective functioning of a social support network to enable positive adaptive outcomes ... which can modify the interpretation of individuals' experiences and empower change."

The impact of socioeconomic burdens on psychological development is analyzed from the perspective of the psychosocioenvironmental conditions surrounding the relationships within the family so that interventions could assure the outcomes would be grounded in context and culture and meeting local communal requirements.

A rigorous methodological approach linked to a wide theoretical comprehension of the communal central concerns enabled this research team to depict an interesting project suited to presenting how a straightforward scientific perspective can contribute to a culturally attuned intervention in psychologically complex developmental processes.

Alicia Oiberman, Manoel Santos, and Cynthia Paolini, from the case study of a region in Argentina, review a discussion on motherhood in the context of poverty. The chapter is a contribution to a better understanding of maternity and child-mother dyads in contexts in which family is still the main axis of human activity but also involves critical psychosocial risk factors. This empirical research stresses psychosocial risk factors regarding the perinatal period, in displaying a perinatal intervention, psychological, social, and cultural characteristics emerge as prominent beyond the biological ones. When mother-child dyads leave the medical center they must deal with a great number of risk factors that endanger further psychological development of both children and mothers, as well as the quality of their relationship.

The psychosocial conditions under which mothers have to deploy the meaningful tasks of raising children are indeed psychologically sensitive. This happens to an extent, and maternal age, socioeconomic status, and literacy ascertain the child's development from early infancy. This fact reinforces the trend for research on the initial processes of mothering and creating bonds not only worthy, but essential to fully understand psychological development at the very start of life.

The evidence-based intervention includes an interview about the perinatal period and a set of analytical categories about psychosocial risk factors during the perinatal time. These data should contribute to an early detection of risk conditions and consequently to a preventive intervention. Concepts about the psychological processes during maternity, such as psychic transparency and life debt, lead to the analysis of sociofamilial risk factors. These could diminish the quality of child mother relationship and even distract the mother from a healthy pregnancy and maternity.

Also within the familial milieu, Jorge Mario Jaramillo, Mirjam Weis, and María Isabel Rendón drive us toward a pivotal concept: the behavioral, emotional, and cognitive components of interactive relationships. Collective and individual levels in this regard are discussed and related to the successful achievement of an integrative self-regulation in social contexts. The adjustment to inherent features of societal requirements represents a basal social capability, which convenes actions, thoughts, and emotions, providing a certain grade of prediction for integration into a developmentally increasingly complex relational network. Family, as the primary socialization environment, leads its offspring to assume specific self-regulative styles that will be reproduced in novel situations beyond the family context.

Nevertheless, cultural values and parenting goals shape the self-regulative styles children should follow; therefore these are differential and specific to context. The authors highlight the until recently prevalent interdependent value of close relationships among Latin American families, which above any other favor "appropriate behavior, sympathy (respecting and sharing other's feelings), and familism (strong family ties, commitment to the family)." These qualities should encourage children to accommodate to communal goals and cohesion. Although the children's willingness to conduct themselves according to this social commitment provides an extraordinary example of the self-regulation paradigm, this might be changing in at least some Latin American countries nowadays. A new orientation appears to be comprising the promotion of more individualized parenting practices, hence independence as societal goal. This could mean a change in socialization practices as well as in intergenerational communication, concerning the specific demands on children to self-regulate under the new developmental scaffold.

Thus, self-regulation is a crucial outcome of familial conditioning for psychological development of children and sorts of buffering scaffold altogether.

The renewing socialization practices and goals are assumed to be present in intuitive socialization theories of mothers. So how the latter influence the developmental guidelines that encompass presumed new self-regulative styles in children of today's changing society arises as the leading question of these researchers. Mothers narrate their points of view about attributions, emotions, parenting practices (behaviors), and socialization goals, implicit in short stories containing hypothetical quarrels or arguments between mother and child, which were categorically codified thereafter. Descriptive and means comparing statistics depict, link, and discuss the findings that show the parenting practices and socialization goals attached. Among other interesting outcomes, interdependence is thus not altogether relinquished, which yet does not allow us to consider that intergenerational conflicts do not suppose new challenges.

A study by Mónica Salazar-Villanea, Tamara Fuster-Baraona, and Mauricio Blanco-Molina analyzes in depth, what it means to be living in families with elderly members in the Latin American and especially in the Costa Rican context. This chapter suits the current concern of the Costa Rican society and its increasingly aging population: an interesting contribution that harvests local production regarding cohabiting styles and examines critically scientific results on this topic produced in the United States and Europe.

A critical review of the individualism/collectivism issue debate guides the idea of interdependence traits, particular to the Costa Rican culture, is presented. On the topic of cohabiting familial environments, the authors identify as a paramount goal to set differences regarding the psychological characteristics of Latino families who migrated to the United States and native families from several native Latino countries in the continent.

Within the context of an interdependently oriented context, and through the issue of mother and father responsibility with regard to the role of grandparents, Salazar-Villanea and colleagues depict the relationships between self and culture.

From the perspective of developmental ecology, focused on studying the cultural contrasts across the life cycle, Blanca Barcelata Eguiarte's contribution to this book addresses the multidimensional variability of individual and contextual factors embedded in family and adolescence. With the prevalence of adolescence issues in her homeland, Mexico, Barcelata Eguiarte stresses a subject that has acquired particular relevance. Besides, this demographic phenomenon is even more notorious in the socioeconomically lower social levels. The study in this chapter focuses on the load of these factors on traditional familial models, and its findings prove to be suitable to substantially expose the outstanding imperative of being in continuing adaptability to the ongoing processes. This psychosocial configuration adds complexity to the course of development and, therefore, to its analysis.

From a systemic perspective of ecological development, the author knots models of familial functioning with models of increasing tension. This allows identification of risk factors as well as protective factors that operate on the individual level throughout adolescence. Specific developmental paths with differentiated outcomes overlap diverse subjectivities. Barcelata argues especially about the strategies of coping and resilience, which psychologically cooperate to buffer adversity, but that both could also enhance individual resources as part of the familial scaffolding. Data from several Latin American countries enable the author to demonstrate the relevance of the indispensable equilibrium between risk and protective factors concerning, for instance, parenting practices and diverse forms of relationship within the family, as essential formulae for reaching a comprehension of ongoing adaptability to adversity as part of the cycle of poverty.

Nayuribe Sáenz, Marcela Ríos, Krissia Salazar, and Ana María Carmiol introduce their research findings about reminiscence and narratives within the child-mother dyad. The discussion highlights the extraordinary relevance for language acquisition and communicative processes, when conveying cultural practices and meanings within the family. To turn life experiences into subjects of intergenerational cultural transmission appears to be a decisive influence in the progressive autobiographical memory, early literacy, and the awareness of being oneself, as well as, in a broader sense, of sociocognitive skills altogether. From a developmental socioemotional perspective, reminiscence is linked with affective bonding, the growth of relationships, and the strengthening of the self.

As for cultural specificity, the authors postulate that dyadic dialogues should be capable of communicating about causes, consequences, and resolution of emotional concerns, most of all regarding negative events. The premise allows us to think of, for Costa Rica and owing to previous research, a hybrid model, which promotes traits of independence as well as of interdependence when comparing cross-cultural studies. The discrepancies between styles rather explain the diversity of parenting practices and socialization goals.

Due to the complexity of the dyads' dialogues in Costa Rican samples, the authors draw on several vectors in the dialogic interaction during the reminiscence. An ingenious but nonetheless rigorous methodological approach thrives as a colorful constellation of the interactive dialogic trade about emotions. The most relevant traits bind together the emotional valence in play and the cultural particularity of the socialization processes.

1
Social Development of Children Living in Poverty in Colombia
An Analysis from an Integrative Perspective

Sonia Carrillo and Karen Ripoll-Núñez

Introduction

The literature on the developmental effects of poverty shows that children who live in poverty are not only deprived of the material, spiritual, and emotional resources necessary for their development, but they are also exposed to social risks, discrimination, and social exclusion (Boyden & Bourdillon, 2012; Presidencia de la República, 2013). Colombia is the second most populated country in Latin America (UNICEF-Colombia, 2017). In 2011, approximately one-third of Colombian children and adolescents live in multidimensional poverty and those who live in rural areas are 2.8 more likely to live in poverty than those in urban areas (UNICEF-Colombia, 2017). In addition to the vulnerability associated with multidimensional poverty, children in Colombia are directly affected by sociopolitical violence related to internal armed conflict. For instance, in 2016, approximately 542 adolescent males (ages 15 through 17) were murdered. Also, in 2016, child and adolescent victims of sexual abuse made up to 86% of the reports at the National Institute for Forensic Medicine (UNICEF-Colombia, 2017). Due to these different sources of vulnerability that may negatively affect children's development in Colombia, it is necessary to adopt an integrative framework to understand variations in their developmental trajectories, risk and protective factors that influence their ways to respond to adverse circumstances, as well as analyze existing research and social policies for children living in poverty.

The purpose of this chapter is to present an analysis of different factors influencing the development of children living in poverty in Colombia from an integrative approach based on an ecological-systemic perspective, a transactional model of the parent-child relationships, and on basic assumptions on children's resiliency. The ecological-systemic perspective on individual development invites researchers and policymakers to focus on several factors at different levels: individual, micro-, meso-, and macrosystems. Poverty affects children and adolescents' developmental outcomes by threatening basic conditions at the individual, family, and community levels (Engel, 2012). For this reason, an ecological perspective is a useful theoretical framework to analyze the development of children living under vulnerable conditions in Colombia. Second, this chapter will rely on the transactional model to analyze the effects of poverty on the parent-child subsystem in vulnerable families, and its effects on children's socioemotional development and well-being. Third, recent literature on resilience will be used to discuss the role of individual as well as environmental factors that mitigate the effects of adversity and protect children from the devastating consequences of vulnerability in their daily lives. Finally, and following the ecological perspective, this chapter will focus on the macrosystem level within which we discuss public policies related to vulnerable families and to children's development in Colombia.

Thus, the present chapter will consist of four sections: first, we present some sociodemographic features that characterize poverty in Colombia in the present moment, and its particular effects on children's and adolescents' development. The second section will involve the presentation of an integrative theoretical perspective to understand the development of children and adolescents living under vulnerable circumstances. Third, the chapter will concentrate on the family microsystem; specifically it will present an analysis of the dynamics of parent-child relationships in vulnerable contexts based on a transactional perspective. The following section of the chapter will discuss some aspects of children's resilience. Recent conceptualizations of resilience focus on an ecological view that includes individual as well as environmental factors. This section will present an analysis of risk and protective factors within the parent-child subsystem that influence children's ability to cope with adversity and to thrive in it. The final section will be dedicated to the presentation of current family- and child-focused policies that impact social development during childhood and adolescence in Colombia. A special focus in this section will be on social policies that target families and children living in vulnerable conditions (e.g., poverty and forced displacement). The chapter will end with recommendations for child development and family researchers as well as policymakers, on issues that need to be addressed in the next decade in order to enhance children's socioemotional development, to design intervention programs to enhance children and adolescents' well-being, and to promote optimal parent-child relationships in this country.

Demographics of Poverty in Colombia

Results from the last Home Survey conducted by the National Administrative Department of Statistics (NADS, 2017a) on poverty indices in the Colombian territory indicated that 26.9% of the population live under the monetary poverty line, and 7.4% face extreme monetary poverty. Also, 17% of the Colombian population lives in multidimensional poverty. This type of poverty refers to five specific dimensions defined by the Oxford Poverty & Human Development Initiative (OPHI); these are: 1) level of education; 2) childhood and youth conditions; 3) work; 4) health; and 5) public services and living conditions (NADS, 2017b).

It is estimated that children and adolescents comprise 30% of Colombia's population, and one in three children lives in poverty (UNICEF-Colombia, 2017). Children living in poverty are at greater risk of dying in the first years of life; it is estimated that children's mortality rates remain at 14 in every 1,000 children (Profamilia, Ministry of Health, 2015). However, there are variations in mortality rates among Colombian ethnic groups, with ethnic minorities (e.g., Afro-Columbian descendants, indigenous groups) having rates as high as 160 deaths for every 1,000 children born alive (Ministry of Health, 2016). Children living in rural areas or from ethnic minorities are 1.5 more at risk of dying early in their lives (Ministry of Health, 2016).

Malnutrition is among the main causes of death in children under 5 years in Colombia. National data show a prevalence rate of moderate to severe malnutrition in 0.09 cases per 100,000 children. A total of 560,000 children under 5 years of age have been diagnosed with malnutrition in the country (National Institute of Health, 2018).

Living in Poverty: An Integrative Perspective

Poverty is one of the most important risk factors to human development. The literature shows the devastating effects of poor living conditions (low household income, unemployment, severe economic and social disadvantages, low education levels, etc.) on children and adolescents' physical, social, cognitive, and emotional development and well-being (Felner & DeVries, 2013). Understanding the social and emotional development and well-being of children exposed to vulnerable conditions such as poverty demands an integrative approach that involves the intrinsic as well as contextual elements that surround individuals. The integrative approach used in this chapter was proposed by Ripoll and Carrillo (2018). It combines elements from the ecological-systemic perspective and the transactional model, to understand children's developmental trajectories. In the case of children living in poverty and other vulnerable conditions, a third element will be added to complement this integrative approach: that is a comprehensive conceptualization of resilience. The model begins with an ecological-systemic view that conceives human development as the effect of relations between individuals' characteristics and elements from the different systems in which they are immersed. As Engel (2012) points out, developmental trajectories for children living in poverty are likely to be influenced by several factors, from the individual level to family and community level. The family microsystem constitutes the main immediate context of influence in children's development (Bronfenbrenner, 1979). Families living in poverty face innumerable constraints that impact their dynamics of functioning, their relationships, and the development of their members. Within the family system, the relations with parents are central to children's lives. The second component in this integrative perspective refers to the transactional model as a base to understand the interactions between children and their parents. In these relations, both parties (parents and children) are mutually affected, and their particular exchange is responsible for their developmental outcomes (Sameroff, 2009). The processes and mechanisms of the parent-child relational subsystem are influenced by the individuals' biopsychosocial characteristics as well as by factors and agents from the different contexts (e.g., immediate and distant) in which this relationship is embedded (Bronfenbrenner, 1979). A final component of this integrative proposal is the concept of children's resilience. The construct of resilience and its contemporary conceptualizations take a key role when discussing poverty and children's development under vulnerable circumstances. Adverse living conditions impose significant challenges to individuals. Children facing adverse situations such as poverty and social conflict may either develop behavior problems and pathologies, or react and use their abilities to survive and thrive (Prince-Embury & Saklofske, 2013). Some authors emphasize the need to move from simple definitions of resilience to a conceptualization of this construct as a "set of processes that alter children's transactions with adverse life conditions to reduce negative effects and promote mastery of normative developmental tasks" (Wyman, 2003,p. 308). Recent developments in the literature highlight the importance of recognizing resilience in a more holistic and ecological view, as a complex construct that involves individual as well as environmental factors (Masten, 2007; Masten & Shaffer, 2006; Prince-Embury, 2012). In the following sections we will present an analysis, of individual and contextual factors influencing children's social and emotional development when living in poverty.

Individual Factors

At this level, researchers have focused on issues such as the role of brain development, as well as the influence of other biological (e.g., nutrition) and environmental (e.g., stress) factors in child developmental outcomes (Engle, 2012). Although brain development is genetically influenced, researchers think of the brain as "experience expectant." This means that it is programmed to receive particular stimuli at specific developmental periods (National Scientific Council on the Developing Child, 2007). For example, the development of visual and auditory functioning is more sensitive during the first three to eight months of life. Perturbations of these processes during critical periods can have long-term effects on the brain's functional and structural capacity (Grantham-McGregor, 2007). Despite the vulnerability of the brain to negative experiences (e.g., malnutrition, neglect), it has considerable plasticity and it may achieve remarkable recovery through timely interventions.

A second group of factors at the individual level include biological and environmental conditions such as birth weight and malnutrition during childhood. Research shows that low birth weight has significant long-term effects on children's development (Lozoff et al., 2006).

Similarly, malnutrition has a negative effect on several developmental areas that include cognitive (e.g., reduced attention), emotional (e.g., how easily a child gets upset), and social (e.g., quality of social relations) outcomes (Walker et al., 2007).

Family-Level Factors

In most societies, parental figures (e.g., biological parents, stepparents, grandparents) constitute the main socialization context in early childhood (Ripoll-Núñez & Carrillo Ávila, 2018). Individual socialization is the process through which children develop a set of emotional, cognitive, and social skills that allow them to function in the community according to the standards defined by their social group (Rodrigo et al., 2014). Recently, integrative theoretical models of parent-child relationships highlight the bi-directional and reciprocal influence of parental figures and children on individuals' development (Bugental & Grusec, 2006; Grusec, 2011; Rodrigo et al., 2014). According to these theories, parental figures instill values and provide models for social behavior that impact a child's developmental trajectories. Also, children as active agents of their development select and interpret their interactions with parents and, as a result, they also influence their parental figures' expectations and behaviors. Some authors postulate that parent-child interactions could be conceptualized as encompassing five different domains: protection, mutual reciprocity, control, guided learning, and group participation (Grusec & Davidov, 2010). According to these authors, effective parenting involves relationship processes and dynamics that foster and maintain adaptive social competencies in each of the domains; parental figures may be more effective in one domain than in others.

Growing up in an economically disadvantaged environment has implications for the relationship between children and their caregivers. First, research shows that living in poverty affects children's development of executive functions that support decision-making, problem-solving, and planning later in life. This is attributed to the environmental characteristics of impoverished communities that foster the development of less reflective and more reactive ways of responding to unpredictable immediate demands (Finegood & Blair, 2017). Similarly, the social and economic constraints that confront parents living in poverty make it more difficult for them to engage in caregiving behaviors that support children's executive function development (Blair & Raver, 2012). Second, children living in poverty are more likely to experience the effects of individual and relational difficulties that affect their parents (e.g., parental depression, marital discord, and increased risk of intimate partner violence) when compared to children from economically stable families (McLoyd, 1990). These factors are likely to increase pressures in the marital relationships such as parenting stress and also may reduce parents' warm and sensitive caregiving toward their children (Finegood & Blair, 2017).

Social Factors

The development of children living in poverty is also adversely affected by the social context that surrounds their families. The challenges of impoverished communities (e.g., low services available, high unemployment, community violence) where families reside constitute a major factor that affects parents' perceptions of stressors and, in turn, lead to negative interactions with their children (Gutman et al., 2005). Among such neighborhood challenges, one that different studies associate with children's difficulties in self-regulation (e.g., impulse control and attention) is community violence (e.g., homicides) (Sharkey, 2010; Sharkey et al., 2012). In Colombia, children who live in economically vulnerable areas are not only more likely to witness violent acts but also to be victims of violence themselves. For instance, children have been victims of landmines (e.g., 10 children in 2006) and homicide (757 homicides in 2016) (UNICEF-Colombia, 2017).

In Colombia, the impact of impoverished communities on children and families is compounded by the internal armed conflict and its effects on the country's social and economic stability. The specific characteristics of the sociopolitical conflict that Colombia has experienced for over six decades set deeper and radical social pressures which have impacted families and children and placed them under different vulnerable conditions. The organization and cohesion of families have been affected, as well as the relationships between parents and children and the development and well-being of all family members (Pachón, 2005; Ramírez, 1998). As a result of the different social pressures associated with the political violence and social conflict, families have disintegrated and people have lost their lands, jobs, homes, and support networks, and the forced displacement phenomenon has significantly increased around the country. According to a general report from the National Information Network (2016), the number of victims from the armed conflict registered in 2016 was 7,603,597 people, and forced displacement was responsible for the biggest number of victims. Currently, the number of victims of forced displacement has decreased to 6,646,395 (Internal Displacement Monitoring Center, 2017). Another consequence of the forced displacement phenomenon is the increase in poverty levels in many Colombian cities which constitutes an important obstacle for children and adolescents' adequate development and well-being (Corredor, 2010; Mendoza & González, 2010).

Parent-Child Relationships: A Transactional Perspective

Children's and adolescents' development and well-being are highly influenced by the dynamics and quality of interactions in the parent-child subsystem. The study of parent-child relationships is grounded in different theoretical approaches that guide family studies. Based on these approaches, researchers have investigated the specific factors that characterize or influence the spectrum of relations between parents and children (i.e., optimal, average, and difficult relations). The analysis of some dimensions of parent-child relations as well as the influence of these relations on children's development requires an integrative perspective. Such a perspective refers to a conceptual framework formed by a set of assumptions that allows for a more comprehensive understanding of a specific phenomenon and consideration of different factors, agents, and contexts that may influence individuals' development (Doherty et al., 1998).

The literature shows compelling evidence of a strong association between secure, harmonious, and supportive parent-child relationships and children and adolescents' social development, life satisfaction, and well-being (Dinisman et al., 2017; Shonkoff & Phillips, 2000; Sroufe et al., 2005; Thompson, 2018). Children's development is affected by a number of factors and socializing agents. However, parents are determinant in their developmental trajectory; they

> are biologically prepared to care for the young as a way of achieving their own reproductive success ... Teach young how to regulate emotions ... Build a warm and affectionate relationships with their children...

are powerful socializers.... and control resources and manage their children's environment to ensure they are exposed to positive social influences. (Grusec, 2011, p. 245)

According to Grusec and Davidov (2010), the interactional dynamics between parents and children and the social, emotional (and sometimes financial) support among family members are some of the more influential aspects on different domains of children's development.

In applying a transactional model to the development of children living in poverty, Engle (2012) postulates that poverty has a continuous effect on the ongoing relationships between children and their caregivers. Such a longitudinal effect has an impact on children's development that may be moderated by parental characteristics. Similarly, children's characteristics may affect parental reactions. As an example, Engle (2012) analyzes the effects on poverty on maternal depression and the ways in which maternal depression has a negative impact on children's development. Such negative effects of mothers' characteristics are exacerbated when the child also has a difficult temperament, because mothers may be less likely to exhibit sensitive, responsive caregiving and more likely to feel depressed. A similar analysis may apply when parents' and children's characteristics interact to buffer the negative effects of poverty. For instance, Engle (2012) postulates that, even in times of economic hardship, parents are more likely to invest in educational resources if they perceive their children to be academically talented. As a result, children's academic achievement improves and, in turn, parental investment in their children is also likely to increase.

Thriving from Adversity: An Ecological View of Resilience

Resilience has traditionally been defined as an individual's responses in the face of adverse or stressful situations. However, contemporary definitions of resilience go beyond individuals' characteristics and include aspects of the different contexts in which they develop; family characteristics and their dynamics of functioning become important elements in the study of this construct (Nichols, 2012; Sheridan et al., 2013). Felner et al. (2000) and Felner & DeVries (2013) suggested that resilience in children and adolescents living in poverty should be conceptualized under a more comprehensive framework. According to these authors, the consequential developmental pathways resulting from being exposed to poverty conditions early in life are the result of complex and dynamic interactions between different factors. In order to better understand resilient children and families in the context of poverty, an ecological perspective is required that considers different exchanges between risk and protective factors within proximal and distal systems in which they are embedded (Felner & DeVries, 2013; Finegood & Blair, 2017; Morris et al., 2007). An integrative approach that incorporates ecological and transactional components combined with elements of recent conceptualizations of resilience, allows a more comprehensive analysis of the immediate (i.e., family) as well as more distant factors (educational institutions, neighborhoods, community) that influence children's pathways of development and well-being.

In the next section, relevant research findings regarding risk and protective factors associated with children and families living in poverty, both internationally and in Colombia, are presented.

Risk Factors for Individuals' Development

Research in Colombia about familial risk factors for children living in poverty has focused on parenting practices, as well as the risks related to abandonment. Studies on parenting practices such as the use of physical punishment and other controlling behaviors (Aguirre, 2000; Aguirre & Duran, 1998; Barreto & Puyana, 1996) have shown that parents living under stressful conditions tend to be less consistent in their demands and, as a result, children find it more difficult to understand and predict their caregivers' behaviors. These studies attribute the use of these disciplinary practices to parents' lower educational levels, as well as to their holding parenting beliefs that justify the use of control and physical punishment. Second, studies on abandonment (Meneses et al., 2012) indicate that due to financial difficulties parents migrate to other areas that offer employment opportunities and this may put children at risk of lack of parental monitoring and abandonment.

Other studies in Colombia have explored the effects of poverty on different areas of child development. For instance, Orozco-Hormaza et al. (2012), in a study with 405 children in Colombia, concluded that children's cognitive development is negatively affected only when their familial context does not provide them with adequate practices to regulate their behavior, and when adults don't offer care and entertainment to their children. However, the family's socioeconomic status by itself does not have an effect on children's cognitive development. Regarding children's socioemotional development, Carbonell et al., (2015) evaluated the quality of the parent-child attachment relationship, as well as other parenting dimensions such as limit setting and parental control. They found that, in order to discipline their children, parents used alternative strategies to physical punishment—such as withdrawal of privileges or scolding—however, parents used corporal punishment more often to discipline girls than they did with boys. Also, mothers' age was negatively associated with frequency of verbal interactions with the child which may account for lower levels in children's cognitive, social, and emotional development. As Carbonell et al. (2015) conclude, other factors such as daily stressors and knowledge about the importance of verbal interaction in children's development may also account for mothers' behavior.

Recently, an analysis of data derived from the Colombian Longitudinal Survey (ELCA, in Spanish) conducted by Universidad de los Andes in different geographical areas of the country revealed that 20% of children under 5 years of age living in poverty are at higher risk of developing socioemotional delay. Such developmental difficulties are correlated with the mother's educational level, parents' increased use of physical or verbal punishment, and parents' decreased use of positive discipline (Bernal et al., 2015). Although children living in poverty are likely to experience higher risk factors, the authors conclude that parents across socioeconomic levels could benefit from parenting education programs.

Protective Factors

Research on protective factors for children and families living in poverty has identified variables, both at the individual and relationship levels. At the individual level, longitudinal studies have identified behavior and personality factors that make children more resilient to adverse conditions, such as poverty (e.g., Garmezy et al., 1984; Werner, 1986). Those factors include: children's a) skill in gaining positive attention from adults; b) possessing a positive view of their experiences; c) ability to maintain a positive perspective on life; d) ability to be alert and autonomous; and, e) having a proactive approach when facing difficulties.

At a relationship level, research on protective factors for parent-child relationships emphasizes the importance of a nurturing relationship between children and their caregivers as a protective factor that can mitigate the developmental effects of family stress and other traumatic conditions associated with poverty (Morris et al., 2017). Nurturing parent-child relationships have a positive effect on children's development of adaptive biobehavioral responses to stress. Also, research evidence indicates that parents can improve the quality of their relationships with their children by maintaining positive daily interactions through activities such as conversations, play, and reading (Morris et al., 2017). In addition to a nurturing relationship, children also need an environment where there are clear limits, guidance, and consistency in parent-child interactions (Morris et al., 2007). In conclusion, research evidence on positive parent-child relationships in families living in poverty has focused on the beneficial effects of parent-child interactions in at least two of the domains defined by Grusec and Davidov (2010): protection and control.

In addition to positive parent-child interactions, research on parenting in economically disadvantaged families indicates that the relationship between parents and other adults (intimate partner, friends, relatives) is key in improving the quality of parent-child relationships (Morris et al., 2017). Perceived social support is associated with positive parenting behaviors and can buffer the negative effect of economic conditions on the quality of parent-child relationships (McConnell et al., 2011).

Some research studies developed in Colombia on children living in poverty have adopted a strength-based perspective that seeks to understand children's resiliency. In particular, the research studies developed by the Research Center on Human Development at Universidad del Norte, in Barranquilla, have focused on children's perspectives on their immediate contexts (family, school, neighborhood) (Amar, 2000). Those studies, based on interviews and observations of over 1,000 participants (4–7 years of age) have found that, in spite of economic adversity, children demonstrate social skills that lead to cooperation, solidarity, and reciprocity in their interactions with others. Also, they suggest that economic adversity stimulates children's independence as well as their conscience about the importance of group affiliation, which are both important skills to deal with the challenges of everyday life in impoverished communities. With regard to family functioning, other studies conducted by the same scholars identified three protective factors in the interactions between family members in these disadvantaged communities: emotional security, affiliation, and positive affect (Amar, 2000). Thus, these studies found that families living in poverty in the Caribbean region of Colombia develop interactions to support children's well-being, protect them from adversity, and foster family cohesion. Most of such interactions between parents and children are characterized by verbal and non-verbal expressions of positive affect and warmth. Also, parents perceive their children as the most important aspect of their family, as a source of happiness, love, and pride. Lastly, these studies have also evaluated factors that foster the functioning of social support networks of families living in poverty. Physical proximity, kin relationships, and trust are three factors that positively influence the cohesion of support networks (Amar, 2000). The results of this study have led to the design and implementation of family education programs at government child-care centers that seek to stimulate children's socioemotional development.

This research is congruent with some of the assumptions of the family resilience model proposed by Walsh (2012, 2016). According to this author, families may be affected in different ways as a consequence of being exposed to different types of stressors or hard conditions. They may either stay in the disruptive state and develop dysfunctional patterns, or follow a pathway of adaptation, surpass the negative events, and thrive from it. Family cohesion, communication strategies, and the pattern of organization inside it are some of the protective resources that will help a family to overcome the stressor and reach their well-being and developmental goals (Del Boca & Mancini, 2013; Walsh, 2012; Zimmerman, 2013). These authors highlight the need to consider these and other family strengths in the design of intervention programs oriented to families and children living in poverty and vulnerable conditions.

Another example of research that has focused on parents' strengths in families living in poverty was developed by Carbonell and her colleagues in her research group on development, affect, and cognition at Universidad Javeriana (Carbonell et al., 2015). This research group has focused on the quality of parent-child attachment relationships in families living in poverty. Similar to other research on parent-child relationships (e.g., Shonkoff & Phillips, 2000), they found that sensitive parenting was positively associated with indicators of children's cognitive, motor, linguistic, social, and emotional development, in their sample of displaced families living in poverty. Also, their results suggest that, even when parents who participated in the study had experienced rejection and severe discipline from their own parents, they were able to exhibit sensitive caregiving toward their children (Carbonell et al., 2015). This finding is particularly relevant to the design of policies and intervention programs, because it shows that parents could improve the quality of their caregiving behaviors if they establish positive close relationships during their adulthood that provide them with the emotional security they lacked growing up in their families.

In summary, an integrative approach that incorporates bioecological, contextual, and transactional components allows a more comprehensive analysis of the different influential factors that affect children's development when they live under vulnerable conditions. The relations these children establish with different agents from the close microsystems (family members, educational institutions, neighborhoods, community), as well as with elements from more distant contexts (health institutions and governmental organizations, public policies) play important roles in their developmental trajectories. The characteristics and dynamics families develop during their different stages should be considered an important input in the design of intervention programs oriented to promote their well-being.

Programs and Policies for Children in Vulnerable Conditions

According to Navarro (2005), one strategy to decrease poverty rates in Latin America has focused on economic growth and its main objective consists in working on the distribution of income and the search for economic equilibrium. A second strategy concentrates on two goals: improving infrastructure (e.g., roads, communications systems) and investing in human capital (e.g., education, skills). This last section of the chapter will discuss policy efforts that have invested in human capital by improving the quality of life of children in vulnerable conditions in Colombia. These social policies for children and families living in poverty have primarily focused on improving access to health services, monitoring children's nutrition, and improving school attendance (Carrillo et al., 2012).

In previous analyses of social policies in Colombia (Carrillo & Ripoll-Núñez, 2014; Carrillo et al., 2012), we have concluded that they can be characterized as focusing on reducing the effects of poverty on children's outcomes, and holding an implicit family perspective (Bogenschneider, 2006). Therefore, parents and other family members are seen as instrumental to programs that seek to improve children's health, nutrition, and school attendance, but the family is not conceived of as a system where transactions between its members can protect children from the effects of poverty. Thus, social programs lack specific goals and actions to improve family functioning in areas that are key to nurture children's development such as parenting practices, family communication, and problem-solving, and couple dynamics (Carrillo & Ripoll-Núñez, 2014; Carrillo et al., 2012).

One of the main functions of families is to guarantee the best possible conditions for an optimal development of its members (Anderson & Sabatelli, 2011).Therefore, families develop different strengths and skills that help them pursue their developmental and well-being goals. Sheridan et al. (2013) suggest that the promotion of resilience should be based on a family-centered approach that follows four main principles: "identifying family needs in their particular context; use individuals' strengths and family positive competences to mobilize resources and promote abilities; use social networks as a source of support, and use help from professionals to enhance or acquire competences" (p. 9).

As mentioned above, policies oriented to vulnerable children and families in Colombia are focused primarily in poverty. As a result of poverty, families lack economic, emotional, and cultural resources, which prevents them from maintaining the integral development and well-being of all its members (Ministry of Health and Social Protection of Colombia, 2012). During the last decade, the Colombian government has made significant progress in the development and implementation of public policies oriented toward helping families who live under vulnerable conditions. One example of these programs, the "Weaving Links, Weaving Dreams, Weaving Life from Early Childhood" developed in 2009 by the Colombian Institute of Family Welfare, the Ministry of Education, and the International Organization for Migrations, focused on the promotion of family resilience as a protective factor for children at risk of involvement with armed groups. Other examples of policies and programs emerged from the National Development Plan for 2010–2014 and 2014–2018 (National Department of Planning, 2010, 2014). One of the main objectives in those plans was to "guarantee minimal competences and strengthening the capacities of people living in extreme poverty for their effective social and productive inclusion" (Velásquez Santa, 2017). One of these initiatives was "Families with Welfare" developed by the Colombian Institute for the Welfare of Families and the Observatory for Peace (2009; Colombian Institute for the Welfare of Families, 2017). This program is oriented toward families living in vulnerable conditions due to economic or social risks and families with children whose basic rights need to be restored. The specific goals of this initiative are congruent with some of the principles of family-centered programs to promote resilience; that is, to identify families' needs and strengths and use them to broaden and enhance their abilities to care for each other, to learn positive strategies to solve conflict, and to use their family network (extended family, neighbors, and community services) for support.

In sum, the existing policies have laid an important foundation for the formulation of programs that focus on family resources for building positive relations and coping skills that promote the well-being of its members. Although these policies have responded to different needs of Colombian families, it is important that the policymakers be mindful of the diversity in the conceptualization of the family and family structures by geographical region, cultural beliefs, and ethnic composition, as well as by age and gender relations.

Final Comments

This chapter focused on the children's socioemotional development within the context of parent-child relationships, when families face the challenges of poverty. Relevant theoretical perspectives to the study of families and children living in poverty as well as research studies on protective and risk factors were discussed. Although the studies reviewed in this chapter on children and families living in poverty in Colombia don't account for all existing research on this topic, it is important to highlight the quality of the research that has been conducted in this country. This body of research includes both contemporary theoretical perspectives on development and a variety of methods to understand the complex interactions between poverty and human development. Based on these strengths of existing studies, it is clear that Colombian researchers are following international tendencies in the study of risk and protective factors for families and children living in poverty. However, researchers should strive to overcome some limitations such as: a) cross-sectional instead of longitudinal and multilevel research designs that allow for the evaluation of causal relations and interactions among factors; b) evaluation of moderating and mediating variables in the relation between poverty and children's development. As shown in existing studies, parenting beliefs, socialization experiences in their families of origin, as well as mother's age and child's gender need to be further studied.

With regard to social policies for families living in poverty in Colombia, an important limitation is their underlying conceptualization of poverty as a one-dimensional construct that focuses mainly on the lack of income. The lack of recognition of the diverse vulnerable conditions families face in different sociocultural contexts have often led to "emergency programs, compensatory measures and partial relief plans in the face of situations of extreme deprivation ... their transitory nature [of these policies] makes their results disappear when the stimulus that generated them stop" (Sunkel, 2006, p.28). Given these public policy constraints, we highlight here the relevance of considering a wider conception of vulnerability when developing intervention programs and public policies aimed at strengthening family well-being and resilience. In this regard, programs should involve those resources and capacities that enable family members to cope with such insecurities, resist them, and generate opportunities to overcome those risk situations (Moser, 1998, cited by Sunkel, 2006).

This is congruent with the ideas proposed by Sen (1999) who favors an approach to the phenomenon from a perspective of capabilities. The capabilities of individuals refer to the possibilities that they have to choose certain courses of action that will lead them to achieve their life objectives or goals (Sen, 1999). This conception of vulnerability should lead to a different emphasis in poverty reduction and eradication programs which goes beyond restoring the minimum conditions for survival (i.e., access to basic services). In other words, a broader perspective on poverty would involve: a) including the notion of capabilities in the study and intervention strategies for families living in poverty; and b) enhancing family resources that contribute to the development of their potential and well-being (Robeyns, 2005, 2006).

The programs and policies developed in Colombia to date have allowed the accumulation of experiences and lessons learned in relation to the design and implementation of interventions oriented to the vulnerable children and families. However, there is still a need to develop alternative models of intervention that: a) are based on research on the characteristics of family functioning in different regions of the country and, in particular, on the strategies they employ to address difficulties associated with poverty and displacement; b) are co-constructed with families and other community actors so that their perspectives on family well-being as the central axis for the development of peaceful coexistence within the family group and with the immediate environment; and c) incorporate a perspective on family resilience that recognizes specific dimensions of intervention such as beliefs, patterns of interaction, and communication.

Lastly, we would like to conclude this chapter by citing Bogenschneider and Corbett (2010) who suggest, we need "research-minded policy makers and policy-minded researchers" to work for the well-being of children and their families. Programs should go beyond the problem or deficit model and adopt positive approaches that consider well-being as the main focus in the construction of healthy and secure family environments.

2
Family-Based Developmental Intervention
Community-Based Participatory Research in a Brazilian Low-Income Neighborhood

Bruna Larissa Seibel, Paul Springer, Cody Hollist, Lisiane Rech, Luiza Piccoli, Carmen Luiza C. Fernandes, Olga Falceto, and Silvia Koller

Introduction

When working with Latino families in any context, it is essential to conceptualize the problem using an ecological perspective. This perspective suggests that multiple factors at multiple systemic levels intersect and influence individuals' well-being (Bronfenbrenner, 1979). In particular, the ecological perspective lends itself well to understanding the structural, developmental, cultural, and familial factors that impact Latino families and individuals (Ayon et al., 2010). From this perspective, we can attune to developmental challenges that children are encountering, while tapping into the strengths associated with Latino culture (Hancock, 2005). This is particularly critical when developing interventions that can be applied to the Latin American context. For example, within the Latino culture, the value of familism is highly valued, and has consistently been found to be a protective factor for Latino families as this cultural value has been linked to positive health outcomes, including lower levels of substance and drug abuse (Carlo et al., 2007; Gil, Wagner, & Vega, 2000; Unger et al., 2002, 2004), and decreased likelihood of child maltreatment (Coohey, 2001). Involvement of the family when addressing developmental issues is especially critical. However, traditional approaches to intervention and treatment often fail to include the family in both gathering data and utilizing them in the intervention process. This we believe is a mistake.

When developing interventions, especially with Latino families, researchers need to be attuned to cultural factors that are in play, and how interventions can impact participant's relationships with their families and community. Literature clearly demonstrates that Latino families value family loyalty, closeness, and the well-being of the nuclear and extended family above the individual (Ayon et al., 2010). Consequently, it is critical to understand the role that families play in the development, and maintenance of a problem, as well as their resources to overcome difficulties. Until this is understood, it is difficult to develop interventions that can make a difference. Approaches such as community-based participatory research (CBPR), are especially sensitive to culture and family developmental issues; as they engage families, communities, and key stakeholders, in not only understanding the problem, but in building community capacity in developing solutions.

The aim of this chapter is to present the "Flourishing Through Education Program," an ecological/systemic intervention program focused on engaging at risk youth and their families, to prevent and reduce school dropout in a low-income community in Southern Brazil. The neighborhood identified for this intervention has some of the highest rates of violence and drug trafficking in Porto Alegre (1.5 million inhabitants), which were closely related to the increase in school dropout rates. To combat this increasing trend, the researchers developed a CBPR project, which included the participation of families and community members in understanding the problem and developing local solutions based on the real needs of this community. This methodology is particularly helpful when addressing community problems, because it focuses on engaging community members in solution building, and elevates them as equal partners in the research process. This process also helps build community capacity by identifying and mobilizing key stakeholders who could help champion the cause that is based on a systemic understanding of the problem as well as allow for a developmental perspective when developing interventions.

To facilitate this process, teams from the healthcare unit, the local public school situated in the neighborhood, as well as community leaders and parents in the community were invited to participate. These individuals became the key stakeholders in championing the cause, as well as partners in this research and intervention endeavor. In collaboration with the key stakeholders, a mixed-method study was designed. This approach was decided on because it was believed that both a qualitative and quantitative approach would help us, first, develop a deeper and richer understanding of the problem; and, second, allow us to utilize quantitative measures to determine the effectiveness of the intervention.

Contextualizing the Problem

While Brazil is the fifth most populous country in the world and has the ninth largest economy, it is a country of inequality and poverty (UN Statistics Division, 2006). In fact, despite Brazil's rapidly growing economy, approximately, 11.8 million people live on less than $1.25 a day (World Bank, 2009), and over 50 million Brazilians are living in inadequate housing (World Urban Forum, 2010). This economic inequality can be seen in every major city in Brazil, and impacts the community, families, and their quality of life.

Several challenges associated with poverty impact the community's ability to address crime, school dropout rates, and quality of life among its residents. These challenges are almost always surrounded by high rates of crime and drug trafficking. With few employment opportunities or extracurricular activities for young residents in poverty-stricken communities, these young residents are being lured into drug trafficking with the promise of regular pay, well beyond the average monthly salary for residents. Compounding the problem with drug trafficking is the violence associated with gang activity to control distribution of power. In 2015, Brazil's homicide rate was between 20 and 25 persons per 100,000 inhabitants, placing it in the top 20 countries in the world (Datasus, 2017). In addition, the lack of governmental resources for healthcare and schooling makes drug trafficking a more attractive solution to the poverty problem for youth.

This is the context in which this study was implemented in the city of Porto Alegre, a city situated in the southern region of Brazil. The community identified in Porto Alegre, was the Vila Jardim, a neighborhood known for its high violence rates, gang affiliation, and drug trafficking. In 2015, when this intervention took place, Porto Alegre ranked 19th on the list of the most violent cities in Brazil, with a homicide rate of 34.73 per 100,000 people (Forbes, 2016).

The Vila Jardim is part of the eastern zone of Porto Alegre, and is considered one of the most dangerous communities in the city. This community is heterogeneous, made up of a mix of inhabitants who migrated from rural regions of Brazil as well as low- and high-income families from other regions of Porto Alegre. Similar to other neighborhoods, this mix of low-income to high-income families created additional tension among community members, with high-income families choosing to send their children to private schools, and to generally disengage from community problems. The community is home to some of the largest and most expensive homes in the city, right next to homemade shacks made from construction scraps, with some homes lacking basic necessities, such as plumbing and running water.

According to municipal data, in the Vila Jardim there were 36.7 homicides per 100,000 inhabitants in 2010. For comparative purposes, in other parts of the city, the average homicide rate was 7.2 during the same time period. In 2014, 66.67% of the deaths of people between the ages of 15 and 29 years (in the Vila Jardim) occurred due to homicides. Of the 31 designated neighborhoods (in Porto Alegre), the Vila Jardim is the fifth most dangerous (Observatório da Cidade de Porto Alegre, 2014).

The elementary school dropout rate is much higher in Vila Jardim than the citywide rate. In 2014, the dropout rate was 3.74% of students in 2014, compared to 1.03%. The illiteracy rate is also much higher accounting for approximately 2.16% in the neighborhood (Observatório da Cidade de Porto Alegre, 2014). The average years of schooling is also disproportionately lower in the Vila Jardim, with students completing an average of 7.63 years of schooling (Observatório da Cidade de Porto Alegre, 2010). It is important to highlight that these averages also include the wealthy population, who have significantly more education, which disproportionately raises the average.

Poverty is clearly a major problem in this community that contributes to such high school dropout rates. Data indicate that the average income for each head of household is 3.95 minimum salaries (a metric used to combat inflation that establishes a monetary value for the poverty line). However, it is important to note that 19.63% of families have incomes below the minimum salary and 51.14% of these families receive only two minimum salaries. To further highlight the disparities between families with means compared to those who are living in poverty, only 7.61% of the families living in the Vila Jardim have an income that exceeds 10 monthly minimum salaries, which clearly distorts community socioeconomic level means (Observatório da Cidade de Porto Alegre, 2010).

Understanding the developmental impact that socioeconomic issues have on young children and families is essential. Literature supports the fact that poverty impacts both psychosocial development and the quality of social and family interactions. Bronfenbrenner (1979; 1996) argues that individuals are part of the environment in which they live, transforming and being transformed in these relationships. Likewise, there seems to be a reciprocal relationship in how learning occurs, in which individuals, families, and the community (and society at large) interact and exchange information for adaptation to the environment (Martins & Branco, 2001; Pearson & Rao, 2003).

Studies have shown there are several community attributes that influence, for example, the quality of family relations, including poverty, precarious housing, and restriction to public health services access, poor social support, and exposure to risk situations (Furstenberg, 1993; Leventhal & Brooks-Gunn, 2000; Pinderhughes et al., 2007; Sampson, 1992; Wilson, 1987, 1991a, 1991b).

Coercive practices in the educational process are also more frequent, especially with children and families who are living in vulnerable contexts (Knutson et al., 2005; Mistry et al., 2002; Pinderhughes et al., 2000; Ribas et al., 2003). The main explanation is that economic difficulties generate adverse living conditions, which in turn impact individuals', families', and community members' psychological well-being—thus, increasing the levels of aggression in family relationships as well as within the community (Conger & Donnellan, 2007; Gershoff et al., 2007; Giles-Sims & Lockhart, 2007; Shor, 2007). It is clear that low-income families who live in poor neighborhoods are more likely to adopt coercive practices due to the perceived need for greater control over their children (Shor, 2000).

Parental neglect has also been linked in part to adverse material conditions, stress generation, exacerbating the challenges of parenting and changes in the life cycle (Kazdin & Whitley, 2003). Thus, it would compose a cycle in which stress would decrease the parental emotional availability and hinder their ability to socialize their children, which continues to increase parental stress and disengagement.

Strengths of the Community

While the Vila Jardim has many challenges, three factors made this community especially appealing to apply the CBPR methodology. First, this community has a devoted and committed healthcare presence, the Posto de Saude. This community medical clinic has been serving this low-income community since 1991. This team has worked tirelessly to meet the medical and mental healthcare needs of the community for nearly 27 years. The healthcare unit is made up of a multidisciplinary team of doctors, nurses, community health agents, administrative staff, hygiene and safety staff, and all are engaged in the community on a daily basis. Examples of the programming developed by this medical clinic include: the Gestation and Puerperium Follow-Up Program, Monitoring of Child Growth and Development, Home Care Programs, Family Therapy, Smoking Cessation, Coexistence and Literacy, Health and Welfare, Mental and Family Health, just to name a few. This team also has a strong history of research and intervention work with the Universidade Federal do Rio Grande do Sul (UFRGS), which over the years has worked to make improvements in several areas related to healthcare and the quality of life of the families resident in Vila Jardim.

Second, the community has a devoted and committed school team that has been struggling to address the high dropout rates in their elementary school. This school has been embedded in the community since 1968. In 2016 the school had 189 students from first to ninth grade. Among the challenges in the school is the diversity of ages in each grade, as it is not uncommon for much older students to be in the first few years of schooling. In addition, the decreasing number of students who continue in school from year to year increases dramatically, with only a few students who start and finish the ninth grade. Teacher reports suggest that a large percentage of students live in a particularly poor area of the Vila Jardim, in which a high percentage of their families are already involved in drug trafficking.

Third, there has been a long history of research and collaboration in the Vila Jardim among the UFRGS and the Grupo Hospitalar Conceição (GHC) the administrative entity that oversees the services of the clinic. This research collaboration led by Dr Olga Falceto and Dr Carmen Fernandes developed into a longitudinal study of family development of the Vila Jardim. This partnership focused on understanding not only the risk factors associated with child development specifically among vulnerable families, but also what the protective and resilience factors were in this population. In the group of students there is a subgroup that is part of a 20-year cohort that started with the perception in the health service that a very large percentage of the babies who were born were weaned early (at less than 6 months) and the index was approximately 30% of live births and that they had breastfeeding conditions and were residents in the territory of the health service. Throughout the four phases of the study, the identification of risk factors and vulnerabilities were consolidated.

A total of five waves of data collection occurred beginning in 1998 and ending in 2017. Results of this longitudinal study led to many important findings that facilitated changes in the delivery of healthcare in the community, as well as adding to an important body of literature for vulnerable families in Brazil. For example, the study shed important light on the impact of marital relationships on maternal depression (Hollist et al., 2007; Stutzman et al., 2009). It also led to the validation of an internationally used instrument to assess the quality of marital relationships among those in Brazilian samples (Hollist et al., 2012). In addition, studies were able to identify how lower cognitive development in students is highly associated with families with psychosocial difficulties and that the quality of the social support network is directly associated with the mental health of the mothers (Falceto et al., 2004; Seibel, 2016).

Finally, the importance of a strong and heterogeneous support network was identified to facilitate strengths and resilience of these families despite the vulnerabilities that they face (i.e. Seibel et al., 2017). Ultimately, what has been impressive about this longitudinal study is that as results were identified, the medical clinic was responsive to suggestions from the researchers, so they could better meet the needs of the community.

In the most recent wave of data collection, a new problem emerged: the violence associated with drug trafficking in the region was leading to high rates of deaths among the adolescent population involved in drug trafficking. Also a connection was found between the high incidences of school dropout and its association with drug trafficking and violence among the adolescents in Vila Jardim.

This new information helped the researchers recognize the urgent need in this community to better understand their vulnerabilities leading to higher rates of school dropout and also deaths of their adolescents, but also to find possible interventions to better assist in their problems. This resulted in the university team proposing a new extension project at the UFRGS, called the "Flourishing Through Education Program." The focus of this project was to develop an intervention that would make a difference in preventing school dropout and drug trafficking in the community. Yet, a methodology or intervention was yet to be chosen. The researchers wanted an intervention that was community driven to build community strengths, in a way that changes could continue long after the researchers had left the community. It was through a collaborative effort with researchers from the University of Nebraska-Lincoln, in the United States, and UFRGS that the decision to implement a CBPR methodology was decided.

Why Community-Based Participatory Research?

CBPR is an approach that is particularly useful when working with disadvantaged populations. In fact, problems associated with disparities of education, poverty, and healthcare among disadvantaged populations are receiving more and more attention worldwide (Minkler et al., 2003). While research looking at these challenges has resulted in quality interventions, much has been ineffective in achieving the desired outcomes because of failure to present the perspective of those who truly understand the problem, the community members. Without including these perspectives we may unwittingly exacerbate problems that disempower community members. This frequently results in interventions that have little long-term effect, because community members are distrustful of the researchers, and their interventions.

CBPR is a research approach that can be used to engage community members as active participants in the research process. This approach maximizes the benefits to the community, as participants are asked to provide their own expertise which is critical in the formulation of the problem, and identification of the strengths and resources in the community and how results and interventions should be implemented (O'Fallon & Dearry, 2002). A hallmark of this methodology is that there is a strong emphasis on looking at research being done "with" community members as opposed to "on" community members (Johnson & Olshansky, 2016). In other words, this approach engages participants as collaborators in the research process (Robinson et al., 2014) where all participants are viewed as equal members of the research team.

CBPR is particularly effective when working with vulnerable populations because it is action oriented, socially conscious, and application focused (Bischoff et al., 2016). More importantly CBPR is a long-term process that emphasizes relationship building and investment in the community being studied. There is a clear understanding that both researcher and community members bring important expertise to the table that is critical in the research process. For example, the researcher contributes their expertise in research methodology and scholarship, while community members bring their expertise in what it means to live in the community and the issues most important to them (Bischoff et al., 2016).

One reason why CBPR can be so effective is because outcomes must be grounded in the context and culture of the disadvantaged community being served (Bischoff et al., 2016). Without this understanding, interventions may never truly meet the local needs of the community being studied. Engagement with community members increases the researchers cultural and contextual understandings, which leads to interventions that alleviate inequality and oppression, while increasing participation. In other words, CBPR allows the researchers to build on the already rich social support network that is present between the school, medical clinic, and families. Systemically (Bronfenbrenner, 1979, 1996), the concept of strong social support networks only empowers individuals, families, and communities in being more competent in supporting themselves and one another in close and meaningful relationships. Utilizing key stakeholders from multiple levels is also a strength of this approach, as both the microsystem and mesosystems are considered as important socializing agents, which broadens the network of the social relations of individuals and contributes to their development (Zamberlan & Biasoli-Alves, 1997). As we build community capacity, by including key stakeholders (including families), those who understand the problem intimately, we can harness the protective functioning of a social support network to enable positive adaptive outcomes (Rutter, 1987; Yunes, 2001) which can modify the interpretation of individuals' experiences, and empower change (Masten & Reed, 2002).

The Process of CBPR

According to Israel and colleagues (1998), there are eight key principles of CBPR that can be applied when working with vulnerable populations: (1) recognizing that the community is the unit of study; (2) building on the strengths already present in the community; (3) continually facilitating collaboration and partnership in each phase of the research; (4) integrating knowledge and action; (5) promoting the alleviation of social inequality by co-learning; (6) using an interactive process; (7) focusing on wellness and an ecological perspective of health; and (8) partnering in the dissemination of the research finding.

Recognizing that the community is the unit of study is essential to CBPR in the need to understand the community in which the individual experiences the problem. This requires the engagement of community stakeholders from a variety of sources, who have had a vested interest not only in the problem but in finding a solution. This should include individuals from a diversity of experiences including teachers, religious leaders, mental health and medical providers, as well as families from the community. The diversity of expertise will allow for a more robust understanding of the complexities within the community, as well as solutions building.

Building on Community Strengths

When working with underserved communities, one error that researchers may make is to not recognize the strengths and resources that already exist. Failing to do so disempowers community members and creates a context where the researcher becomes elevated as the expert and they begin to impose their view of the solutions. Conversely, building on community strengths empowers community partners, and brings resources that may be critical to developing interventions and solutions. More importantly building on community strengths and resources creates a sense of competence and hopefulness among community members, as members begin to see themselves as capable of addressing the needs within their community.

Continual Collaboration and Partnership

A hallmark of CBPR is a fostering of collaboration among researchers and community members; however, in order to collaborate effectively, individuals need to see that the researcher cares about the community, and that they truly want to include the community in the research process. Unfortunately, in many communities, there is an inherent mistrust of researchers. It takes time and active engagement to bring the right people to the table who can teach the researcher about the context and culture of the community. Entering the community and developing the trust of key stakeholders is only the beginning of the collaboration. In many instances the researcher will need to suspend their biases and expertise in order to learn from the community members, and to elevate them to equal partners in the research process. Traditionally in CBPR, focus groups have been an important means to foster collaboration. Through this process, the research team can begin to elevate everyone's voices and perspectives in such a way that they can begin to define the research problem and identified goals for the community. It is critical that all solutions and advancement of local initiatives be community driven.

Integrating Knowledge and Action

As the researcher and community members work together, it is critical that whatever data are gathered, via community assessments, focus groups, or individual interviews, lead to interventions that mobilize existing resources and community members with specific expertise that can make an impact on the identified goals for the community.

Promoting the Alleviation of Social Inequality by Co-Learning

As researchers and community members learn from one another, they begin to develop research questions that are critical in the data collection process. In fact, Bradbury and Reason (2008) argued that the knowledge community members acquire and how they put that learning into effect is a key indicator of success in this approach. One can argue that co-learning actually builds community capacity, and empowers community members to make a difference that leads to social and/or community changes in underserved communities.

CBPR Is an Iterative Process

Ultimately, CBPR is an iterative process of engagement, problem identification, solution generation, planning, implementation, and feedback (Robinson et al., 2005). In other words, each phase of the research process informs the others, leading to a continuous learning process. Consequently, researchers and community members need to be flexible enough to adapt solution generation and interventions based on data that they are constantly receiving from participants and community members.

Focusing on an Ecological Perspective

As a means to help take a more holistic approach when entering communities, it is helpful to take an ecological approach (Bronfenbrenner, 1976). This approach includes looking at environmental, social, interpersonal, psychological, and biological factors within every community. Being overt with this perspective will also help community members and participants to think outside of the box at what factors may be contributing to problems, and what solutions may be utilized.

Partnering in the Dissemination of the Research Findings

Finally, because community members participate in the research process, it is important to recognize that these data are owned by all members of the team. Consequently, researchers should consult the CBPR team prior to submitting materials for publication, in addition to including members of the team to participate in future manuscripts or dissemination of the work. This ongoing feedback of data is a critical aspect of this work, as it acknowledges the contributions of all (Israel et al., 1998).

How CBPR Was Planned and Applied: "Flourishing Through Education Program"

The Flourishing Through Education Program was designed with the purpose of developing a community-driven intervention focused on addressing the dropout rates of students in the local elementary school. The researchers recognized that if the interventions were going to make a difference then the proposed action must be accepted and supported by the community, and that it would have to enhance the psychosocial protective factors for these youths and families. As a result, the solutions needed to build on existing resources, so as to build community capacity and competence in addressing future community problems.

What was different from this project than the previous research studies done in this community was that we engaged local community members (including families) to better understand the community problem, prior to generating solutions. Whereas past studies typically included the medical and university system only, this study aimed to increase its reach by including additional agencies and community members who could expand understanding of the social, environmental, interpersonal, and psychological factors that contributed to the high dropout rates (facilitating an ecological perspective).

CBPR was identified as the perfect methodology for achieving the aims of this project. Through the implementation of CBPR we sought to understand, in partnership with the community, what the real challenges and barriers were for families, children, teachers, and healthcare professionals in addressing their dilemmas; as well as what resources might exist that could help us understand and tackle this problem from a different angle. By taking a more ecological perspective we were able to start thinking outside of the box, and recognize what key resources exist and how we can collectively apply them in seeking solutions to the demands we were encountering.

It was determined that a mixed-method analysis would help us better understand the problem, and facilitate the greatest engagement of community partners in the research process. Both quantitative and qualitative questionnaires were developed for four different groups of people, which would help paint a clearer picture of the problems of the community and its potential solutions. These groups included: (1) teachers and the administrators at the school; (2) a team of professionals and agents of the community health center; (3) community leaders, and families living in the region; and (4) a sample of teenagers from the community. Due to the violence during the data collection process, the research team was unable to interview and assess all of the community leaders, families, and teenagers living in the region. However, the data that we did collect provided an important voice in guiding the direction the team took. We believed that these voices were critical to developing interventions that were sensitive to the family needs and unique culture of the community. How better to understand the problem than by asking those were are "intimately" faced with this problem on a daily basis; which is a strength of the CBPR methodology. As we move forward in this project, we hope and expect to access these groups in the future.

The mixed-method design used convergent analysis, since qualitative and quantitative data collected and analyzed together provided a more detailed and in-depth understanding of the processes (Creswell, 2013). The questionnaires were collected using an iPad. This format made it easier for participants to complete the questionnaires and increased their sense of anonymity in the process. The researchers used a platform called Qualtrics, which enabled direct tabulation of the data, which facilitated the analysis process. The methodology also included a focus group with the school team and the healthcare team.

The data collection started with the application of the questionnaires with the key community leaders and adolescents. However, due to the increase in violence and territorial disputes over drug trafficking in the region, the collection process with the adolescents had to be suspended. Despite this challenge, preliminary results indicated that the violence in the community was not only creating a context in which families felt unsafe, but also made children more vulnerable to becoming involved in drug trafficking and dropping out of school. With these data, the research team became convinced that interventions needed to involve both the healthcare professionals and teachers in some way, so families would feel supported. It also was clear that interventions needed to be developed and implemented so as to improve the psychosocial processes of the children and families, and occur in a location free from the influence of drug traffickers, so families would feel safe to attend.

Data from the healthcare team confirmed that the high rates of school dropout and financial and social inequalities were two of the most significant obstacles in the community. The healthcare workers who lived in the region also acknowledged the powerful role that the drug traffickers and gangs played on the future of young children, and on family safety. Consequently, the social inequality present in the neighborhoods as well as the "professionalization" of drug trafficking were identified as the most significant key risk factors for the research participants.

Because of the families' high rates of poverty, drug traffickers offered children the opportunity to make quick and easy money, in exchange for loyalty and protection. Once the child began trafficking, called "airplaning" (e.g. those who transport the drugs without generating suspicion from the police), it became nearly impossible for them to stop. Those who attempted to quit, were met with violence, threats to their families, and even death. Unfortunately, for families in extreme poverty, with low educational levels and few job opportunities, drug trafficking provided one of the only stable incomes for survival.

Data from the school teachers also validated what the healthcare team reported. In summary, the financial and social inequalities were not only causing deterioration in the health and wellness of their students and their families, but were affecting how the students and families felt about education. As we explored the data more thoroughly we were surprised to discover the negative impact this had on the teachers' own physical and mental health. For example, 35% of the teachers explicitly stated that their physical and mental health was being affected by their work. In fact, over 60% of the teachers reporting experiencing physical and/or verbal aggression from their students, with an additional 30% reporting that they even experienced aggression from parents. The teachers indicated that they were at a loss as to what they could do, and realized that if nothing was done, student dropout rates would only increase.

The CBPR team realized that if we wanted to make a difference we needed to improve the psychosocial well-being of not only the children and families, but also of the teachers. Both the families and teachers needed additional support for interventions to be meaningful and gain traction. As a community-based team we determined that the first source of intervention should begin with the school teachers. Based on extensive literature, we knew that improving student-teacher relationships and parent-school engagement, we would improve our likelihood of combatting the high dropout rates. We also recognized that as we increased community engagement as a whole in the child's educational experience, it would serve as an additional protective factor for these students.

There were several reasons why we decided to use the school as the main point of intervention for these families. First, the school was the only place in the community in which we could develop and implement interventions free from the influence of the drug traffickers (due to the violence in the community). Second, the school was well established and had excellent relationships with families in the community, even among families that were involved in drug trafficking. As a result, the school was a "neutral" environment for families, free from conflict and could involve all members from the community. Third, the healthcare unit was already involved within the school, as these two buildings were adjacent to one another. Therefore, programs could be jointly created with the teachers and healthcare professionals, thus increasing the likelihood that the community would "buy-in" to the work being done in the schools. Elevating the school and its importance among community members and families was a very important first step to the community, since the students needed to see the school as a safe place, and an institution that could help them develop skills, while having other options than dropping out and selling drugs.

As the CBPR team immersed itself in the data as a guide for what interventions needed to be developed; we realized that the teachers were experiencing high rates of burnout and depression. We were concerned about asking the teachers to do more for their students and families when they felt so depleted and overwhelmed. We also recognized that the school teachers were capital to enhancing the student's experience in school. Because of this, the team felt that if we wanted to make a difference in the psychosocial well-being of the children, we first needed to help the teachers feel more empowered, so they had capacity to help their students have hope in their lives. The first strategy we implemented was in offering psychotherapy to the teachers, in the form of weekly individual sessions and monthly group sessions. This intervention promoted much needed space for teachers to improve their mental health, as well as providing a safe environment for the teachers to begin to support one another. This allowed the teachers to further develop a culture and community among themselves where they could support one another. This intervention also sent an important message to the teachers and helped them feel valued and validated in the work they were doing. Over time, as their overall well-being increased we began identifying interventions that could make a difference for the children and families that included the teachers' involvement.

This identification process occurred in the form of focus groups that included teachers, healthcare providers, and community activists. This focus group allowed the researchers to begin the development of collaboration with the community as equal partners in the research process. This increased community participation, as these groups felt more invested and caught the vision of how they could make a difference. As a result, they felt more ownership of the project, and that their opinions and ideas were valued. The results from these focus groups allowed the team to recognize the perceived barriers the community was struggling with as well as their strengths, which was necessary in identifying solutions that could make a difference.

Through this community-based participatory process, the community identified several initiatives that it believed would make a difference in the students' and families' lives. These initiatives while implemented on school grounds had the support of all the CBPR members, including the healthcare team members, administrators, teachers, and community activists. The first interventions utilized the school teachers and administrators in identifying students who demonstrated behavioral, emotional, or learning difficulties. Developmentally, the team recognized that in order to assist these students, an intervention needed to be developed to assist in offsetting the negative contextual factors these children were experiencing in their lives. With the permission of their parents, the students were identified and arrangements were made for them to receive psychological counseling, through the Instituto da Familia, a local marriage and family therapy center in the community. These services were provided at no cost to these students, and sent a clear message to the student and their families that the school was not giving up on them. Families felt supported, as resources were being given to their struggling students, which increased their engagement in school. As these students began utilizing the services, they reported feeling more connected with their school teachers, and an increased interest in the subjects being taught. The skills that they were being taught in therapy also had a trickle-down effect in their family relationships. Physical and verbal aggression in the school also dropped dramatically, which further enhanced the learning environment. While this intervention did not fix all of the problems, it helped students develop skills to cope with the environment they were in and to utilize new skills. This provided a strong foundation for the next intervention.

The next intervention was aimed at developing educational programming, both during and after school, that would engage students and families, and help them see the school as a resource, as opposed to a place they only visited four hours a day. The CBPR team felt that in order to develop programming that would be meaningful; they would have to elevate their students' voices and discover their interests. A survey was developed in which students were asked for their input on programs that would be of interest to them (e.g. those in the fourth through ninth grade). Once the data from the students were evaluated, the CBPR team worked with the local university and other members in the community to develop quality activities and programs that would not only be sustainable but would be viewed as important for students as such. Programming included: music and reading classes, as well as art and mural projects. For example, a "life planning workshop" was developed with the help of the students so they could explore professional opportunities that existed. Students were given resources related to governmental grants and free courses, so they could also see the potential that existed outside of their communities. As a result of this program, students reported a greater sense of belonging to the school, and many reported that school was a place where they felt safe and could pursue their dreams. In many ways, students felt like they could be active participants in their education, and that others took their suggestions, thoughts, and needs into account.

In addition to these workshops, a partnership with the Department of Education and Agronomy at the UFRGS was established. This collaborative endeavor, jointly carried out with the University of Nebraska-Lincoln led to the development of a school and communal garden. The CBPR team was particularly interested in developing this intervention because research has shown that gardening experiences for children has been shown to increase relaxation, decrease emotional disturbances (Habib & Doherty, 2007), and can increase interpersonal skills (Robinson & Zajicek, 2005). In addition to improving the socioemotional health of the children, we saw this as an opportunity to create a safe space for the community to learn how to plant and grow their own food. The CBPR team wanted this garden to be a source of pride for community members, and a place where families could also learn about healthy eating and family meals. This garden became a place where students' learning could extend beyond the textbook and help students feel closer the land and the environment in which they lived.

As time went on the garden space began to be used across multiple subject areas such as plant handling, mathematics, and biology. The garden was also made available to other members of the community. For example, an elderly group in the community contributed to the maintenance of the sites. They also assisted in identifying and collecting medicinal herbs and recipes which were offered to the children and their families. The families were also invited to contribute to the garden. As families left the violence of the community and entered the school garden, parents were better able to share and teach their children in a safe space.

The third intervention came out of data that suggested there is a need for the revitalization of school spaces. Respondents of the survey reported that the school was visually uninviting, which added to the negative feelings for the students and teachers. As a way to motivate students to feel more welcomed, several "revitalization" projects were developed. These included painting murals in the school, as well as several planting projects (e.g. plants, flowers, and fruit trees). Students and families were then invited to participate in revitalizing and in renovating this space. Through this process students and parents became more engaged in their education, as they felt more of a sense of ownership in the school (through this new space). The school also became a space where families felt more welcomed, which also increased their investment in the school.

In collaboration with the healthcare unit another intervention was developed called the Graffitiing Generations project. This project came out of an idea presented by several healthcare members of the team, and was broadly shared with the community, so they could receive feedback on how they could best implement the project. While initially the community was skeptical of this idea, they quickly saw the benefit of this space. Together with several professional graffiti artists, who donated their time, the community worked together to revitalize this space, improving the cultural identity, self-esteem, and collectivity of the community residents. Community members have commented on how the new space has helped others become more invested in the community and one another. Families have been utilizing the space, which has increased communal interactions and bonds.

Finally, based on additional data, the CBPR teach wanted to extend an intervention to the community, to assist other at risk children and residents who might not be in school. This intervention was aimed to help increase young residents' awareness of job potentials that could exist for them, outside of trafficking. This led to the development of the first community-based manicure workshop. The aim of the workshop was to expose young people over the age of 14 to a potential career choice that would require minimal job training, yet provide a stable income. This intervention was received with enthusiasm by the community, and planted the seeds of future occupations that young students could pursue. The hope was that, by exposing students and young adults to opportunities previously out of their awareness, it would encouraging them to stay in school, while providing adults with skills that they could use to supplement their income.

Additional initiatives are being developed by this community-based team, in partnership with the neighborhood schools. Several of these initiatives include the construction of a sports complex, a judo workshop for children and adolescents, and yoga workshops for adults. The educational garden project will also be expanded, providing training for educators in the region.

Conclusion

All of these projects and interventions were born out of the implementation of the CBPR methodology with the focus of reducing school dropout rates, while strengthening family involvement and relationships. Almost all of the interventions were developed with the understanding that long-term change could only be effected if parents and families were involved in the interventions. Additionally, the team recognized that the basic psychological processes that children were experiencing, due to poverty and violence, had to be addressed. The CBPR methodology provided an avenue in which key stakeholders from the community, schools, and health clinics could come together and mobilize their existing resources to facilitate protective factors within the child/adolescent's and families' everyday life conditions. As parents and community members became more involved in the schools, student engagement increased. The CBPR team was able to mobilize these strengths that existed in the students' life more explicitly to help them feel supported and important in their educational endeavors. Students have reported that their basic psychological well-being has not only improved through opportunities to go to therapy, participate in the school garden, and increased school programming, but that they have felt heard by their teachers and other adults in the community. Previously in the schools, students were not asked to provide feedback, and so they felt they had little opportunity to be heard and better themselves. Through the CBPR process, students were asked for input and participated in bettering the school, which increased their investment in their own education. They were also able to see "real and tangible" other options, outside drug trafficking, for them in their lives.

As researchers, we felt that the CBPR process was essential in facilitating collaboration among partners. This assisted in expanding the perspective of the problem and integrating new knowledge, from an ecological perspective, into real and meaningful action that could make a difference in the psychological processes of the children and adolescents. This was accomplished as community partners (including the students) were made equal partners in the research process. This facilitated ownership not only of the problem, but of potential solutions that could be implemented to overcome these challenges. It also created buy-in by every team member, as they shared a common vision and goal. It is important to acknowledge that these interventions all occurred within a 24-month period of the implementation of this methodology. This is a striking and impressive testament to the power of this action-oriented research methodology—especially in a community where there was little hope for creating change. What is equally impressive is that these interventions involved the students and parents within the community during a time when there had previously been little investment from these groups. In this process, students and parents were empowered not only to facilitate change, but to have opportunities to enhance their own relationships with one another through meaningful activities. While it is still unclear what the long-term impact will be of these interventions on the children's and adolescent's life, we are confident that, as these programs continue, they will further enhance the psychosocial well-being of the students and families who participate.

3
Motherhood in Poverty, a Perinatal Intervention Device to Detect Psychosocial Risk

Alicia Oiberman, Manoel S. Santos, and Cynthia I. Paolini

Motherhood is a phenomenon that transcends biological aspects, acquiring a psychological, social, and cultural value.[1]

In Argentina, there are 6,808,769 women and 6,489,373 men from 14 to 49 years of age. Of these, 54% of the women and 47.7% of the men are "heads of household" (they are the only economic household provider) and within this group 2,988,314 women and 2,357,709 men live in homes where there is at least one son or daughter.

According to data obtained from the 2016 census, 32% of Argentinians are poor and 6.3% are indigent.

In Argentina, the average age in which women usually have their first child is at 23 years old. However, it has been observed that socioeconomic status is a very important factor that influences the age at which a woman becomes a mother. Thus, it can be spoken of two differentiated groups related to their age at the beginning of the maternity process: one is a group of women that begins to have children from the age of 30, belonging to a medium and high socioeconomic status; and the other, a group that initiates motherhood around the age of 20.

It was found that when a woman lives in an extremely low socioeconomic condition (indigence) it is more likely that she will become a mother, on average, three or four years earlier than those women who are in medium to high socioeconomic conditions (not poor) (Lupica, 2011).

---

[1] The present study did not receive financial support.

Alicia Oiberman, et al., *Motherhood in Poverty, a Perinatal Intervention Device to Detect Psychosocial Risk.* In: *Family and Contexts of Development.* Edited by: Mariano Rosabal-Coto and Javier Tapia-Balladares, Oxford University Press. © Oxford University Press (2025). DOI: 10.1093/oso/9780197675144.003.0004

Furthermore, level of education also plays a role and may influence the age at which women start having children (Lupica, 2011). A delay of one year to beginning motherhood has been observed as they move from a lower educational level to an immediately higher one. The exception occurs when they move from the "incomplete university level" to the "full university level," where a delay of practically three years has been observed. Thus, women with more years of formal education (full university) become mothers, on average, seven years later than those who have fewer years of formal education: 27.2 years and 20.6 years respectively (Lupica, 2011).

Regarding childhood, it has been pointed out that half of the populations in poverty are children aged between 0 and 14 years old. The number of people who live in poverty reaches almost 13 million citizens, of whom six million are children (Tuñon, 2015).

It should be noted that 14.7% of women (438,522) and 3.1% of men (72,071) are single parents—separated, divorced, widowed, or single—who live with their children and are the only economic household provider. Single parenthood could lead to a situation of disadvantage and inequality for many women and men in Argentina (Lupica, 2011).

The aim of this chapter is to describe a perinatal psychological device that allows the detection of psychosocial risk situations at the time of birth; and to present the results of its application in a hospital from the city of Florencio Varela—Province of Buenos Aires, Argentina—that provides healthcare and assistance to families in low socioeconomic situations.

The Motherhood Process as a Stage of Child Development

By the end of the nineteenth century, in the decade from 1880 to 1890, the breadth and scope of the research and the theoretical progress that had taken place led to the emergence of a new science: developmental psychology. For this reason, the nineteenth century was called "the century of the child," an expression that arose in part from the fact that, in the second half of this century, child psychology had begun to develop as a science, with scientific bases.

Until the late 1960s, developmental psychology studied the development from childhood to adolescence, because in the beginning it was thought that the development process was something that ended in adolescence. This old conception has been modified in recent years, in light of new theories and research on human development (Baltes & Schaie, 1973; Riegel,

1976, 1979). Developmental psychologists have been gradually accepting that their object of study includes the whole life of a person, and the processes of psychological change that occur in it (Palacios, 1993).

Consequently, developmental psychology is no longer confined solely to the study of development during childhood and adolescence, but to the study of the processes that occur throughout the lifespan of the human being, from birth to death. This unmistakably implies a paradigm change: the conception of a human being who develops all through life. This paradigm change led to the emergence of a new model of human development, the life cycle model (Baltes, 1987). There has been an extension and deepening of the field of study of developmental psychology, to include adulthood and, even more so, the so-called third age. There has also been an expansion toward development in the young child. Therefore, we are facing a synchronous growth that has affected all ages of life in general (Bermejo, 1994).

> This scientific interest in the development of the young child that began in the 1960s has grown to the point that in the early 1980s it constituted a vast area of study within the psychology of development called: "The development of the young child." This area of study focuses on the development during the first three years of life and the belief that early childhood (0 to 3 years) is a critical period for further development. (Mallol & Riba, 1994)

The growing interest in the study of the development of the baby also implies a new change of paradigm regarding the possibilities of the baby. The baby is no longer thought of as a passive little child without any abilities other than reflexes, but rather as an active individual (Brazelton & Cramer, 1991).

This change of paradigm in the conceptualization of the baby substantiates the relevance of the first years of life for further development and leads to a growing interest in the evaluation of child development in early infancy, aiming at prevention and early intervention. This change would not have been possible if a reconceptualization of the baby had not occurred at the same time, because it was not even thinkable when the newborn was considered as completely passive (Doménech & Gómez de Terreros, 2003). Research supports the conception that the young child, the baby, has a much broader level of organization and competence than previously thought.

Moreover, much progress has been made in the study of capacities of the newborn and in the first months after birth, and more recently, since the twenty-first century, the belief that the prenatal stage is of great incidence and relevance has also been established in terms of later development. Currently, this development is conceived not only as a process that occurs during childhood and adolescence but that begins much earlier, at the prenatal stage.

For this reason it is extremely important to consider the process of motherhood as an inseparable part in the process of child development. Since it is impossible to think of the baby as an individual isolated from his or her parents and the circumstances and context in which develop the processes of pregnancy, delivery, and puerperium. Those factors influence directly and indirectly the prenatal and postnatal development of young children. We understand the process of motherhood as a developmental stage during the lifespan, the first stage in the development of a child.

The Motherhood and Mothering Process: Theoretical Basis

The process of motherhood—including pregnancy, childbirth, and puerperium—represents a vital and developmental crisis that affects the entire family group.

The woman will be able to overcome that crisis according to: her personal history, her psychosocial situation, the characteristics of her personality, and the place that this child occupies in the historical linkage of that family (Oiberman, 2000).

Motherhood and fatherhood are vital and represent developmental crises which produce psychological changes in women and men who are going to become parents.

The way in which mothers and fathers go through this crisis depends on a multiplicity of factors.

Historically, there has been a passage from the concept of imposed motherhood to chosen motherhood. Contraception arising from the 1970s has given women the possibility of delaying motherhood, as well as deciding whether or not to get pregnant and choose motherhood. However, in our society, having a baby entails both a choice and a social and biological imposition (Knibiehler, 2001; Oiberman, 2005). There are many implicit social impositions that lead most couples to reproduce with the feeling that they have made a free choice. The main effector of this normative imposition would be the previous generation. This imposition does not seem to be linked to religious beliefs; however, it could be another independent source of demand to procreate (Oiberman & Santos, 2015).

Several authors have described the psychological processes that occur in the mother and how these may affect the caregiving she provides to her newborn child. Donald Winnicott (1958, 1981, 1987) conceptualized the mother's empathic ability to understand and respond appropriately to her baby's needs. Winnicott has called this unconscious mechanism of regression the "Primary Maternal preoccupation." This psychological condition of the mother is a state of extreme sensitivity that allows her to fully identify with the needs of the baby in order to be able to satisfy them.

For this normal process of motherhood to occur, the woman must be psychologically healthy, which is based not only on her psychic state but also includes her social and family context.

This maternal (psychological) state is complemented by a state of absolute dependence from the baby. It is the continuous care of the mother for the baby that allows the development of that child to begin, without compromising the baby's "body-mind" unit. Consequently, the function of maternal care in these early stages will especially be the "holding." The holding function is a basic factor of maternal care that corresponds to an emotional holding of the baby.

When this holding function fails, Winnicott calls it "environmental failure." Here the concept "environment" refers to the mother and the care she provides to the baby. At the earliest stage of infancy, when the child is in a state of "absolute dependence" on the mother, such a failure can have very serious effects on later biopsychological development, causing an experience of maximum vulnerability (Winnicott, 1981).

Spitz (1973) proposes a similar concept, referred to as "deep sensibility." The mother acquires a deep sensibility—referred as "almost magic" toward her baby—where the mother, during pregnancy and the immediate period following childbirth, finds once again a coenesthetic perception that is normally absent in other periods of life (Spitz, 1973).

Also, Rene Spitz in 1965 postulated that affective experiences during the first year of life influence the child's subsequent development. The early establishment of a healthy affective bond between a mother and her child will positively impact the development of the child (Spitz, 1973).

Monique Bydlowski (1999) was a psychoanalyst who proposed two original concepts regarding pregnant women: psychic transparency of pregnancy and life debt. These concepts help us to understand some aspects of maternity and psychoaffective development.

Life debt refers to the woman's aptitude to transform herself into a mother and, according to Bydlowski, it implies a recognition of gratitude toward the person who originally gave life to that woman, her own mother.

Psychic transparency adduces an aspect of mental functioning during pregnancy in establishing transference between therapist and patient, where there is access to the preconscious, and more spontaneous and richer free associations can be observed, specially related to infancy and parental images. Furthermore, it has been proved that hormonal changes during pregnancy influence and modify maternal behavior particularly socialization and cognition (Russell et al., 2001). The pregnant woman goes through a series of regressions and evolutions that lead to the identification with her own mother—the almighty mother from the first years of life—and to the identification with the baby that she once was (Bydlowski, 1999).

A key relevant concept in developmental psychology is based on the attachment theory postulated by Bowlby (1989), where the need to create a baby-caregiver relationship is affirmed as essential for healthy development to occur. The development of this type of bond will allow the establishment of a secure attachment pattern, which will influence the development of the personality and the way in which the child will later face the world. Thus, the establishment of a secure base will be essential for the optimal functioning of mental health.

Peter Fonagy made important contributions in this field that are considered by several psychologists as integrating fundamental constructs and theories, such as attachment theory and psychoanalytic theory (Delgado et al., 2015). One concept of relevance for clinical psychology is the concept of mentalization, which can be defined as the natural human imaginative capacity to perceive and interpret behavior in self and others as conjoined with intentional mental states, such as desires, motives, feelings, and beliefs (Allen & Fonagy, 2014) or as "holding mind in mind." And according to this construct, the infant's ability to mentalize supports the self-regulation capacities.

Other relevant and related contributions were made by Edward Tronick (Cohn & Tronick, 1989; Tronick et al., 1978): his still-face experiment and mutual regulation model. His contributions help us understand the specificities in self-regulation processes in infants—particularly when mothers are unavailable—emphasizing the importance of early mother-child interactions to promote the development of the infant's emotional capacities (Delgado et al., 2015).

Cohn and Tronick (1989) affirm that *"the major functional components of the mother's behavior are its affective quality and its contingent relationship to the baby's behavior"* (242) and that it has been observed in families with multiple risk factors that this process is altered when the mother disrupts their normal interaction leading to the baby being forced to self-regulate, with its consequences seen in the subsequent development of the child.

In summary, the phenomenon of motherhood involves a critical process, in terms of developmental crisis, in which there is an intense mobilization of the most primary aspects and a reorganization of identity.

These changes need to be elaborated internally. The past and present history together with the mother's personality structure and the characteristics of the baby are factors that configure the qualities of the bond between the mother and the baby, being essential for a healthy development of the child.

Emotional Support of the Pregnant Woman

In the course of the history of motherhood, several subjects helped the mother in the process of childbirth. They provided support to the pregnant woman, not only from a physical point of view but also emotionally.

Until the sixteenth century, female midwives—women—had a privileged role in providing psychological support through words and different amulets. But in the eighteenth century the perspective changed and male obstetricians—men—privileged saving the body of the mother and the child, leading to the medicalization of childbirth. Later, from the twentieth century, specialized medical practitioners, neonatologists, began to intervene with the emphasis on saving the premature or pathological child.

It was only after the twenty-first century that the first projects of perinatal psychologists found a starting point (Dayan, 2015; Molénat, 2001; Oiberman, 2005). Since the 1960s, the relationship between psychosocial factors and complications in childbirth began to be suspected (Molénat, 2001). In the decade of the 1990s, the link between an increase in premature births, "life events," and the perception of stress was taken into consideration (Glangeaud-Freudenthal, 1994). And from the beginning of the twenty-first century, an understanding of its underlying neuro-endocrinological and immunological mechanisms was achieved (Dayan, 2015; Salvatierra, 1998).

The antecedents and historical foundations of perinatal psychology date back to the ancient matrons, the obstetric psychoprophylaxis, and the "doulas," who accompanied the mother during childbirth so that she could go through this event without fear. However, the postpartum was disregarded, leaving the puerperium period "acephalic."

The birthing classes started by the Russian School (Nikolaev, 1957), the works of Leboyer on birth without pain (1978), the contributions of Als in the units of neonatal intensive care in the United States (1978, 1986), the study carried out in Spain by Salvatierra about psychobiology of pregnancy (1998), the contributions of Racamier on puerperal psychosis (1978), and Molénat's (1992) publication in France regarding the training of health professionals in the maternity wards, all constitute the antecedents that allowed the development of perinatal psychology.

Another relevant contribution in this field is the assessment scale of psychosocial risk, specific for women during pregnancy and puerperium (Priest et al., 2008). It has been pointed out by Zhang et al. (2013) that negative life events can lead to emotional alterations during pregnancy such as depression and anxiety. In the same line, Alvarenga and Frizzo (2017) studied the life events that might affect mental health during pregnancy.

In Argentina, the contributions of Videla and Grieco in the maternity unit of San Isidro during the 1970s (Videla & Grieco, 1993) and the development of the perinatal psychology program at the University of Buenos Aires (Oiberman & Santos, 2015; Fiszelew & Oiberman, 1995; Vega, 2006) provided fundamental tools for this specific area of psychology.

The scientific and technological advances in obstetric and neonatal medicine during the last 40 years brought a reduction in perineonatal morbidity and mortality, but at the same time they increased the medicalization of birth.

This led to the World Health Organization, in a meeting held in Fortaleza, Brazil, in 1985, to make a statement called "Birth Is Not a Disease." From that moment on, a path of changes in relation to childbirth care models began, with initiatives to "humanize" perinatal care.

Thus, the current proposal of "Safe and Family Centered Care in Maternity Hospitals" has emerged and proposes perinatal care as a common area of united work between several specialties: obstetrics, pediatrics, neonatology, nursing, psychology, social work, genetics, diagnostic imaging, and nutrition. These perinatal health teams, working from a family-centered approach, promote that women and their families take an active care role during pregnancy, delivery, and with the newborn child—whether born healthy or with any pathology that implies his or her hospitalization in a neonatal intensive care unit (Santos, 2010, 2018).

This consists fundamentally in a change of paradigm in this assistance: adding the humanistic to technology; founding real progress in comprehensive perinatal care.

Therefore, the inclusion of perinatal psychology in the field of perinatal healthcare has allowed us to address the problem of critical birth situations by introducing a psychological perspective and providing psychosocial intervention strategies to this interdisciplinary work.

Perinatal psychology is a specific area within early infancy psychology, which belongs to the field of developmental psychology. It contributes and enriches the area of developmental psychology by incorporating the particular moments of pregnancy, childbirth, and puerperium, as well as incorporating fetal development as a part of child development during the lifespan.

Perinatal psychology works simultaneously with two subjects: the pregnant woman/postpartum and the baby.

The contributions and approaches that support this inclusion into the area of developmental psychology are based on a conception that regards the importance of the first 1,000 days of life (pregnancy plus the first two years of life) as fundamental to the subsequent development of the child (Victora, 2012).

Perinatal psychology, as part of developmental psychology, responds to the opportunity for interventions aimed at primary prevention in early child development (Victora, 2012).

The psychological work in the perinatal area aims to enable, through early detection and intervention, that the first interactions between the mother and the baby are an expression of health for both members of the dyad. Therefore, within this paradigm, a place of insertion for perinatal psychologists is created.

The work of perinatal psychologists involves the creation of specific psychological strategies for maternal-neonatal care, in many cases working with mothers who come from an environment with high social vulnerability.

Perinatal Psychosocial Risk Screening Study

Objective

The aim of this research was to detect psychosocial perinatal risk at the time of medical discharge from the hospital of the mother-baby dyad, applying a Perinatal Intervention Device (PID): the Perinatal Psychological Interview (PPI) and the Psychosocial-Perinatal Risk Categories, in order to detect psychosocial risk during the perinatal period and develop protocols that take into consideration the psychosocial discharge from the hospital of the mother and the baby.

Methodology

In order to achieve the above mentioned goal, we carried out an exploratory study which would lead us to a better understanding of perinatal social risk situations at the time of medical discharge from the hospital.

Instruments

The PPI was administered and the Psychosocial-Perinatal Risk Categories were applied (cross-sectional study: administered once before discharge from the hospital).

Perinatal Psychological Interview
The PPI (Oiberman & Galíndez, 2005; Oiberman, Fiszelew et al., 1998; Oiberman, Scholam et al., 2000; Oiberman, Misic et al., 2011) is a psychological instrument that assesses psychological, physical, and socioemotional aspects of pregnancy and puerperium.

It has been developed and studied regarding its validity, comparing experimental and control group (Oiberman, Fiszelew et al., 1998).

The psychological aspects assessed by the PPI include the following variables: planning and acceptance of the pregnancy; prenatal care check-ups; emotional presence of the baby during pregnancy in the mother's imagination, dreams, choosing a name; if she could feel the movements of the baby during pregnancy; labor and delivery fears; being worried (afraid) about the baby's health during pregnancy; any presentiment of premature childbirth; anxiety; anguish; delivery as a life event.

The physical variables taken into consideration are: hospitalization during pregnancy; hypertension; bleeding; gestational diabetes; contractions; others mentioned by the mother during interview.

Also, 22 life events integrate the assessment of socioemotional aspects which the mother could have been exposed to.

The life events were classified and grouped in five different types of life events: problems in the relationship with her partner; social problems; death-related problems; current problems; and problems with any other son(s)/daughter(s).

The PPI is incorporated into the perinatal medical record of the patient. In this way, the healthcare professionals can see the socioemotional situation of the patient and take these variables into consideration in cases where a postponement of the obstetric or neonatal discharge could be required.

Psychosocial-Perinatal Risk Categories
Several specific risk categories related to psychosocial factors and situations during the perinatal period were identified (Oiberman & Santos, 2015).

Subsequently to the PPI, the perinatal psychologist analyzes the findings—related to psychological, physical, socioemotional aspects and problems that emerged during the PPI—and evaluates the presence or absence of psychosocial-perinatal risk situation.

The Psychosocial-Perinatal Risk Categories are the following:

- **Risk due to non-nesting**: These are situations in which the mother does not give an affective place to the unborn baby (psychic pregnancy is affected). These are usually unplanned pregnancies and/or pregnancy without medical control. During pregnancy, the mother says she has not imagined the baby. She has not chosen a name for the baby. In these cases, pregnancy is experienced as a stressor (pregnancy as a life event in itself). This can lead to difficulties in the beginning with the emotional bond with the baby and accented ambivalence.
- **Social-familial risk**: These are cases in which there is a family environment of risk (social life events: violence in the couple, drug addiction, a family member in prison); abandonment of other previous children. It can generate difficulties in starting an emotional bond with the baby.
- **Risk due to mourning**: Deaths of children or relatives, previous abortions, etc., that are resignified during pregnancy or childbirth. Childbirth can be experienced as a life event, as a fear of dying. In these cases there may be difficulties in starting an emotional bond with the baby and accented ambivalence.

- **Risk due to denial of pregnancy**: These are situations in which the mother denies the pregnancy: psychological denial (the mother does not realize that she is pregnant) and biological denial (for example, the mother does not perceive movements of the baby, does not notice the increase in the size of her belly, etc.).
- **Risk due to extreme poverty**: This is where mothers live in extreme poverty.
- **Risk associated with institutional situations**: This is where delivery/giving birth is a life event: lack of available hospital beds force the mother to make a "pilgrimage" in search of a place to give birth. Situations of referral of the baby to be hospitalized in a neonatal unit in another hospital (for example, the local neonatal service had to be closed due to intrahospital infections), which imply a mother-baby separation.
- **Psychological risk**: Psychological disorders: depression, psychosis, phobias, denial of own or baby's pathology, etc.
- **Physical risk**: Health problems or diseases before getting pregnant that could lead to complications during pregnancy and/or delivery. For example: HIV, syphilis, epilepsy, etc. The mother could experience the delivery/giving birth as a life event and/or it could lead to difficulties in beginning an emotional bond with the baby.
- **Adolescent pregnancy risk**: These are cases in which both parents are adolescents and there is an indicator of difficulty in beginning an emotional bond with the baby (Oiberman & Santos, 2015).

Procedure

The procedure consisted in first administering the PPI, the interviewing of mothers by a specialized perinatal psychologist (there were four psychologists working at Mi Pueblo Hospital).

Subsequently, the findings of the PPI were registered in the corresponding protocol/optic design (Oiberman, Scholam et al., 2000), which allowed the team to summarize these findings in a visual and practical manner, making the detection of relevant aspects easier and faster.

After this, the Psychosocial-Perinatal Risk Categories could be applied and identified (Oiberman, 2013). The specialized perinatal psychologists study and analyze the relevant findings during the PPI and categorize it in one of the Psychosocial-Perinatal Risk Categories (or as "No psychosocial-perinatal risk detected").

Hence, the above mentioned tools and procedure allow for an assessment and its consequent clinical decision-making process related to the identified risk situation. For example: postponement of obstetric or neonatal discharge; referral to specialized health services such as social work / social services; a link-up with appropriate external health services for specific treatment; or specialized follow-up of the case; etc. In cases where no psychosocial-perinatal risk situations are detected, no specific intervention related to these variables are indicated or recommended.

Participants

The unit of analysis were dyads mother-newborn baby—healthy and with pathology.

The sample is composed of 2,160 mother-baby dyads.

The interviews were administered in the period April 2011 to September 2017: in the maternity unit and the Neonatal Intensive Care Unit (NICU) of Mi Pueblo Hospital, based on the following inclusion criteria:

1. Maternity unit: Healthy mothers (without postpartum pathology) and healthy babies.
2. NICU: Healthy mothers (without postpartum pathology) whose babies were hospitalized for neonatal pathology or prematurity (babies in NICU = 59% of the sample).

Characteristics of the Social Situation in Mi Pueblo (in English, "My People") Hospital

The social characteristics of this particular hospital will be briefly described, due to its relevance in relation to the goals of this study.

Mi Pueblo Hospital in the city of Florencio Varela started operating in December 1992. In the year 2010 some building renovations were done, the pediatrics and neonatal departments were built and the maternity unit was partially remodeled. The hospital maternity unit currently has 120 beds. The name of the hospital "Mi Pueblo" was granted in recognition of the Civil Society which impelled its creation by imagining it only as a maternal and children's hospital. This is why, despite being a general hospital, the community of Florencio Varela usually calls this hospital "El Materno" (or "The Maternity").

Currently, 52,000 pediatric consultations take place in this hospital (according to data from the year 2015), which represents more than 4,000 consultations per month. Unfortunately the offer of healthcare services in this location (including hospitals and primary care centers) is extremely low or not provided, and sometimes issues must be resolved outside the district. Another possibility is to appeal to the private medical system, but its costs are inaccessible for many patients and that represents an obstacle to achieving free access to the healthcare system. Therefore, most of the time, Mi Pueblo Hospital represents the only real possibility for medical attention in cases of pregnancy or childbirth.

According to the 2010 census data Mi Pueblo Hospital had to respond to demand from 255,000 inhabitants, corresponding to the Florencio Varela city population at that time. However, the population had now reached 425,000 inhabitants, projecting a growth of 3% per year. According to this estimation, today's population would be close to 500,000 inhabitants, of which 132,000 inhabitants live below the poverty line, and 60,000 of them are children (Porto, 2011).

Results

From a total of 2,160 dyads assessed in this study between 2011 and 2017, it was observed that 748 (34%) were evaluated as being at risk, in at least in one category of the psychosocial perinatal list of risks, while in 1,410 (65%) dyads there was no risk detected (Table 3.1).

Categories of Psychosocial Perinatal Risk in 748 Interviews: Social-familial risk, 246 (33%); risk due to non-nesting, 137 (18%); psychological risk, 85 (11%); adolescent pregnancy risk, 78 (10%); risk due to mourning,

Table 3.1 Dyads at risk and no risk ($N = 2,160$)

Dyads at risk / no risk	N (%)
Risk	748 (34,6%)
No risk	1,412 (65,3%)
Total	**2,160 (100%)**

65 (9%); physical risk, 57 (7.6%); risk associated with institutional situations, 26 (3.5%); risk due to denial of pregnancy, 22 (3%); risk due to extreme poverty, 19 (2.5%); cases of multiple risks (women who belonged to more than one category of risk), 13 (1.7%).

It could be observed that the highest percentage of risk situations corresponded to cases of social-familiar risk, followed by risk due to non-nesting. Both categories imply 51% of the total detected risk.

Association Analysis

In the analysis of the results, a significant association between dyads at risk and unintended pregnancy was found.

Those dyads at risk represented a significantly higher frequency of unintended pregnancy (60.3%) compared to dyads without any risk among which 49% were cases of unintended pregnancies. This difference was statistically significant ($p = .000$) (Table 3.2).

A significant association between risk and non-acceptance of pregnancy was also found. Non-acceptance of pregnancy were cases of women who said they had not accepted the pregnancy or had difficulties at the beginning of pregnancy to accept it.

We found a significantly higher frequency of non-acceptance of pregnancy in those dyads at risk (5.52%) versus those who did not present any risk (1.01%). This association is highly significant ($p = .000$) (Table 3.3).

And finally, a highly significant association between risk and non-controlled pregnancy (i.e., not having attended routine medical checkups during pregnancy) was found ($p = .000$).

Table 3.2 Dyads at risk by intended or unintended pregnancy ($N = 2,002$)

	Unintended pregnancy	Intended pregnancy	Total
No risk	640 (49.0)	666 (51.0)	1,306 (100.0)
Risk	420 (60.3)	276 (39.7)	696 (100.0)
Total	1,060 (52.9)	942 (47.1)	2,002 (100.0)

$Chi^2(1) = 23.4371$ Pr $= .000$

Table 3.3 Dyads at risk by acceptance of pregnancy (N = 1,963)

	Non-acceptance of pregnancy	Non-acceptance at the beginning of pregnancy	Acceptance of pregnancy	Total
No risk	13 (1.01)	131 (10.0)	1,149 (88.9)	1,293 (100.0)
Risk	37 (5.5)	142 (21.2)	491 (73.3)	670 (100.0)
Total	50 (2.5)	273 (13.9)	1,640 (83.6)	1,963 (100.0)

$Chi^2(2) = 87.0070$ Pr = .000

Table 3.4 Dyads at risk by controlled pregnancy (N = 2,019)

	Uncontrolled pregnancy	Controlled pregnancy	Total
No risk	22 (1.6)	1,308 (98.4)	1,330 (100.0)
Risk	79 (11.5)	610 (88.5)	689 (100.0)
Total	101 (5.0)	1,918 (95.0)	2,019 (100.0)

$Chi^2(1) = 91.9456$ Pr = .000

As can be observed in Table 3.4, within the group of dyads at risk we have found a higher frequency of non-controlled pregnancy compared to the group of dyads with no risk where the frequency of uncontrolled pregnancy was significantly lower.

Discussion and Conclusions

The PPI is applied in the NICU and in the mother-baby hospital rooms.

This device has been specifically designed to intervene "in situ" at the beginning of the mother-baby bonding process, by performing a preventive task.

The objective of perinatal psychological assistance is to carry out preventive interventions in maternal and child mental health.

The first step toward the possibility of intervening preventively is the early detection of social risk situations.

For this reason, we aim to evaluate the psychosocial dimension of motherhood through PPIs and defining perinatal psychosocial risk categories. The assessment and detection of a social risk situation may involve:

- The postponement of medical mother-baby discharge.
- The referral to zonal social services.
- The referral to zonal health units near to the mother-baby's home.

Motherhood and mothering are complex processes that involve biological, psychological, social, and cultural factors, which interact and combine determining the characteristics of the perinatal situation of each dyad mother-baby.

Due to the importance of a healthy bonding process for the development of the child and the physical and psychological health of the mother and baby, it is necessary to detect psychosocial perinatal risk situations that can affect the course of these processes.

The perinatal psychological device presented in this chapter allows the detection of risk situations in the moments related to childbirth.

From the analysis of the results obtained in this study, we could determine that when other significant problems emerge during pregnancy, the mother feels that there are obstacles that deflect her from developing an adequate and healthy pregnancy/motherhood process.

The detection of these risk factors allows early interventions aiming to prevent perinatal-related difficulties that could compromise the healthy development of the dyadic bond and the critical consequences of this for the health of the child and the mother.

In concordance with the concept of psychic transparency (Bydlowski, 1999), counting with a specific instrument to detect psychosocial risk situations will allow preventive interventions that will benefit the child.

Risk factors are defined as those conditions and/or characteristics that increase the probability that a person could develop a particular disorder in comparison with a randomly selected person from the general population. Precursors to the study of this concept were found in Argentina by Casullo (1998) who carried out studies related to risk.

In accordance with the proposition of Priest et al. (2008), the aim of detecting risk is to facilitate the referral of patients in order that these patients can receive assistance, for example, through preventive programs, early intervention programs, and specific assistance programs designed to reduce the adverse effects in the fetus due to possible consequences of maternal and infant health (Priest et al., 2008).

The present study is founded on the idea that perinatal psychology is an area of developmental psychology, as fetal development is considered the first stage in child development.

Also, it aligns with Victora (2012) and the recent studies of UNICEF who consider the first 1,000 days of life as fundamental for further development (Lake, 2017).

In this way, this chapter aims to present a contribution to psychology from a preventive perspective of early infant development.

To conclude, we would like to emphasize the importance of transforming words into a connecting bridge in perinatal healthcare; realizing that the medical act in perinatology can be transformed with words and a clinical attitude: seeing and performing our professions beyond the simple act, technical action, or protocols, but moreover understanding that in front of us there is a person who feels, suffers, struggles, tries to overcome personal situations, and is asking for support at a crucial moment of their life: childbirth. This realization is pivotal during this particular developmental moment of their lifespan, and it can make a difference.

4

Colombian Mothers' Intuitive Theories Regarding Their Children's Self-Regulation

Jorge Mario Jaramillo, Mirjam Weis, and María Isabel Rendón

Self-regulation is a developmental task of great relevance in all cultures. In fact, all children need to learn to regulate their behavior, emotions, and cognitions on their own in various situations. This is essential to adapting successfully to the demands of social groups and to achieving important goals for individual development (Jaramillo et al., 2017). Recent studies have shown that ability and motivation to self-regulate are positively related to school achievement (Cadima et al., 2015; Montroy et al., 2016), satisfactory social relationships (Eisenberg et al., 2016), and high levels of emotional well-being (Moffit et al., 2013).

Baumeister and Vohs (2007) defined self-regulation as "the self's capacity for altering its behaviors ... [which] greatly increases the flexibility and adaptability of human behavior, enabling people to adjust their actions to a remarkably broad range of social and situational demands" (p. 115). More specifically, self-regulation involves focusing and maintaining attention, initiating or inhibiting actions, thoughts, and emotions, as well as monitoring the results to achieve a particular goal (Blair & Raver, 2015; Kelley et al., 2015; McClelland & Cameron, 2011; McClelland et al., 2010; McClelland et al., 2015).

Children begin to develop self-regulation in the preschool years, usually in the context of their family relationships (Whitebread & Basilio, 2012). Parents often lead children in adopting beliefs and values which are strongly rooted in their culture and serve as major motivations for self-regulation (Grusec & Goodnow, 1994; Trommsdorff, 2009). Moreover, parents also model and shape behaviors through socialization practices that later might be adopted by children to self-regulate successfully in different situations (Díaz & Eisenberg, 2015).

As beliefs and values change depending on the history, the living conditions, and the adaptation requirements of different groups, it is assumed that the development of self-regulation varies depending on the cultural context (Jaramillo et al., 2017). Trommsdorff (2009) states that according to whether socialization goals are aimed to promote primarily independence or interdependence, there might be notable differences in the way self-regulation is socialized. Western Europe and North America are recognized as cultural contexts in which socialization has traditionally been directed toward *independence*. When independent values are prioritized, an underlying socialization goal for the development of self-regulation is to strengthen the individual self in such a way that children can increase their levels of individual performance and achievement. In Asian countries, on the other hand, where *interdependent* values might influence socialization goals to a stronger extent, children develop self-regulation in order to preserve social harmony (Trommsdorff, 2012). Thus, the underlying cultural values and parenting goals have implications for the types of self-regulatory behaviors that children develop. For instance, in some contexts in India and Nepal it is common to teach children to suppress the expression of negative emotional states in order to avoid generating conflict or disturbing other people. Instead, in North America and Germany children are usually encouraged to express positive and negative emotions as the expression of emotions is supposed to represent children's individuality and their capacity to affirm themselves in front of others (Heikamp et al., 2013).

Keller and Kärtner (2013) state that the dimensions of independence and interdependence represent useful prototypes for the description of socialization goals. However, variations in the application of those prototypes should be taken into account. For instance, variation in parenting behavior has been shown in cultural communities with similar socialization goals. Moreover, there is intracultural variation as socialization represents individual acquisition processes, in which other variables as for instance parents' educational level and socioeconomic status (SES) also play important roles (Greenfield, 2014; Harwood et al., 1995; Harwood et al., 2000; Jaramillo et al., 2013). Studies on intracultural variance in socialization goals, parenting practices, as well as studies assessing historical change and acculturation processes are needed in order to better understand transitions between independent and interdependent values (Citlak et al., 2008; Kağitçibaşi, 2005; Keller, Borke, & Yovsi, 2005). In contexts in which typically interdependence has been valued highly, rapid changes and transitions toward industrialization and economic growth might lead to a combination of independent and interdependent values (e.g., Trommsdorff & Kornadt, 2003) and to an autonomous-relational orientation in socialization goals (Kağitçibaşi, 1996, 2005). Research on socialization goals and practices in the Latin American context is still relatively scarce. In the last decade of the twentieth century, there were various research projects conducted in the North American context, in which socialization goals and practices of Latin American mothers were compared with those of Anglo-American origin. The Latin American mothers included in these studies were generally from the Central American area, mainly from Puerto Rico, and although different methodologies were used, they were mostly based on semi-structured interviews and on observations in the natural environment. The results of these investigations consistently showed that in the Latin American context interdependent values tended to prevail over independent values (Harwood et al., 1999; Miller & Harwood, 2001). Moreover, Latin American mothers place emphasis on the child growing up in close contact with other family members, in such a way that it is common for other persons in the extended family (usually women) to be involved in the care and education practices of their children. This was shown for instance in a study conducted by Leyendecker, Lamb, Schoelmerich, and Fracasso (1995), in which middle-class mothers of Anglo-American and Central American origin were asked to describe the activities of their young children of the last 24 hours. Further, mothers promote the formation of a strong family bond by guiding children and accompanying them in their activities, even during play (Leyendecker et al., 2002). Several researchers have described respect and appropriate behavior, sympathy (respecting and sharing other's feelings), and familism (strong family ties, commitment to the family) as typical Latin American values. It is supposed that the underlying socialization goal is the ability and willingness of the child to act in harmony and in accordance with the expectations of the community to support the maintenance of social cohesion (Halgunseth et al., 2006; Harwood et al., 2006; Rosabal-Coto, 2012; Triandis et al., 1984).

However, more recent studies conducted in Costa Rica, Colombia, and Brazil suggest that socialization goals in Latin America might be changing. Keller, Kuensemueller, et al. (2005) compared a group of mothers from a rural Cameroon context with rudimentary technology and community production systems, with Costa Rican and German middle-class mothers. They observed mothers' interactions with their 3-month-old children and found that German mothers had a strong orientation toward independence, whereas Costa Rican mothers tended to promote interdependence in their children, and this latter orientation was even stronger in mothers from Cameroon. In a similar study several years later, Costa Rican and German mothers had both increased in their emphasis on independence, while there were only minimal changes observed in Cameroonian mothers (Keller, Borke, & Yovsi, 2005). The increasing emphasis on independence might be rooted in technological and economic developments. It is supposed that the greater the technological development and involvement in economic globalization of a country, the stronger the emphasis on independence in maternal socialization goals (see also Greenfield, 2009).

A study on socialization goals and practices of mothers of 3- and 4-year-old children conducted in Bogotá and its peripheral rural area showed that the socialization goals related to interdependence tended to prevail over those of independence in Colombian mothers. However, an increase in valuing independence was observed in mothers who are more closely connected to the processes of globalization and technological development. That is, young, urban, middle-class mothers with a higher academic educational level showed higher independence values than mothers of lower socioeconomic classes with less connection to globalization and technology (Jaramillo et al., 2013). Thus, without decreasing the emphasis on interdependence, Colombian mothers were found to be increasingly concerned to promote independence in their children in order to prepare them for today's complex world.

Moreover, studies conducted in Brazil suggest a growing tendency for independence in parents' socialization goals and practices, combined with the aim to achieve a balance with interdependent values, in order to promote the development of an autonomous-relational self in their children (Macarini et al., 2010; Seidl-de-Moura et al., 2013).

Regarding parenting practices, several studies, which were conducted in the last two decades in Latin American countries, found that today's parents give their children more time for spontaneous play (Aguirre, 2000) and express affection and appreciation to their children in daily life more often and with a higher intensity than in former times (Aguirre, 2000;

Bernal et al., 2009; Jaramillo et al., 2010). On the other hand, there is a tendency to diminish the use of punishment as a means to persuade children to behave in socially expected ways, combined with a greater willingness to use dialogue and negotiation instead of unilateral imposition of authority as a means to discipline children (Aguirre, 2000; Ares & Bertella, 2015; Cardona-Oviedo & Terán-Reales, 2017; Darling et al., 2008; Jaramillo et al., 2010). These changes could be related to demographic and cultural transformations such as the progressive decrease in the number of children per family, which promotes more individualized parenting practices (Cienfuegos, 2014; Sunkel, 2006); the increase of parents' educational levels that allow them a broader knowledge about the processes of child development, the growing recognition of children's and adolescents' rights (Comisión Económica Para América Latina y el Caribe, 2014), as well as a growing technological development and involvement in economic globalization of Latin American countries, as described by Greenfield (2009).

As can be concluded from the previous studies, socialization goals as well as parenting practices of mothers in Latin America might have changed. However, little is known about the underlying implicit theories of mothers through which socialization goals might influence contemporary parenting practices (Trommsdorff et al., 2012). Research in the Latin American context on the underlying intuitive socialization theories of mothers in their present realities has been scarce. Moreover, socialization goals and parenting practices regarding children's self-regulation have rarely been studied in Latin American contexts. As self-regulation is an important developmental task, and parenting practices influence its development, it is crucial to find out how today's mothers in Latin America think and feel in situations that demand children's self-regulation. Therefore, this study aims to gain new insights about intuitive socialization theories of mothers in Colombia in such situations. These intuitive theories include socialization goals and practices as well as attributions and emotions of the mothers. According to the literature, mother's intuitive socialization theories affect their parenting practices as well as the development of children's self-regulation (Trommsdorff et al., 2012). Thus, the question arises which are the socialization goals and concrete behaviors of mothers in situations that demand self-regulation in their children. Moreover, mothers' attributions in these situations as well as their emotions might play important roles. Therefore, the study seeks to answer the following research question: Which attributions, emotions, behaviors, and socialization goals do mothers in Colombia, a changing cultural context in Latin America, report for situations that demand children's self-regulation? Are maternal behaviors and maternal socialization goals related to mothers' SES and educational level?

Method

Participants

The sample consisted of 69 mothers, who were contacted through the school their children attended. A prerequisite to participating in the study was to be the mother of a son or daughter in the first, second, or third year of primary school. The age of the children ranged between 7 and 10 years (27 children were 7 years old, 35 children were 8 years old, five children were 9 years old, and two children were 10 years old). To estimate mothers' SES, we used the official classification by strata of the Colombia state for the assignment of public services. We considered strata 1 and 2 as low SES and strata 3, 4, and 5 as middle SES. In this study, 34 mothers (49.3%) had a low SES and 35 mothers (50.7%) had a middle SES. Mothers reported their highest level of education on the International Standard Classification of Education 1997 (ISCED-97) scale (Organisation for Economic Co-operation and Development, 1999), which we adapted to the Colombian education system. As can be seen in Table 4.1, the majority of the mothers with a low SES had either not completed or completed secondary school (baccalaureate) as their highest educational level. Only five mothers with low SES had completed a technical school certificate and only one had completed university education. Of the mothers with a middle SES, the majority had completed university education or postgraduate studies and only some of them had either not completed or completed their baccalaureate as their highest educational level. We categorized mothers' educational level as low or high. A low educational level includes the categories incomplete primary education, completed primary education, incomplete secondary education / baccalaureate, and completed secondary education / baccalaureate. A high educational level includes the categories incomplete technical school education, completed technical school education, incomplete university education, completed university education, incomplete postgraduate studies, and completed postgraduate studies.

Table 4.1 Mother's educational level and socioeconomic status

Mother's SES	Incomplete primary education	Completed primary education	Incomplete secondary education /baccalau- reate	Completed secondary education /baccalau- reate	Incomplete technical school	Technical school certificate	Incomplete university education	Completed university education	Incomplete postgrad- uate studies	Postgrad- uate studies
Low status	0	2	10	13	1	5	0	1	0	0
Middle status	0	0	2	2	1	1	0	11	4	13
Total	0	2	12	15	2	6	0	12	4	13

Notes: N (Number of mothers) = 69

Procedure

All mothers were informed in detail about the purpose and the procedures of the investigation. Further, they all provided written informed consent prior to their participation, knowing that they could refuse or revoke their consent at any time. Mothers participated in individual interviews, which were recorded. The duration of the interviews ranged between 20 and 30 minutes.

Measures

A brief version of the Socialization-Situation Test (SOSIT), a semi-structured interview created by Kornadt and Trommsdorff (1990), was used to assess mothers' intuitive theories. In this study, intuitive theories were captured by mothers' attributions, emotions, maternal behaviors, and socialization goals in hypothetical situations which would require self-regulation by their children. To assess attributions, emotions, behaviors, and socialization goals of mothers, we presented the mothers with three hypothetical situations that would require children to regulate their behavior and emotions in order to respond adequately to social norms or expectations. The situations were read to the mothers in the interview. The situations were the following:

1. Park Situation: You have spent some time with your child in the park. It's time to go home but your child does not want to finish playing and says, "I'm going to the swings."
2. Telephone Situation: You are waiting for an important call from a friend. As soon as you start talking, your child starts to complain: "You have to play with me."
3. Shopping Situation: Your child accompanies you to make purchases. Very soon she sees a toy she wants to have. You tell her that you cannot buy it and you want to continue with the purchase, but your child stays in front of the showcase, shouts, and complains: "I want this toy!"

For each situation, the following four questions were formulated to the mother, in order to assess her attributions, emotions, parenting practices (behaviors), and socialization goals:

1. "Why does the child behave in this way?" (maternal attributions)

2. "What do you feel in this situation?" (maternal emotions)
3. "What would you do in this situation?" (parenting practices or behaviors)
4. "Which aim are you pursuing with your behavior?" (maternal socialization goals)

The category "maternal attributions" assesses how mothers explain the behavior of the child described in each of the hypothetical situations. To what cause do they attribute the child's behavior? Attributions to the child, the mother, other people, or the community were taken into account.

The category "maternal emotions" refers to emotions that the mother would experience because of the behavior of the child described in each of the hypothetical situations.

The category "maternal behaviors" asks the mother about her behaviors which she would display in each of the hypothetical situations to promote self-regulation in her child. This category includes the following subcategories:

- Power assertive techniques: Disciplining with physical contact, disciplining without physical contact, criticism, physical punishment, physical and verbal punishment, verbal punishment, and psychological control.
- Problem-focused behavior: Reasoning, modeling, guidance, or instrumental support, negotiation, evaluation of the conditions and decision, giving in to the child's desires.
- Emotion-focused behavior: Comforting, distraction, reappraisal.

The category "maternal socialization goals" assesses what the mother seeks to achieve through her behavior in the situation. This category includes the following subcategories:

- Time perspective: Short-term goals, long-term goals, non-specific time perspective.
- Purpose of socialization: Harmony orientation, prosociality, empathy, respect for other's needs, coping with disappointment, meeting role expectations, achievement orientation, search for the child's well-being.

- Reference of the goals: Reference to the child, reference to the mother, reference to others, reference to community or society.

Data Analysis

The answers of the mothers were analyzed regarding the attributions, emotions, behaviors, and socialization goals in each situation. The interviews were recorded and transcribed in order to perform content analyses using the software Atlas Ti 6 for qualitative data processing. We calculated the frequencies of mothers' expressions of attributions for each category and their respective subcategories for each of the three situations. To examine associations of mothers' SES and educational level with maternal behaviors and socialization goals, we used the Chi-square test.

Results

Maternal Attributions

When answering the question "why does the child behave in this way?" most of the mothers described reasons and behaviors typical for children of that age that would prevent them from self-regulating as expected by adults. In some cases, mothers' mentioned behaviors that might lead to a lack of self-regulation in their child. Table 4.2 shows the types of causes to which mothers attributed the behavior of their child in the three hypothetical situations.

Overall, mothers most often attributed the child's behavior to the child's motives (57.01%). When referring to the motives of the children, the mothers mentioned the children's need to spend time playing and doing what they like or having fun, such as going to the park. Moreover, they mentioned the desire of the children to share more time with their mothers, wanting mothers to pay attention to them and to confirm how important they are for them. Some mothers mentioned the intention of children to contradict or challenge authority by disobeying or trying to force the mother to do as they (the children) wish.

Attributions to the child's behavior (20.17%) were the attributions which were mentioned second most frequently across the three situations. When

Table 4.2 Maternal attributions

		Park situation	Telephone situation	Shopping situation	Total	Percentage
Attribution to the child	Child's emotions	6	3	0	9	3.94%
	Child's behavior	11	6	29	46	20.17%
	Child's motives	47	56	27	130	57.01%
Attribution to the mother	Mother's emotions	0	0	0	0	0%
	Mother's behavior	6	2	9	17	7.45%
	Mother's motives	0	0	0	0	0%
Attribution to others		4	0	6	10	4.38%
Non-specific attribution		4	4	8	16	7.01%

Notes: N (number of mothers) = 69. Total number of mother's expressions of attributions = 228. The "Total" column indicates the number of times mothers referred to each of the attribution categories. The column "Percentage" presents the percentage for each category in relation to the total number of attributions described by the mothers referring to the behavior of the child, mothers described the difficulty they experience in interrupting an activity that the children enjoy and the children's tendency to seek the immediate satisfaction of their desires. Undesirable behaviors of children were mentioned, too, such as caprice, rebellion, and disrespect of authority, trying to impose their own will, possessiveness, and ignoring norms.

Sometimes, mothers attributed the child's behavior to their own behavior (7.45%). In these cases, mothers for instance pointed out that they often do not spend enough time with their children and do not share enough fun activities with them, such as playing or going to the park. Moreover, "bad parenting" was mentioned as a cause of undesirable behaviors of children. For instance, practices such as pleasing the child in everything he wants, giving him everything he asks for, or not devoting attention to him when he is expressing or requesting something.

Maternal Emotions

Mothers named a wide spectrum of emotions which they would experience in the hypothetical situations in which their child does not self-regulate. The emotion which was by far the most frequently mentioned was anger (or rage), followed by frustration, and sadness. In Table 4.3, a list of the emotions mentioned by the mothers is presented. Emotions are ordered according to the frequency they were mentioned. As can be seen, the list also includes some positive emotions such as joy, empathy, admiration, and tranquility. These emotions were mentioned mostly in relation to the situation of the park, which was interpreted by some mothers as an opportunity to share more time with their child or satisfying their children's need for activity, play, and fun.

Maternal Behaviors

Mothers reported most often using behaviors which focus on the problem (68.12%) and among these problem-focused behaviors, reasoning (30.35%) and negotiation (23.51%) stand out. For instance, mothers reported giving reasons to their children, so that they can understand the meaning and importance of regulating their own behavior in the situation. Moreover, mothers reported that they would seek agreements with the child through

Table 4.3 Maternal emotions

Emotions	Park situation	Telephone situation	Shopping situation	Total	Percentage
Anger	17	29	30	76	37.25%
Frustration	3	2	11	16	7.84%
Sadness	2	3	7	12	5.88%
Shame	0	0	5	5	2.45%
Discomfort	0	3	2	5	2.45%
Tiredness	3	1	0	4	1.96%
Confusion	2	2	0	4	1.96%
Joy	3	0	0	3	1.47%
Stress	1	1	0	2	0.98%
Concern	0	1	0	1	0.49%
Surprise	0	1	0	1	0.49%
Nuisance	0	1	0	1	0.49%
Anguish	1	0	0	1	0.49%
Quietness	1	0	0	1	0.49%
Insecurity	0	0	1	1	0.49%
Empathy	1	0	0	1	0.49%
Burden	0	1	0	1	0.49%
Admiration	0	1	0	1	0.49%
Impatience	1	0	0	1	0.49%
Unspecified emotions	19	18	12	49	24.01%
General positive emotions	3	0	2	5	2.45%
General negative emotions	4	4	5	13	6.37%

Notes: N (number of mothers) = 69. Total number of mothers' expressions of emotions: 204. The "Total" column indicates the number of times mothers referred to each of the emotion categories. The column "Percentage" presents the percentage for each category in relation to the total number of emotions described by the mothers

dialogues, so that both parties give in to some degree and take into consideration the interests of the other party. Other behaviors that were found within this category were to evaluate the specific situation before making a decision and to give in to the child's desire (the latter was mentioned most often in the telephone situation). In these cases, the mothers interpreted the situation according to the desires of the child and these become the priority criteria in finding the best possible solution. Thus, the situation does not require the child's self-regulation anymore, since it is the mother who reorients her own behavior.

Mothers also reported that they would use power assertive techniques to control their child's behavior (27.38%). The power assertive technique which was reported most often was discipline without physical contact. That is, the mother imposes her authority on the child using language as a means to persuade him to obey. Some mothers used discipline with physical contact or psychological control to impose their will. Very few mothers reported physical or verbal punishment (see Table 4.4).

Mothers barely mentioned using emotion-focused behaviors (3.45%). Within this category, distraction as a means to modify the emotional experience of the child in the situation was reported most often (see Table 4.4).

Figure 4.1 shows the behaviors that were described by the mothers most frequently in the three hypothetical situations which demand children's self-regulation. As can be seen in the figure, the frequencies of mothers' behaviors to regulate the behavior of their children were similar in the three situations. In all three situations, reasoning was mentioned most often, followed by negotiation, discipline without physical contact, and evaluation of the situation before deciding, in this order.

Analyses with the Chi-square test showed that negotiation was significantly associated with SES in the shopping situation ($\chi^2 (1) = 12.28; p < .05$). Further, negotiation was significantly associated with mothers' educational level in the park ($\chi^2 (1) = 6.724; p < .05$) and in the shopping ($\chi^2 (1) = 6.194; p < .05$) situations. In the shopping situation, more low-SES mothers mentioned negotiation strategies (71.4%) than middle-SES mothers (25.8%). Additionally, more mothers with a high educational level used negotiation strategies in the park situation (60%) than mothers with a low educational level (27.6%). In contrast, in the shopping situation, more mothers with a low level of education named negotiation strategies (65.5%) compared to mothers with a high level of education (34.3%). Furthermore, there was a significant association between mothers' educational level and the behavior of giving in to the child's desire in the park situation ($\chi^2 (1) = 3.862; p < .05$). More mothers with a low level of education were willing to give in to the child's desire (17.2%) than mothers with a high educational level (2.9%).

Maternal Socialization Goals

When asked "Which aim are you pursuing with your behavior?" most of the mothers' responses described long-term goals that they want to achieve in

Table 4.4 Maternal behaviors

General category	Sub-category	Park situation	Telephone situation	Shopping situation	Total	Percentage
Power assertive techniques	Disciplining with physical contact	4	0	6	10	2.97%
	Discipline without physical contact	20	24	19	63	18.75%
	Criticism	1	0	0	1	0.29%
	Physical punishment	0	0	4	4	1.19%
	Physical and verbal punishment	1	0	0	1	0.29%
	Verbal punishment	1	0	2	3	0.89%
	Psychological control	4	1	5	10	3%
Problem-focused behavior	Reasoning	30	29	42	102	30.35%
	Modeling	1	0	1	2	0.59%
	Guidance or instrumental support	1	2	2	5	1.48%
	Negotiation	20	28	31	79	23.51%
	Evaluate situation and decide	13	3	6	22	6.54%
	Give in to the child's desire	5	10	4	19	5.65%
Emotion-focused behavior	Comforting	0	0	0	0	0%
	Distraction	4	5	5	14	3.16%
	Reappraisal	0	0	0	0	0%
	Non-specific behavior	0	1	0	1	0.29%

Notes: N (number of mothers) = 69. Total number of mother's expressions of behaviors. The "Total" column indicates the number of times mothers referred to each of the behavior categories. The column "Percentage" presents the percentage for each category in relation to the total number of behaviors described by the mothers

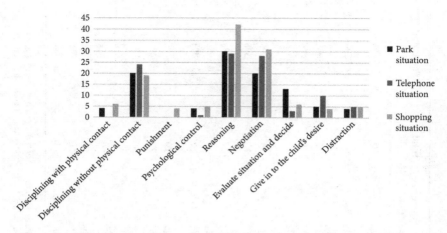

Figure 4.1 Most frequently mentioned behaviors of mothers in the three hypothetical situations of self-regulation

the education of their children (72.68%). However, there were also a considerable number of mothers (27.31%) who focused on the concrete situation and defined goals that they would seek to achieve in the specific situation (i.e., short-term goals).

The long-term goals mentioned by the mothers mainly referred to promoting the child's learning. Hereby, the following long-term goals were mentioned most often: obedience and respect for the authority of the mother; respect for the elderly and their personal spaces; respect for other's needs; meeting role expectations; distinguishing good from evil; following rules; recognizing that things have to be earned and that not everything can be obtained immediately; recognizing the consequences of one's actions; understanding that there are time limits and boundaries for everything and that you have to respect them; acquiring discipline.

Within the long-term goals, the purposes of socialization which were most frequently identified in mothers' statements related to the child's meeting of role expectations; coping with frustration and disappointment; respect for other's needs; and empathy. Although less frequently, mothers also mentioned the search for the child's well-being; the development of abilities; and harmony orientation (see Table 4.5).

The results of the Chi-square test showed that the expression of short-term goals was significantly associated with SES in the park situation (χ^2 (1) = 4.095; $p < .05$) and with educational level in the shopping situation

Table 4.5 Maternal socialization goals

General categories	Specific categories	Park situation	Telephone situation	Shopping situation	Total	Percentage
Time perspective	Short-term goals	21	23	9	53	27.31%
	Long-term goals	42	42	57	141	72.68%
	Non-specific time perspective	0	0	0	0	0%
Long-term goals: purpose of socialization	Harmony orientation	7	0	0	7	3.50%
	Prosociality	1	0	0	1	0.50%
	Empathy	2	7	3	12	6.00%
	Respect for other's needs	3	22	3	28	14%
	Coping with disappointment	10	7	31	48	24%
	Meeting role expectations	27	14	17	58	29%
	Enhancing capacities in the child	5	2	4	11	5.50%
	Seeking the child's well-being	13	4	6	23	11.50%
	Non-specific purpose of socialization	5	7	0	12	6%
Long-term goals: rationale / reference to	To the own child	58	56	62	176	93.12%
	To the mother	5	4	3	12	6.34%
	To other persons	0	0	0	0	0.00%
	To the community or society	0	1	0	1	0.52%

Notes: N (number of mothers) = 69. Total number of mother's expressions of socialization goals: time perspective = 194; purpose of socialization = 200; reference of goals = 189. The "Total" column indicates the number of times mothers referred to each of the categories of socialization goals. The column "Percentage" presents the percentage for each category in relation to the total number of socialization goals described by the mothers

(χ^2 (1) = 4.807; p <.05). More low-SES mothers expressed short-term goals (50%) compared to middle-SES mothers (24.1%) in the park situation. Further, more mothers with a low level of education expressed short-term goals (25.9%) than mothers with a high level of education (5.9%) in the shopping situation.

For long-term goals, there was a significant association with SES in the park situation (χ^2 (1) =3.996; p <.05), indicating that more middle-SES mothers expressed long-term goals (72.4%) compared to low-SES mothers (46.4%). The expression of long-term goals was also significantly associated with mothers' educational level in the park (χ^2 (1) = 4.753; p < .05) and shopping situations (χ^2 (1) = 4807; p < .05). In both situations, more mothers with a high educational level expressed long-term goals compared to mothers with a low level of education (park situation: 73.5% of mothers with high educational level, 46.4% of mothers with low educational level; shopping situation: 94.1% of mothers with high educational level, 74.1% of mothers with low educational level).

Further, the socialization goal of promoting respect for other's needs was significantly associated with SES (χ^2 (1) = 4.685; p < .05) and educational level in the telephone situation (χ^2 (1) = 5.784; p < .05). More middle-SES mothers (65.5%) expressed the goal of promoting respect for other's needs compared to low-SES mothers (36.0%). Further, more mothers with a high level of education (62.5%) expressed the goal of promoting respect for other's needs compared to mothers with a low educational level (30.8%). Enhancing the child's capacity was significantly associated with educational level (χ^2 (1) = 5.284, p < .05) in the shopping situation, in which more mothers with a high educational level (17.6%) mentioned strategies to enhance their children's capacities compared to mothers with a low educational level (0%).

Discussion

This study aimed to gain new insights on intuitive socialization theories of mothers in Colombia in situations that demand their children's self-regulation. To this end, the attributions, emotions, concrete behaviors, and socialization goals of the mothers in such situations were explored. Mothers most frequently attributed the behavior of the child in the hypothetical situations of self-regulation to motives and behaviors typical of children at that age. Thus, it seems that mothers try to put themselves in the place of the child in order to understand the child's behavior. In accordance with the trends which have been reported in recent literature on changes in parenting in Latin American countries, many of the mothers in our Colombian sample emphasized the need and desire that children have to play (see Aguirre, 2000), to have fun outdoors, to share time with their parents, and to receive affection and attention (see Jaramillo et al., 2010). Moreover, mothers reported the difficulties of their children in delaying the satisfaction of their desires due to their stage of development. In other words, mothers recognize the individuality of the child and try to consider and respect the needs of the child in their parenting behaviors.

Further, it is noteworthy that although most mothers experience negative emotions (anger, frustration, sadness) in relation to their children's difficulties in self-regulation, in their parenting practices (maternal behaviors) reasoning, negotiation, and discipline without physical contact predominate. Thus, the mothers in this sample seem to prefer the use of dialogue over punishment as a means to resolve conflicts with their children and to promote children's self-regulation. These results seem to contradict the results of studies which compared parenting practices of Anglo-American mothers and Latin American mothers two decades ago. Those earlier studies concluded that Latin American mothers used power assertive techniques to a high extent, such as giving orders, explicitly guiding the behavior of children, and disciplining with physical contact to lead them to behave in the expected way (Carlson & Harwood, 2003; Harwood et al., 1999). Parental practices might have changed in the sense that mothers nowadays use more dialogue, recommendations, and negotiation and mothers might even consider to change their decisions in a flexible way, giving in to children's desires when they offer compelling reasons (Aguirre, 2000; Ares & Bertella, 2015; Jaramillo et al., 2013).

Moreover, the findings on maternal socialization goals showed that for most mothers it is a priority to promote the development of an "Ought Self" in their children (Higgins, 1998). In the present study, this was manifested through different statements of mothers in which they highlighted the importance of children behaving as they should, adequately fulfilling their role, and responding positively to the expectations of their parents or society. Moreover, mothers highlighted socialization goals as obedience, respecting elders, meeting role expectations, and respect for other's needs, which coincide with the traditional Latin American socialization goals of respect, sympathy, and familism, which are supposed to be rooted in interdependent values (Halgunseth et al., 2006; Harwood et al., 2006; Triandis et al., 1984).

These findings indicate that although parenting practices might have changed in the sense that mothers use more reasoning and negotiation in order to guide the behavior of their children, they still emphasize the importance of socialization goals that promote interdependence (Jaramillo & Ruiz, 2013). Thus, socialization goals of mothers in this study might coincide with Kağitçibaşi's (1996, 2005) description of the autonomous-relational orientation and fit with the tendency of a combination of independent and interdependent values that has been observed in several countries in transition toward industrialization and large-scale economies (Greenfield, 2009, 2014; Keller & Kärtner, 2013; Trommsdorff & Kornadt, 2003). Thus, todays' Colombian mothers might still emphasize traditional socialization goals rooted in interdependence values and at the same time use parenting practices that seem to stem from independent values.

Moreover, our results show that although mothers mentioned mainly long-term goals when describing the purpose they would seek to achieve in each of the three situations of self-regulation, there were significant differences regarding mothers' SES, educational level, and type of situation. We found that mothers with a low SES and a low educational level mentioned short-term goals more frequently than mothers with a middle SES or high educational level. Further, mothers with a middle SES and high educational level mentioned long-term socialization goals more frequently than mothers with low SES or low educational level. This shows that highly educated mothers as well as mothers with a higher SES focus more on long-term goals than less educated mothers or mothers with low SES. This might be rooted in the fact that mothers with low SES often indeed are forced to care more about the near future than mothers with higher SES, for instance because they have more troubles affording everyday expenses and they have fewer opportunities to take care of their future by taking precautions.

Interestingly, the differences between mothers with high and low educational levels as well as between those with low and middle SES regarding negotiation strategies depend on the situation. While in the park situation highly educated mothers mentioned negotiation more often than mothers with less education, the pattern was reversed in the shopping situation. The results show that the mothers of our sample in general think that negotiation is an important parenting practice, which they seem to use a lot. However, there are differences in how and when Colombian mothers think that negotiation is a valuable strategy, depending on their SES and their educational level. While in the shopping situation, for highly educated mothers and middle-SES mothers, negotiating is perceived as less adequate than in the park situation, for the less educated and low-SES mothers it is the other way around. One reason might be financial aspects of the shopping situation, which might be relevant for low-SES mothers only. It could be hypothesized that low-SES mothers show solidarity with their children in shopping situations because they often cannot satisfy their own shopping wishes due to financial constraints. Low-SES mothers might feel sad or guilty because they actually often cannot afford toys as well as other shopping desires. Thus, they do not perceive the child's behavior in this situation as a "tantrum," but as a reasonable expression of frustration. Consequently, negotiation might be used by low-SES mothers in this situation because they seek to reduce the feeling of frustration in their children.

Another reason for this reversed pattern might be that the situations are qualitatively different. In the shopping situation, it might be less effective to negotiate and there might be fewer opportunities to discuss all pros and cons with the child because of time, money, and room constraints. Further, it might be important for mothers to show consistency with rules in this situation, which is important for the long-term promotion of self-regulation in their children. In contrast, the park situation might give more opportunities to spend quality time with children and it possibly represents fewer drawbacks to discussing and negotiating with the purpose of enhancing children's abilities to discuss as well as giving them room to discover and learn their own self-regulation strategies. In fact, mothers often reported that they perceive leaving children more time to play in the park as an opportunity to share time with them in a situation that they like. These results suggest that it is important to pay more attention to the different types of situations that mothers share with their children in everyday life and to the meanings that these situations have for them, when we study practices that mothers use to promote the development of children's self-regulation. Both situations and their meanings change depending on the way of life and the theories and values that mothers apply in the socialization of their children. Documenting and understanding this variability could help to achieve a broader and more accurate view of the different means through which parents promote the development of self-regulation in their children.

Moreover, the differences in maternal socialization goals and practices based on mothers' SES and educational level might be rooted in differences in mothers' underlying cultural values. Just as former research in Colombia found higher independent values in mothers with higher educational levels and a higher SES (Jaramillo et al., 2013), the differences based on educational level and SES of the present study might be partly explained by differences in valuing independent and interdependent values. Thus, these results might illustrate intracultural variation in the socialization practices and goals of todays' Colombian mothers.

5

Multigenerational Cohabitation and Relationships in the Family

Losses and Gains for Children in the Interaction with Grandparents in Latin America

Mónica Salazar-Villanea, Delia Tamara Fuster-Baraona, and Mauricio Blanco-Molina

Introduction

Child-rearing and child development characteristics vary within and between cultures and at the historic times in which they occur, or what Bronfenbrenner called, the chronosystem (1994). Nowadays and in a sociodemographic context of increased longevity and decreasing fertility rates, it is important to highlight in this chapter the developmental trajectories, potential benefits, and multigenerational significance of the experiences of intimacy, mutual influencing, closeness, and distancing that cohabitation with grandparents has for Latin American children. As people are living longer and with better health, they are more likely to spend time grandparenting, and because fewer children are being born, children are more likely to receive more care from a grandparent (Phillipson, 2010).

Grandparenting can occur in at least three possible ways: in the relationship of non-resident grandparents with their grandchildren; in the context of multigenerational families (co-resident grandparents), the most common way in Latin America; and when grandparents take custody of their grandchildren.

Literature on the occurrence of this last way of grandparenting, known as grandfamilies or kinship families, in which grandparents are primary caregivers to their grandchildren, has shown an emphasis on the diversity of social-interpersonal, cultural, and policy-related contexts and targeting for interventions, since the past decades have seen a growth in the numbers of children raised by grandparents without a parent at home, as immigration has become a more important social issue in the United States (Hayslip et al., 2019).

Results reported on Latin American grandfamilies living in the United States demonstrate the value of grandparenting as a survival strategy, a protective factor for children, and a family's strength in managing crises and transitions within a context of loss, associated with the economic needs of immigration, lack of community support, and the need for cultural identity reference (Beltran & Cooper, 2018; Goodman & Silverstein, 2005).

The main purpose of this chapter is to amplify the scope of grandparenting significance for children raised in Latin America, illustrating some of the effects of grandparenting and the developmental gains and losses of multigenerational co-residence. Specifically, the chapter will deal with the interaction with grandparents within a multigenerational cohabitation that can happen in interdependent and collectivistic contexts were familism is a value and a protective factor for children, such as Latin America; and that is the context in which Latin American children are being raised. Thus, recognizing that familism is not a homogeneous construct and that the diversity embedded throughout our countries need further studies to acknowledge different ethnic group particularities, indigenous populations' traditions, and distinct socioeconomic and political backgrounds.

In Costa Rica, it is estimated that in one in three homes where a child younger than 6 years of age is present, at least one adult member other than a parent is present as well. Of those homes, 18% are households where the grandparent is the actual head of family (Carmiol, 2015). In Chile, 40% percent of grandparents live with a grandchild (Grundy et al., 2012). Co-residence with grandparents is reported to be relatively high in Nicaragua (55%), Costa Rica (41%), and Mexico (45%), in comparison to the United States (27%) (Gibbons & Fanjul de Marsicovetere, 2017).

Bronfenbrenner's (1979) theory of development can help us understand how grandparents and grandchildren's development are dependent on each other and how context shapes development. For Bronfenbrenner, a complex array of factors—including individual thought processes, interpersonal relationships, organizational structures, public policies, and community systems and situations—influence how humans behave. The intergenerational domain is a part of the "psychosocial environment." However, this intersects with other spheres of the environment. The individual is viewed as being embedded in closer circles of relationships (microsystems), as well as wider and distal circles such as the political, economic, and cultural systems (macrosystem). There is a social context within each of these domains of influence and there are multifaceted relationships between the domains (Kaplan et al., 2017).

Within the microsystem, the narrowing of social networks in the later years of life encourages an adaptive and normal aging emotional regulatory effort. As people age, they tend to seek the optimization of affective relationships, with relatively greater time invested in intimate friendships and family relationships (Carstensen, 1995; Hayslip & Champa, 2007). Furthermore, and as part of what Bronfenbrenner (1979) called the macrosystem, culture plays an important role in how people in old age spend their lives. In Latin American countries, "aging in place" or "growing old at home" is the expectation as a normative process, even when facing frailty, disability, or dementia with advancing age. Along with this, there is an absence of government support and accessible formal specialized care options, and instead families assume the caring responsibility (Domínguez Guedea et al., 2013).

This multigenerational cohabitation has been related to *familism* as a collectivistic cultural value in Latin America. Familism promotes interdependence in informal support networks and results in enduring ties that increase positive affection. As Gibbons and Fanjul de Marsicovetere (2017) affirm, the centrality of the extended family in the cultural values of Mexico and Central America cannot be overstated: grandparents help and support family members, serve as role models, and impact socialization and the transmission of culture for the new generations.

In developed countries with high mobility and more individualistic cultures, such as the United States, it is less common for children to live with their extended family (Rogoff, 2003). In contrast, it was found that in most developing countries of Latin America such as Colombia, Mexico, Costa Rica, Argentina, Venezuela, Chile, and Brazil, multigenerational co-residence is increasing (Ruggles & Heggeness, 2008). This could be due to socioeconomic reasons like housing shortages, migration processes, an increasing female labor force, and declining employment opportunities for the young (Ruggles & Heggeness, 2008). Or it could also be due to the concurrence of individualistic and collectivistic traits, nuanced and interwoven in interdependent cultures.

Alternatively, cultural values such as familism might promote the cohabitation of three generations in Latin American countries and the caring of children by grandparents. Therefore, taking care of children by older adults might be the result of a normative value and not the result of personal choice (Grundy et al., 2012).

Familism is frequently observed in Latin America, and is considered to be a protective factor against mental problems. It promotes growth and development among children, since the family unit is defined in terms of respect, support, obligation, and reference (Valdivieso-Mora et al., 2016). In the process of socialization, the cultural value of familism can be understood through the interdependent and heteronomous family change model of Kağitçibaşi (2005).

This model suggests that interrelatedness arises as a psychological arena for positive affect and subjective well-being derived from people's cognitive and affective evaluations of their lives. Older adults living with children might experience feelings of optimism, solidarity, meaningfulness, and loyalty to significant others (Oliveira et al., 2017; Parveen et al., 2014).

Familism has been theorized as a sense of connectedness or strong identification with nuclear and extended families (Smith-Morris et al., 2012). It also refers to the cultural value that one's family is expected to provide necessary emotional and instrumental social support when needed (Calzada et al., 2012).

It has even been proposed that, within multigenerational family relationships, the systemic links are constituted through their members' histories. This may involve the inclusion of physically non-present members of the family network, as well as older people living elsewhere, deceased relatives, ancestors' spirits, and so on. These systemic links thus provide a highly redolent social context for human development over the life course (Marsico et al., 2015).

Nevertheless, it is ethically important to recognize that there is great diversity among families and communities in Latin America, with different political and sociocultural conditions. And various ways in which support is given within each lifestyle. In a changing and aging society, dichotomizations, such as "individualist" versus "collectivist groups," or the assumption that familism is a homogeneous construct, obscure the significant and rich variations embedded throughout our countries. It must also be acknowledged that family care activities will differ by gender, generation, and geography. Women are still the main providers of most of the emotional and instrumental care in daily life. Research on familism, mainly developed in the United States with its Latin American migrant population, might be omitting diverse and heterogenous family systems within a common cultural shared value. In this sense, it must be clearly stated that the characteristics and dynamics of families are modified according to their context, so the relations of Latin American migrant families in a country such as the United States may not necessarily correspond to the typical interactions of their peers in their country of origin.

Losses and Gains in Interactions with Grandparents in Latin America

Living and growing within a multigenerational family cohabitation becomes a scenario for development within Latin American cultures in which the interaction with grandparents is fundamental in a context of family diversity and societal change.

The role of grandparents in Latin American societies has been underrepresented in the scientific literature, which is mostly published in the United States through the study of Latin American migrants. Grandparenting research has typically been uncommon in developing countries (Schwalb & Hossain, 2017).

The multigenerational co-residence domain, as part of the psychosocial environment for development, intersects with other spheres of the environment since families are embedded in a community, in a society, and in eco-systems (Kaplan et al., 2017). Besides cultural aspects, other macrosystemic aspects such as the economy and social structure are determinant in multigenerational cohabitation.

In Latin America, this context involves a sociopolitical reality with not only income inequality, but also diverse social problems like diminishing access and quality of public services, citizen insecurity, discrimination, violence, migration, and corruption. These intersections ultimately result in decrease developmental opportunities for one-parent homes headed by women.

Possible developmental gains and losses of the multigenerational family interactions across different domains are detailed below.

Growing Old at Home as a Familistic Paradigm

It is well known that informal social support typically decreases as age increases (Acuña & González, 2010; Castellano, 2014). However, when reciprocity and balance is present in the family's support and care system, the well-being of all members tends to increase (Stuifbergen & Van Delden, 2011). This kind of responsiveness to one another's needs is the foundation of multigenerational solidarity as the generations who live together exchange different types of support (affective, instrumental, or economic) at different times, their relationship evolving and covarying through time.

Bengtson et al. (2002) understand family solidarity through six interrelated components: (1) contact, (2) exchange of support, (3) norms of obligation, (4) value similarity, (5) relationship quality, and (6) opportunity structure. For multigenerational cohabitation, family solidarity implies trustworthiness between members of different generations (Lüscher et al., 2013). Their interdependence is based on how their lives—across the generations—are inextricably linked (Kaplan et al., 2017). Often taken for granted, strong family ties are arguably the most crucial building block in creating an enduring and solidary society, precisely because families are the main source of continuing care (Suitor et al., 2011).

Given the economic disparities in our aging Latin American society, multigenerational connections within families play a critical role in terms of resilience and success at the individual, family, community, and societal levels. In this demographic scenario, the societal expectation for adult offspring is to take care of their parents in old age, the so-called intergenerational contract. In this "familistic paradigm," typically represented by the Mediterranean and Ibero-American contexts, family members organize, finance, and provide care services (Doyle & Timonen, 2009).

Interdependence becomes a norm in multigenerational households in Latin American contexts. Even when other options are available, such as external caregiving, the family may remain the core care provider for older parents and young children. It is important to consider, however, that such formal care is usually expensive and inaccessible to most of the population with medium and low incomes.

As an informal social support, family living is one of the worldwide predictors of positive affect and subjective well-being; it is related to benefits in health and longevity (Diener, 2012). In Costa Rica, for example, data have shown the presence of a possible protective role for this positive affect in old age, related to a healthier aging: Costa Ricans differ from an American-based sample in their self-reported affective profiles. The positive affect of Costa Ricans was 10 points higher than in the US sample (31.3 vs. 40.6, out of a possible 50), while negative affect was equivalent in both samples (Salazar-Villanea et al., 2015).

In Latin America, research has focused on the losses that caring for elderly family members has on the psychosocial well-being of the family's middle-aged generation. These losses are attributed to increased financial obligations and overall negative impacts on health and quality of life for the middle-aged family members (Fernández & Herrera, 2016). As part of the informal support system within the family, the main caregiver is often a middle-aged woman, daughter, or daughter-in-law who accrues losses in her own developmental trajectory (Brenes, 2009; Dias et al., 2015; Montero et al., 2014; Morlett et al., 2015; Russo, 2016; Silva-Ferreira & Rodriguez-Wong, 2008).The implications of these factors on children's development and attachment have not been extensively studied in Latin America.

Unbalanced family care with no reciprocity and that is perceived as a mandatory obligation is associated with overload and loss (Fernández & Herrera, 2016). In this regard, Thrush and Hayder (2014) showed that in low- and middle-income countries, a psychological burden or subjective overload is the most commonly reported. There is an increased probability of interpersonal conflicts due to deprivation related to personal time, isolation, or fatigue, especially when in conjunction with financial worries.

Grandparenting as a Solidarity Family Strategy

Grandparents both give and receive help from adult children and grandchildren in multigenerational cohabitation. Grandparent-grandchild relationships become necessary in an environment of great sociodemographic change (Beltrán & Rivas-Gómez, 2013; Tobío Soler, 2011). The elderly become caregivers within the household and, as multigenerational studies have indicated, this co-residence of older people and children is beneficial when solidarity strategies diminish the stress of a high-intensity care provision (Oliveira et al., 2017). In Brazil and Peru, it has been found that children living with their grandparents have better grades, better health, and are taller than children not living with grandparents, especially if grandparents receive public payments from the government, showing that economic support to the elderly trickles down to the young (Rentería-Pérez et al., 2007).

However, when it comes to caregiving of grandchildren, there are gender differences: grandmothers, especially maternal grandmothers, are more involved in child-care than grandfathers (Dunifon & Bajracharya, 2012).

Also, it is a role defined by age: younger (and healthier) grandparents are more able to take care of children than older ones (Dunifon & Bajracharya, 2012). Other factors affecting grandparenting are physical distance (how far parents and children live from each other) and the relationship parents and grandparents have (Dunifon & Bajrachaya, 2012).

It has been reported, for example, that in collectivistic and interdependent cultures being a "grandmother" is perceived as a parental responsibility that continues even when the sons and daughters have become independent. The impact of multiple roles on well-being has been studied in terms of the quality of roles (rather than the number of roles) and the satisfaction derived from them. In this sense, child-care seems to reinforce the grandmother's perceived value and status within the family. Younger generations recognize a sense of purpose and usefulness deriving from the emotional significance associated with companionship, the recovery of family history, and their role as counselors and economic supporters (González-Bernal et al., 2010; León et al., 2016; Triadó et al., 2008; Urrutia et al., 2016; Villar et al., 2012; Weisbrot & Giraudo, 2012). Hoyuelos Planillo (2004) distinguishes twelve roles grandparents can play in the relationship with their grandchildren: caretaker, playmate, storyteller, provider of historic sense and continuity to the family (by telling stories from the family's past), transmitter of moral values, model of aging and dying, alternative models (contrasting to the parents model), mediator between parents and children, helper during crisis, providers of unconditional love, confidants, and providers of tenderness. As it can be observed, some of these roles are complimentary or even alternative to the roles parents play, therefore, grandparents enrich the lives of children in a way that would not exist if they were not present. Furthermore, grandparents can compensate for inadequate care from parents. However, they can potentially interfere with parents' practices and rules by "spoiling" the child.

Effects of Relationship with Grandparents

The emotional support given by grandparents to their grandchildren seems to be higher during childhood, with a tendency to decline during adolescence, and becoming significant again during young adulthood (Klein, 2015; Pinazo-Hernándis & Lluna, 2011; Prato et al., 2012; Rentería-Pérez et al., 2007). Grandparenting contributes to the transmission of family stories that favor a sense of belonging, generativity in adults, and well-being in childhood and adolescence (Lázaro-Ruiz & Gil López, 2005; León et al., 2016; Merrill & Fivush, 2016). However, in Latin America the mediating role of grandparents in the relationship with the mother and father (the middle generation) has not been studied enough, even though other studies recognize it as a key factor (Bol & Kalmijn, 2016).

Empirical evidence in Latin America relates multigenerational cohabitation with an increased old age generativity resulting from the upbringing and caring experiences and with increased emotional support benefits for the grandchildren. In monoparental families the grandparent-grandchild relationship is the best example of multigenerational solidarity (Hernández-Cordero, 2016; Pinazo-Hernándis & Lluna, 2011; Quecha-Reyna, 2015; Tobío Soler, 2013). In general, child-care produces added satisfaction for grandparents as a result of having a closer relationship with their grandchildren (Zapata Posada et al., 2016) and Latin American parents might consider grandmothers as providing better quality care than day-care centers or preschools (Partidas, 2004).

On the other hand, child rearing can become the sole responsibility of grandparents when parents leave their children behind and migrate to other countries in hopes of improving the family's economic situation (Sánchez-Molina, 2004). Migration has created global families with members living in more than one country (Phillipson, 2010); the older adult often stays in the home country. As Dias et al. (2017) describe, the economic hardship and job-related migration of Brazilian parents causes grandparents in many families to take full responsibility for grandchildren. In a study from Colombia, grandmothers took the role of caregivers sometimes against their desire when their own children migrated. Since they were housewives and did not enjoy a pension or retirement savings, they were financially dependent on their offspring (Micolta León & Escobar Serrano, 2010).

Another reason for grandparents to take a more active role in child rearing occurs when their children become parents at a young age. In Latin America, a large number of adolescents become parents (UNICEF, 2007). Because teenage mothers may continue with their education but are not economically independent and not considered to be prepared for parenthood, grandmothers assume more responsibility for child rearing (Zapata Posada et al., 2016), in addition to providing economic support for both their children and grandchildren. Young grandmothers may simultaneously be employed, parenting their own daughter, and grandparenting; in some cases, these young grandmothers also have elderly care responsibilities. In this case, a young grandmother, for example, could be in her middle age, between 35 and 45 years old, having in her care responsibility for three different generations (her own children, grandchildren, and senior parents).

Other reasons for grandmothers to take full responsibility for caregiving include the parents' death due to criminal or political violence, child abuse, or diverse difficulties experienced by the parents (drug abuse, psychiatric problems, incarceration, among others) (Hayslip & Kaminski, 2005). This support has been especially important in countries suffering from political violence. In the case of Argentina, a country that suffered under a dictatorship during the 1970s, grandmothers had an important role in protecting the rights of children. The Asociación Civil Abuelas de Plaza de Mayo (Grandmothers of the Plaza de Mayo) continues to work in locating children kidnapped during the repression and returning them to their surviving biological families (Ortiz Cochivague, 2012).

Child rearing in these circumstances can have negative effects on older adults. For example, Colombian grandmothers felt that, because of childcare, their plans for the future were truncated (Zapata Posada et al., 2016). In the case of grandmothers living with their children who were adolescent mothers, conflicts might occur over the best way to raise the latter's children (Zapata Posada et al., 2016). Providing economic help for grandchildren can be detrimental, although this could depend on gender. In Chile, it was found that providing time and material help was associated with better mental health for the grandfather, but not for grandmothers (Grundy et al., 2012).

Further research must be done to understand the developmental gains and losses for grandchildren. A study in Peru showed that co-resident grandparents might use more traditional parenting techniques, such as physical punishment for discipline or traditional forms of healing (like rubbing a guinea pig over the body) over occidental medicine, which could create conflict with parents (Mechan Salazar & Díaz Manchay, 2013). It has been found in the United States that children raised by custodial grandparents are at a higher risk of having mental problems compared to the general population (Smith & Palimieri, 2007). This could be due at least in part to the fact that being cared by grandparents is the result of previous difficulties with parents, that these children have experienced the trauma of losing their parents, and that they are usually living in poverty (Dunifon, 2012).

However, being raised by custodial grandparents is a better option for children than institutionalization (Hayslip et al., 2019; Hayslip & Kaminski, 2005), and adolescents of single mothers fare better when a grandparent is also present at the home (Deleire & Kalil, 2001). Finally, living with grandparents can also allow children to maintain a connection with their traditional culture (Gibbons & Fanjul de Marsicovetere, 2017; Mechan Salazar & Díaz Mondary, 2013). Many children say their grandparents' love and stability allowed them to succeed in school, stay out of trouble, developing strong morals and religious values (Dolbin-MacNab et al., 2013). In a Latin American context in which children whose families don't assume custody are raised in institutions that do not always provide good childcare, being raised by an extended multigenerational family or custodial grandparent might be considered a better alternative.

Conclusions and Challenges

Research literature on familism, multigenerational cohabitation, and family relationships in Latin America is limited in amount and scope, both for quantitative and qualitative approaches. The available theorizations published in Spanish are from research in Spain, and the empirical data that have been published are primarily based on studies with the Latin American migrant population living in the United States. Generalizations may obscure the diversity of Latin American countries, with different ethnic group particularities, indigenous populations' traditions, and socioeconomic and political backgrounds. Although with a Latin American identity, migrants in a new context change their daily interactions, relationships, and practices. For example, one study showed that Mexican mothers in the United States, as a result of their migration, changed their eating habits, by having more ready-made food, as well as their child-rearing practices, including not allowing their children to play outside because of safety concerns (Fuster, 2011).

Low income, low education, and previous trauma associated with migration experiences, as well as mental illness or substance abuse, will probably continue to be correlated to lower outcome measures of behavioral, emotional, and physical well-being of children in Latin American grandfamilies studied within the United States. But, grandparenting in multigenerational cohabitation, as the most natural context for development for children in Latin America, has been found to provide a favorable family environment for children to live in, distributing parental functions and resources and promoting children's well-being. Research suggests that children who have been the beneficiaries of positive affect in multigenerational caregiver relationships in early childhood experience greater gains in familistic cultures, where it is common to live in extended-family households.

Thus, ethnicity, cultural diversity, and socioeconomic status are powerful variables in better understanding how children respond to grandparents as attachment figures within multigenerational family structures, with potential affective benefits that persist into adulthood.

Definitively, more research needs to be done on child's development and well-being, studying positive roles in the interaction between grandparents and grandchildren.

Revalidating care in the multigenerational cohabitation family system—in other words, framing it as positively responsiveness to the needs of others in the family instead of a negative burden—has been proposed as a strategy to maintain the solidarity of the family in our interdependent Latin American culture. Multigenerational solidarity becomes fundamental for development as a possible protective factor for children's development in Latin American countries within adverse and diverse political, economic, and social circumstances. Especially in an aging Latin America where there is no government-sponsored, well-structured, accessible formal care options for younger or older people. Paradoxically, developed countries with independent cultural values are increasingly calling for multigenerational co-residence and relationships; for instance, university students living with older adults, or elderly residences and child-care centers sharing spaces and activities. This could respond to an instrumental and economic strategy to optimize benefits, seeking to implement an interdependent policy in an independent rational context, where the emotional framework, affective closeness, and intimacy do not sustain those relationships.

The affective search for positive contact with others and for family closeness has different meanings at different times of life. Likewise, the possibilities of giving and caring are diverse at different points in the life cycle. These interactions have direct effects on the socioemotional development during life course considering the ecological system of multigenerational cohabitation in Latin American families. This could also be influenced and determined by gender in Latin American context.

Developmental gains in multigenerational co-residence are more likely to happen when there is reciprocity and balance, although this reciprocity may not be synchronous since different types of support might be given by different family members at different times throughout life. For example, affective, instrumental, and economic contributions of family members may not occur simultaneously; a family member can contribute in the affective domain at one time of their development (childhood), and economically in another (adulthood).

As it has been illustrated in this chapter, and following Bronfernbrenner's (1979) Ecological Theory, human development is a product of interactions within a nested arrangement of concentric structures: the micro-, meso-, exo-, and macrosystems, where each one is contained within the next. Different microsystems, such as interpersonal relationships, dyads, and roles within the family (i.e., grandparents-children, grandparents-grandchildren), interact in the multigenerational family mesosystem of relationships with people of the same generations (i.e., spouses, different kinds of peer groups), and at the same time, there are other external influences or environmental aspects that do not depend directly on the person and dyads, such as interactions at their community, workplaces, school class, and so on. Finally, all these systems interact at the upper level of the concentric structures or macrosystem, referring to cultural or subcultural values (i.e., familism, individualism, and collectivism), ethnic issues, religions, socioeconomic factors, or public policies. Considering that Latin America is not a homogenous region—geographically, ethnically, or sociopolitically—the picture of family interactions between generations and these ecology systems is complex. The study of the effect of multigenerational cohabitation on family relationships and child development is still incipient regarding its ecological validity and even more in its theoretical basis.

However, one particularity of the Latin American experience of grandparenting can be mentioned. In a family-oriented culture (macrosystem) that promotes the involvement of extended family in child-care (especially for grandmothers) and that experiences lack of institutional support in child-care from governments, Latin American families might be more likely to solve child-caring needs internally (within the microsystem) than through institutions (macrosystems), either temporarily (while the parents work) or permanently (custodial care). Although child-care might have positive effects for both grandparents and children, such as maintaining and reinforcing family liaisons, it might also put grandparents under strain.

Bronfenbrenner (1979) coined the term ecological transitions for those events when the person's role and position change. Seeing their children become independent adults after a prolonged period of care might provide a sense of relief and achievement to middle-aged and elder adults. But for custodial grandparents around the world, going back to raising children might feel like a regression. For these reasons, supporting grandparents' task in child-care, especially for those who are more disadvantaged (older, poorer, sicker, and more isolated) should be a priority for governmental agencies. One of Bronfenbrenner's most important contributions has been to remind us that children's development is the product of different settings beyond the family unit.

In the new context of an aging world, Latin American psychology must theorize about changes within the family, considering development beyond the early stages of life. There is a lack of empirical evidence to support political transformative actions and more robust evidence is mandatory in this regard in future research.

6
Family Mechanisms Underlying Adolescent Development in Facing Changes and Adversities

Blanca E. Barcelata Eguiarte

Introduction

One of the most popular and useful approaches to human development is the ecological perspective (Bronfenbrenner, 1977), based on assumptions and principles or general theory systems applied to the sciences of development (Lerner, 2011).[1] This approach may have had a great influence on the main child and adolescent development theories, on their theoretical and methodological implications to understanding the complex interaction within the person-environment system. Therefore, child and adolescent development is the result of dynamic interactions across multiple ecological organizer systems (microsystem to macrosystem). The aim of the sciences of development is to understand the complex variabilities in developmental trajectories and outcomes for children, adolescents, and families in diverse conditions and contexts (Lerner, 2011). Consequently, researchers have focused on the complex interaction of person-context which implies that a wide variability of personal and contextual factors include the family, which is considered one of the most important proximal factors for the adaptation and mental health of children and adolescents. This perspective includes cross-sectional, longitudinal, and cross-cultural research aimed to study and to explain the variability in the individual trajectories and outcomes across time, domains, and cultures (Magnusson & Stattin, 2006). This implies an interactional paradigm of developmental that supposes that, particularly,

---

[1] This research was supported by PAPIIT IT300223, DGAPA, National Autonomous University of Mexico.

Blanca E. Barcelata Eguiarte, *Family Mechanisms Underlying Adolescent Development in Facing Changes and Adversities*. In: *Family and Contexts of Development*. Edited by: Mariano Rosabal-Coto and Javier Tapia-Balladares, Oxford University Press. © Oxford University Press (2025). DOI: 10.1093/oso/9780197675144.003.0007

adolescence is a stage of the life cycle in which family plays an important role in the adaptation process and could be a proximal determinant, functioning as a mediating factor between the adolescent and distal factors, for example poverty. So, studying adolescent development in normative as well as non-normative conditions is needed; however, little research with children and adolescents, and families is reported in the literature with the Latin American population.

Families and Adolescents: An Overview of the Latin American Context

According to the World Health Organization (WHO, 2017) every five persons in the world are adolescents and in Latin America they represent 30% of the population. In Mexico, adolescents represent the widest strip of the population pyramid (National Population Council, 2015). In several Latin American countries, including Mexico, there exists a wide range of cultural contexts that frame child, adolescent, and family development; nevertheless, some macrostructural conditions seem to be common to all of them, such as poverty, linked to high marginalization and low human development rates for a significant population percentage in the area (Boltvinik, 2013). As Kliksberg (2014) argues, in diverse countries of Latin America, such as Bolivia, Ecuador, Guatemala, Mexico, and Peru, poverty represents a challenge for many families and a risk to child and adolescent development, including urban poverty which has also increased in the metropolitan areas of large cities (Boltvinick & Damian, 2016).

Therefore, the poverty in Latin America means families with children and adolescents frequently have to face chronic financial stress. High unemployment rates, for example, have contributed to higher levels of poverty, with around 51% of people living in poverty, which in turn has led to increased migration, a growing informal economy, and increasing inclusion of former housewives in the workforce (Barceló, 2007; Kliksberg, 2005; UNICEF, 2021; WHO, 2014). The consequence of this is a transition from the traditional nuclear family to diverse family configurations and dynamics in order to face the globalized world demands. In the 1970s, in Latin America the main family configuration was the nuclear family, in which the mother was primary caregiver and responsible for raising the children (Kliksberg, 2005), nowadays both fathers and mothers can be equally responsible for the rearing of children. The National Institute of Statistics and Geography (2020) informs us that in Mexico there are about 126 million people, of which around of 31% are adolescents aged 12 to 29 years, while young people between the ages of 15 and 29 living in Mexico represent 25% of the country's total population (National Council of Population, 2020). In addition, around of 99 million people live in a family, of which 71% are nuclear families, 28% are extensive, while 2.5% do not live in family. Of these families, 53.8% are biparental, 18% mono-parental, and 28.2% represent other kinds of family structure, suggesting that the family is continually changing, which is influencing directly or indirectly its dynamic and functioning. According to the World Bank (2021), Mexico is one of the low-middle-income countries (LMICs), where the vast majority of adolescents are living under of the poverty line. Moreover, the current economic crises have affected more than half of the population through the family. So, 58.7% of the population represents the economically active population (EAP), with increasing unemployment affecting the standard and quality of life for the whole family and its members. Census of Population and Housing (CONAPA, 2020) highlights an increase in the number of Mexican homes that are economically provided for by both parents, and furthermore, four out of every 10 homes are economical supported only by women, as sole household income provider for the family.

In this sense, the study of adolescent development can be better understood by assuming an integral and systemic perspective of human development, not only to explain some personal and family proximal factors, but also to include other kinds of distal factors such as poverty, health, and education policies, which could represent serious obstacles for the integral development of adolescents and families in Latin America and Mexico.

Theoretical Framework of Family and Adolescent Development

The developmental psychopathology perspective of child and adolescence development (Luthar, 2006), more recently also known as the ecological-transactional or organizational perspective (Cicchetti, 2010, 2013) due to its influence from the premises of the ecological model of human development proposed by Bronfenbrenner (1977), considers that adolescent development is the result of the interaction of diverse ecological systems (Cicchetti, 2010).

The adaptive or maladaptive outcomes in terms of mental health are the result of a transactional process across multiple levels with proximal factors (person, family) and distal factors (school, neighborhood, sociopolitical, and cultural contexts) (Aaron & Dallaire, 2010; Cicchetti, 2010) of which family plays a central role in adolescent development (Conger & Conger, 2002). This perspective is part of a macroparadigm which some researchers call the "sciences of development" (Lerner, 2011), and considers that the family is: 1) a system in transformation with the ability to adapt to diverse demands across the life cycle, in order to ensure continuity and psychosocial growth for every member (Carter & McGoldrick, 2005; Minuchin & Fishman, 1981); and 2) a semi-open system in interaction with other wide external systems, so that those happening in economic, cultural, or political context affect its members. The family is a natural group and at the same time an organizational system, defined by its number of members, positions, and interactions, inner and outward, revealing its members' way of gathering together to face certain situations and defining its functioning, mobility, or transformation capacity along the life cycle (Carter & McGoldrick, 2005; García et al., 2015; Patterson, 2002). Family functioning is a complex process, the product of transactional rules between its members, which allows organizing and self-regulating in a dynamic way. There are diverse models of family functioning, for example the Olson's Circumflex Family Model (2000) or the McMaster Family Functioning Model (Miller et al., 2000), both of which nevertheless refer to the main mechanisms of: 1) family cohesion; 2) communication; 3) flexibility; and 4) conflict and problem-solving. They share the same assumptions that high family cohesion, open communication, flexibility, and a capacity to solve problems can increase the adaptation and resilience of the whole family and its members, including adolescents.

Family cohesion refers to the engagement or affective link level between the family members which develops a sense of belonging and support among members; a healthy level of cohesion contributes to enhancing a central developmental task during adolescence—accomplishing a sense of their own identity (Carter & McGoldrick, 2005; Olson, 2000). An "excess" of family cohesion can lead to an excess of emotion, while the contrary, a low cohesion, can represent emotional disengagement with a consistent perception of neglect and lack of family support for the adolescent (Minuchin & Fishman, 1981; Olson, 2000). Communication includes every kind of verbal and non-verbal expression (Davis & Cummings, 2006) as part of the daily interactions in the family system, having both an instrumental and emotional function. The communicational patterns among family members reflect the family's functioning, and are associated with adaptive and non-adaptive behavior in children and adolescent (Fitzpatrick, 2004; Rueter & Koerner, 2008). Adaptability or family flexibility is defined as the skill of the family to fit and react in an appropriate way to change: the ability to face situational stress, non-normative life events, or those due to transitional normative situations in the life cycle of the family or its members (Olson, 2000; Walsh, 2006). This process involves organizational rules that improve a family's fitness to adapt to change and transitions that can involve daily tasks in family development (Carter & McGoldrick, 2005; Miller et al., 2000).

The Family Stress Model (ABCX) proposed by Hill (McCubbin & Patterson, 1982) constitutes another theoretical-methodological framework that explains how some families react to critical and adverse situations, according to, for example, life event characteristics and the family's vulnerability level. Family stress theory (McCubbin & Patterson, 1982) as well as the theory of family resistance (Patterson, 2002) propose that the combinations of family functioning elements, and other resources like coping and social support, contribute to dealing with daily or major events like chronic illness, unemployment, sexual abuse, or natural disasters (Figley, 1982; Patterson & Garwick, 1994; Walsh, 2006). On the other hand, the Family Stress Model (Conger & Conger, 2002) proposes that a focus on the family's economic conditions contributes toward explaining how economic strains can directly or indirectly impact adolescent development through a deterioration of marital relations and parenting. On the basis of Conger's model, recently Wadsworth and colleagues (Mistry & Wadsworth, 2011; Santiago et al., 2012; Santiago et al., 2011; Wadsworth et al., 2016) have shown evidence of the negative impact of poverty on development, and its association with externalizing and internalizing symptoms. They have focused on understanding the complex relationship between stress, coping, and family factors as mediators and moderators between poverty and adaptive and maladaptive adolescent outcomes; most of this research has been developed based on the American population.

However, personal variables like perceived social support, coping strategies, and self-efficacy could be protective factors, buffering the negative effects of stress and risk on adolescents given that they are used as resources since they may play a mediating role between family economic strains or parental conflict and the adolescent outcome. Thus, several multifactorial research projects focus on family and adolescent adaptation processes in normative and non-normative situations that involved stress or some type of adversity, include coping and social support (e.g. Bokszczanin & Makowsky, 2007; Santiago et al., 2012; Wadsworth & Santiago, 2008).

Family as a Risk-Protective Factor in Adolescent Outcomes: Prior International Research

From the "ecological-systemic perspectives" (Cicchetti, 2010; Lerner, 2011; Sameroff & Rosenblum, 2006), particularly from the developmental psychopathology perspective, understanding trajectories and adolescent developmental outcomes requires taking into account a particular adolescent's family context. Adaptation and resilience are complex processes, in particular the latter, because it implies adaptation under adverse, stressful, and risk situations involving non-normative or unexpected events in the life cycle of adolescents and families (Carter & McGoldrick, 2005; Masten & Cichhetti, 2010). Research models in resilience, particularly the risk-resilience model, suppose that development involves an interplay between diverse personal and environmental risks and protective factors within the ecological system of the adolescent (from macrostructural to individual systems). So, abuse and neglect in the family (Cicchetti, 2013), lack of communication, low family cohesion, negative parenting practices, or mental illness are all considered family risk factors since they are associated with emotional and behavioral problems. However, some characteristics of adolescents, like their use of productive coping strategies or their perceived social support from another significant person can act as moderating variables, buffering and minimizing the negative consequences of the family situation on developmental outcomes. On the other hand, a supportive and warm family can be protective when faced with social and personal negative factors, for example impulsivity, negative peers, or a violent neighborhood (WHO, 2014). Thus, some family characteristics can work as a proximal risk, whereas others can provide a protective function acting as mediator and moderator between proximal and distal factors (Anderson et al., 2013).

Thus, it is central to know how families face normative and non-normative situations (Rutter, 2012), in terms of adaptation to everyday and ordinary situations, and resilience in extraordinary and unexpected situations. For decades, the studies on stress and family resilience theories have shown that chronic family stressors come from the combination of different family adversities that work at different risk levels (Cicchetti, 2010; Conger & Conger, 2002; Masten & Cicchetti, 2010; Rutter, 2012; Sameroff & Rosenblum, 2006). The stressors associated with structure and family functioning—such as: a) low socioeconomic status; b) parents with low schooling; c) parents with low occupation profiles; d) low living standards; e) the unemployment of the main provider; f) lack of stability in family configuration; g) precedents of mental illness in one or both of the parents; h) sexual abuse; i) intrafamily violence; j) anti-social behavior and crime; k) alcohol and drugs use by parents; l) precedents of suicide behavior in the family—tend to increase the effect of other internal or external stress sources, creating a synergistic effect and giving rise to discontinuities in adolescent development.

Further, stressful family events often have a negative impact on adolescents' mental health. Thus, abused children in a neglected family environment are more likely to exhibit biological and psychological problems, such as neurodevelopmental deficits and violent behavior (Cicchetti, 2013; Freisthler et al., 2006). Also chronic physical and sexual abuse in childhood and adolescence by a family member has been linked to later suicidal behavior (Olshen et al., 2007; Trepal et al., 2006). Regarding family functioning, there is evidence that a tense family environment with communication problems, little support, and low cohesion is associated with emotional problems (Davis & Cummings, 2006); and the absence of parental support predicts anxiety (Bokszczanin & Makowsky, 2007). In contrast, open and flexible communication patterns, particularly with parents, are related to positive parenting strategies (i.e. DeVore & Ginburg, 2005; Fitzpatrick, 2004; Karreman et al., 2009). Also, a cohesive family as well as perceived social support are related to emotional well-being and adaptivity even in adverse situations (Crespo et al., 2011; Perosa & Perosa, 2001).

On the other hand, economic hardship associated with poverty and marginalized settings affects the adolescent's development in families, who also have to face diverse stressful events, since poverty creates a cascade of stressors (Rutter, 2012). Living in conditions of poverty also implies chronic stress, associated with internalizing and externalizing problems (Leventhal & Brooks-Gunn, 2000), which also impacts on the biological domain with serious consequences in terms of significant disorders in the adolescent's development (Walker et al., 2011). Nevertheless, there are adolescents who, despite risk and adverse experiences, contrary to the predictions, report positive adaptation and development trajectories, which means they are resilient (Luthar, 2006; Rutter, 2012). Family can give support to an adolescent of low achievement or who has been assaulted. In this process, family can be crucial for their positive adaptation or resilience.

Sameroff and Rosenblum (2006) establish that there are families who represent different risk levels. The high-risk families are those who provide few protective resources. Several studies (e.g. Conger & Conger, 2002; Leventhal & Brooks-Gunn, 2000; Wadsworth et al., 2016) indicate a set of useful indicators of socioeconomic level to identify poverty: 1) family income level; 2) schooling and occupation of parents; 3) mother's age at first pregnancy; 4) family structure and size.

Multifactorial research aimed at studying adolescent and family mechanisms of adaptation with low economic resources and conditions of poverty (e.g. Santiago et al., 2012; Santiago et al., 2011; Wadsworth & Santiago, 2008) include aspects of family functioning. Although other aspects also are linked to the context, its support networks, and coping strategies which can come up between the risk conditions, showing that they can be protective factors and give positive endings as a result; such is the case with their coping, their perception of the particular life events, and their social support. Thus, the family system, in addition to representing a multi-factor environment through its subsystems linked to exosystems, offers parental support and a warm climate that promote resilience, operating on a continuous risk-protection(Aaron & Dallaire, 2010; Conger et al., 2010; Everall et al., 2006).

In synthesis, the international literature shows that family context plays a central role in the adolescent's development in normative and non-normative situations that might represent risk and adversity. The functional families are those with high levels of cohesion and flexibility, open communication, good parenting practices, and skills to cope with internal and external stressors. A good family functioning provides a healthy family environment generating condition for positive adolescent development and adaptive outcomes.

From Risk to Protection in the Family Context: Sharing Experiences in Latin America and Mexico

Many Latin American families are inserted in what is known as the "circle of poverty" as proposed by Birch and Gussow (Garmezy, 1991), generating transgenerational psychosocial problems, since poverty is associated with other risks and is considered a chronic stressor that is added to and associated with other stressors in the form of a cascade, as Rutter (2012) points out. So, as was mentioned, families have to face diverse natural challenges, many of them associated with factors in the macrosystem such as poverty and low human development indexes (HDI), like kidnapping, displacement, migration, violence, delinquency, and crime (UNICEF, 2011). Kliksberg's (2005, 2014) studies show multiple faces and types of families, most of them living in marginalized settings associated with diverse stressful life events; however, they show that Latin American families and adolescents overcome the adverse experience by being resilient, as shown in the research findings.

Distal economic, social, or political variables are associated with migration, family abandonment, and other problems of family functioning which, in turn, are related to violence and delinquency during adolescence. These kinds of factors in the macrostructure seem to test the capacity of the family system to adapt to new circumstances. Therefore, the configuration and structure of families have been changing, through adaptive processes, showing resilience in most of cases of Latin American families. Nuclear or intact family is no longer the most frequent sort of family, the single-parent configuration has become common, as well as the extended family, trying to cover specific and contextual needs of Latin American families. The question is, how do families manage all these situations? The answer is not so simple, and the responses are along diverse systems.

In the last decades, research in Latin America has been growing, showing the importance of family context to child and adolescent outcomes from the "sciences of development" (Ierulle, 2015; Tapia et al., 2012). Family issues like abuse, violence, divorce, mental disorders, impulsive behavior, depression seem to be related to proximal factors but also to distal factors such as poverty and marginalization, since there is an interaction of protective and risk factors along the ecological systems, which is demonstrated in the literature.

A study prepared by Benjet et al. (2009) in Mexico showed that approximately 68% had experienced at least one adversity or were living in chronic adversity conditions and 7% had brought some type of adversity. Around of 60% of adolescents living in the metropolitan area of Mexico City reported more than three poverty indicators and about 30% also presented significant stress levels associated with family issues (Barcelata & Lucio, 2012). The studies of Barcelata et al. (2012b) have been consistent in showing how a higher number of negative family events, in addition to less cohesion and communication, might make the difference in clinical and school samples of adolescents in marginalized settings of Mexico City. Moreover, resilient youths tend to have a more cohesive family and they perceive more family support than non-resilient adolescents do. These data relate to low socioeconomic classes, in which exist a higher number of negative events than in other socioeconomic classes (Lucio et al., 2001). However, many studies show that there are adolescents capable of being competent and resilient, although resilient adolescents presented a low number of stressors and better ways of coping, but the central variable is the family. In other words, a better family environment in addition to active coping mechanisms were the main resilience predictors (Barcelata et al., 2012a). These findings are similar to others (Arenas et al., 2008) who reported that parental support and open communication can be the basis for designing intervention programs with Mexican school adolescents and parents.

Colombian youths living in similar circumstances, for example, Amarís, Paternina, and Vargas (2004) highlight the importance of family cohesion and sense of belonging to adolescents in circumstances like violence and displacement, or under economic pressures and unemployment (Martín et al., 2007). Other studies with Colombian families with adverse experiences show that coping aimed at solving problems contribute to dealing with stress (Amarís et al., 2013), however, families with adolescents in divorce proceedings tend to use less active coping and more coping focus on emotion (Cadavid & Amarís, 2007). Research with Chilean families (Gómez & Kotliarenco, 2010) shows that families react in different ways, developing diverse trajectories of family functioning, along the life cycle, facing stressful experiences and life events through dynamic process by steps. The chronic nature of poverty is a major and multidimensional stressor that influences adolescent development through multiproblem families (Grotberg, 2004).

Many families in the context of poverty and psychosocial risk are characterized by family functioning difficulties and negative parenting as the presence of rejection and hostility for parents increase emotional and behavioral problems, since the perception of having family support is associated with high cohesion and communication and low conflict (Barcelata et al., 2013; Quiroz et al., 2007). Besides, a lack of financial resources has created a situation where parenting practices extend to other family members (e.g. grandparents) and even public institutions who try to "rescue" children and adolescents, changing in a significant way the adolescent trajectories (Ierullo, 2015; Luna et al., 2010). Early pregnancy continues to be associated with marginalized families and settings (Barcelata et al., 2014);

sexual abuse, mostly carried out in the victims' own families (Beltrán, 2009), as well as child sexual exploitation (Amarís et al., 2007); and other problems related to the use of alcohol and other drugs such as tobacco (Ramírez & Andrade, 2005). In psychosocial risk populations, the presence of rejection and hostility for parents is a variable that increases emotional and behavioral problems, since family support perception is associated with high cohesion and good communication and low conflict (Barcelata et al., 2013; Quiroz et al., 2007).

Negative parental rearing patterns are also related with low economic status, and low educational and cultural resources in parents, as well as to emotional and behavioral problems as some studies show in Mexico. Andrade et al. (2012) showed how parents with depressive children used psychological control as a way of controlling the adolescent's behavior. In contrast, positive parenting styles, such as open communication characterized by parent's relating with warmth and affectivity, are associated with a lower number of internalized and externalized problems, and better adjustment and mental health (Betancourt & Andrade, 2011; Méndez et al., 2013; Ruvalcaba et al., 2016). Behavior control can be positive for children and adolescents, except in the case of psychological control since this can imply a sort of indirect means of behavior management according to the wishes of parents, consequently making behavior problems more likely. Other studies about family risk and suicide behavior factors in adolescents (Rivera & Andrade, 2006) report that family unity and support as well as higher freedom to express emotions and less perception of family difficulties were protective factors. Family can be also a risk or protective factor with behavior in terms of use of alcohol and drugs, as studies in Ecuador and Mexico have demonstrated (e.g. Ramírez & Andrade, 2005; Rodríguez et al., 2007). The findings suggest that the level of family cohesion is a mediating variable, in addition with the level of parental communication when exploring resilience in adolescent users and non-users of drugs.

On the other hand, research about migration (another important issue worldwide in recent years) effects on families, like forced displacement, "ambiguous losses" (Falicov, 2002), child neglect (Aguilera et al., 2004), and family environment demonstrated the negative effects on family and adolescent development, but also provided indicators of positive adaptation and resilience. For example, a father's absence in immigrant Mexican families in the United States of America was a stronger factor for stress compared to other variables (Aguilera et al., 2004). Here families present restructuring and resilience indicators derived from the transformation processes and efforts to cope with challenges that this absence implies, the absence of the "head of family," forcing women to take a more active role in the home economy, and also to assume new empowering roles to face other challenges (Pick et al., 2011). A subsequent study (Rivera et al., 2013) showed that the family's dynamic in Mexican migrants of the state of Michoacán (Mexico) led mainly by women was characterized by a supportive social and community climate, despite stressful life events, and their adolescent sons presented a high level of individual resources, such as sense of humor, but the best predictors of positive adaptation were open communication and family cohesion.

Márquez (2008) provided a model of the relation between parenting styles and academic-social adjustment in school adolescents, reporting a link between supportive parenting styles, a positive family climate, and academic competitivity, in similar way as was lately reported by González, Guevara, Jiménez, and Álcazar (2017). Also, low academic profiles showed positive interrelations with rejecting parenting styles and a negative family environment, in which the relationship with the mother was essential.

Summarizing, from an "ecological-systemic perspective" also known as the "sciences of development," and particularly "developmental psychopathology" studies of adolescent development in some countries of Latin America highlight the flexibility and capacity of adolescents and their families to face many adversities.

Family represents the most stable primary group for growth even during adolescence, but the adolescent's developmental trajectories and outcomes do not depend on this proximal context, so it is important take into account some critical considerations, because adaptive mechanisms are not always the same. So, explaining the processes of adaptation and resilience means studying several specific models of resilience, as some researchers have suggested (Masten, 2001; O'Dougherty et al., 2013), which can be useful in understanding adaptation in spite of the adverse condition in which many Latin American families live.

A compensation model of resilience, based on the risk-resilience model (Masten, 2001), assumes that positive adaptation results from the balance of risk and protective factors, because some protective factors are stronger than the risk factors. For example, in families with a neglectful father, frequently mothers or grandparents can provide family support that adolescents need;

or a sense of cohesion and community can help them to resist the pressure and stresses of life for migrant Latin American families; and also a combination of personal and family resources can contribute to resilience (Aguilera et al., 2004 Jiménez Arrieta et al., 2012; Rivera & Andrade, 2006).

In some cases, the challenge-resilience model seems to be capable of explaining how adolescents and families face many adversities. The stress inoculation model proposes that a few adverse experiences could improve resilience in adolescents and families, working as a "vaccine" for later and more intensely stressful experiences, preparing the adolescent to learn functional strategies to cope with other similar experiences (Masten, 2001). A moderate exposure to stressors or to a minor adverse experience can increase their capacity for adaptation in a major adverse situation, as some studies show (Amarís et al., 2004). On the other hand, within, the framework of risk is the cascade model (Masten & Cicchetti, 2010; Rutter, 2012) that supposes the sum of cumulative and subsequent vulnerabilities and risk variables negatively affects developmental trajectories and, consequently, outcomes. It could be that this model better explains issues associated with alcohol consumption, family maltreatment, neglect, and abuse, all problems of high prevalence among Latin American adolescents and families (Rivera et al., 2013; Rodríguez et al., 2007).

Conclusions

Childhood and adolescent developmental sciences are a broad umbrella of diverse ranges of models useful for analyzing the family as a proximal risk-protective context for the development of adolescents living in adverse and conditions of significant risk. Wide international evidence from this perspective shows the importance of proximal factors like family, as well as distal factors such as poverty and marginalization, which can represent a risk for adolescent developmental outcomes, depending on a complex interaction along the different systems. This model has been lately adopted in Latin American research, since a high proportion of children, adolescents, and families are living in high-risk conditions.

The studies of Latin American families have focused on adolescent and family development and adaptive processes to normative and non-normative situations, analyzing the relationship between stress, risk, and resilience in different directions: a) toward the study of the negative impact of stressful life events and severe stressors on adolescents or whole families, for example, analyzing the adaptation processes facing them in major events or trauma (e.g. Amarís et al., 2004; Beltrán, 2009; Cadavid & Amarís, 2007); b) measuring family stress derived from a multiple adversity context, examining the relation between major events, chronic and daily stressors, and its relation with family stress perception, personal stress, and negative adolescent outcomes (Amarís et al., 2013; Andrade et al., 2012; Barcelata et al., 2012a, 2012b; Barcelata et al., 2014; Estévez et al., 2012; Santiago et al., 2012; Santiago et al., 2011); c) attending to the study of family functioning and parenting styles or rearing, with special attention on communication processes, cohesion, and flexibility, analyzing their relationship, or mediating or moderating role, facing significant stress or risk conditions (e.g. Amarís et al., 2004; Arenas et al., 2008; Barcelata et al., 2014; Falicov, 2002; Márquez, 2008; Rivera et al., 2013).

This brief overview shows that Latin American adolescents and their families have to face multiple risks in diverse ecological systems, and how they can be resilient. Family is, perhaps, the most important system offering risk or protective roles, since it is associated with mental health problems but also with positives outcomes. So family is a proximal context that usually works on the basis of a risk-protection continuum for the adolescent. So, family-adolescent interaction implies the covariation of specific psychological processes and different context levels including the cultural dynamic. On the other hand, adolescence represents plenty of opportunities and resources that can be promoted and enhanced. Coping is an individual and family protective factor when it is using in a productive way; social support, particularly family support (mother and father) and a generally good, functioning family (demonstrating openness, flexibility, cohesion, good parenting, etc.) can be the best protective factor for a good adaptation in adolescence to different settings, including situations of risk and adversity. Many children and adolescents in Latin America are resilient: they have a more functional family environment, have higher parental supervision and perceive higher parents support and perceived positive parenting. In spite of contextual conditions for families, children, and adolescents being similar in Latin America including Mexico, cultural diversity within and between countries generates differences and inequalities in the developmental opportunities of adolescents, even within each country. This implies many risks, opportunities, and challenges for the social and economic sciences, as well as sciences of human development. More research is needed to understand the many adolescent trajectories and developmental outcomes.

The ecological-transactional model offers a wide theoretical and methodological framework for research with practical implications particularly relevant for research in Latin America due the wide variations of macrocultural factors across the continent and microcultural contexts even within a country. This can be useful in understanding the interplay of beliefs, cognitions, emotions, and behaviors in both individual and family systems. Evaluation and intervention from a preventive perspective with empirical evidence should be carried out in different settings. However, every region of Latin America should be taking account of the diversity of families which have to face specific challenges in order to propose approaches and viable mental health actions for making families, children, and adolescents resilient, keeping in mind the different microsystems in which they live.

Finally, another important component for adaptation in Latin American adolescents and families is the role of culture; for example, it seems that collectivism can be a cultural variable that seems to work as a protection factor, which can generate a sense of coherence and cohesion intra- and inter-families, contributing to the positive development of adolescents. Research could be the basis for planning public health action, as some programs developed in Colombia in schools supported by the Ministry of Education (Flórez-Alarcón, 2005; Flórez-Alarcón & Hewitt, 2013) have shown. A healthy-school program has aimed, for example, to reduce alcohol abuse in the school setting by children and youths.

Latin American researchers have to face many challenges in order to development their own theoretical and empirical models. Studies have been carried out across multiple settings, with different theoretically and methodologically specific models, according to populations, groups, contexts, and resources. However, it is important to integrate experiences and findings with those carried out in other countries. New and more programs are needed based on research evidence designed from a preventive perspective in family and school interventions given the lack of mental health public services. On the other hand, more multidisciplinary research is needed aimed to understand adaptation and resilience processes in Latin American youths and families, most of them living in conditions of high social-economic pressure. So, research is needed in diverse Latin American countries; despite similarities across countries, there are specific factors, most of them related to socioeconomic and cultural issues, that can lead to differences in responses to and ways of coping with poverty and adversity, as the evidence has shown (e.g. Wadsworth et al., 2016), even in the "same culture." Longitudinal studies are also needed because the effects of early experiences are not always evident in cross-sectional studies. Then, too, it is important to work with more positive models, such as a competences model, aimed to promote social, emotional, and cognitive competence in adolescents and families, which will represent the accumulation of resources or competences they use to face challenges in a changing world.

7

Emotion Talk during Reminiscing

A Comparative Study between Mother-Son and Mother-Daughter Dyads from Two Different Educational Backgrounds in Costa Rica

Nayuribe Sáenz, Marcela Ríos, Krissia Salazar, and Ana M. Carmiol

Interactions between parents and their children are key scenarios during the process of development and its results (Vygotsky, 1978).[1] Language plays an essential role in such interactions in being the main instrument of culture and, therefore, an enhancer of skills as well (González-Rey, 2010). Reminiscing, or talking about past, personal events brings these two features together: it is guided by adults and it involves language, which, in turn, makes it into a daily arena of great relevance for early childhood development.

Studies about reminiscing arose from efforts to document individual differences in memory development. Early findings revealed that the way caretakers reconstruct past personal experiences through conversations with children affects the way they code and retrieve the details of the event (Fivush et al., 2006). At present, the effects of reminiscing on the development of early abilities such as autobiographical memory (Fivush, 2011), early literacy (Reese et al., 2010), self-awareness (Song & Wang, 2013), theory of mind (Taumoepeau & Reese, 2013) and socioemotional development (Fivush, 2007; Laible, 2004) are well known. The purpose of this study was to describe how Costa Rican mothers reminisce with their 4-year-old children, with a special interest in identifying how they refer to the emotions involved in the events under discussion.

---

[1] Authors' note: We would like to thank the participating mothers and children. Portions of this research were developed as part of individual honors theses conducted by the first three authors at Escuela de Psicología, Universidad de Costa Rica. Preparation of this chapter was supported by a grant from Vicerrectoría de Investigación, Universidad de Costa Rica, awarded to the fourth author (723-B7-219).

Nayuribe Sáenz et al., *Emotion Talk during Reminiscing*. In: *Family and Contexts of Development*.
Edited by: Mariano Rosabal-Coto and Javier Tapia-Balladares, Oxford University Press. © Oxford University Press (2025). DOI: 10.1093/oso/9780197675144.003.0008

Talking about emotions is important for child development (Dunn et al., 1991; Hughes et al., 2014; Ornaghi et al., 2015). Labeling, explaining, and rationalizing emotional experiences of our own or of others promote socioemotional development in the preschool years (Fivush et al., 2003; Goodvin & Romdall, 2013; Lagattuta & Wellman, 2002). During conversations, speakers attribute emotional states, and discuss their causes and consequences and the way to solve negative emotions. This promotes children's ability to evaluate, interpret, and understand emotions (Nolivos & Leyva, 2013).

Reminiscing allows for exchanges that can encourage the creation of affective bonds, the development of the self, and the relationship with others (Leyva et al., 2014; McDermott & Peterson, 2003). Different findings indicate that securely attached children tell stories that are more complete, consistent, and coherent (Kelly, 2015), especially when such stories deal with difficult emotional experiences (Fivush & Vasudeva, 2002; Laible, 2004, 2010). Other results highlight the relationship between reminiscing and self-awareness (Fivush, 2007), inasmuch as talking about emotions of their own and of others helps the child to evaluate and understand the event from a personal perspective, and in its relation to the perspective of others as well. It also helps children understand their feelings about the event, allowing them to create connections between past experiences and their understanding of the present, hence facilitating a more comprehensive understanding of their own selves.

Conversations about negative events can be particularly elaborate, reflexive, and explanatory. This supports the argument that social conflict is an opportunity to promote social understanding (Dunn et al., 1991). Unlike conversations about positive events, discussions of negative events imply tensions. Consequently, talking about them requires effort to regulate the intensity, direction, and duration of the conversation. Empirical evidence indicates that discussions about negative events involve a greater deal of mentioning of the causes and consequences of emotions than discussions about positive events, as well as more connections between mind and emotion (Lagattuta & Wellman, 2002). For this reason, conversations about negative events constitute favorable scenarios for caregivers to help children understand how to face and solve conflictive experiences (Fivush et al., 2003). One goal of the present study was to analyze the amount and type of emotion talk produced by mothers and their children when talking about negative and positive past events. Based on the findings previously described, we expected dyads in our sample would refer more often to the causes, consequences, and resolution of emotions during negative than during positive events.

The sex of the child has also been identified as a variable that explains individual differences in emotion talk during reminiscing. Nevertheless, findings are not entirely conclusive (e.g., Goodvin & Romdall, 2013; Laible, 2004, 2010; Van Bergen & Salmon, 2010). Fivush et al. (2003) found that Anglo-American mothers made more efforts to solve negative emotions with girls than with boys. On the other hand, Melzi and Fernández (2004) found that, when discussing positive events, Latin American mothers asked more questions about emotions, their causes, and consequences to their sons than to their daughters. Such differences could be explained by the variations in traditional gender roles across cultural contexts. However, the evidence is still too scarce to provide a definite answer. This study attempted to identify differences in the way Costa Rican mothers reconstruct past personal experiences with their sons and daughters. Based on the available evidence, no *a priori* hypotheses about the pattern of results concerning emotion talk as a function of children's sex were made.

Cross-cultural evidence has identified differences in the way caregivers from different contexts reconstruct past emotional experiences with their children. When reminiscing about emotional events with their preschool children, Anglo mothers use more elaborate and evaluative conversation styles than Asian mothers (Fivush & Wang, 2005). In addition, they are more explanatory and focus more on discussing the causes and resolutions of emotions. A plausible explanation for this difference could be the variations in the cultural orientations about the self in both cultural contexts. While Anglo societies have been characterized for encouraging an independent self, Asian societies focus on promoting the development of an interdependent self. Thus, while Anglo mothers promote the development of autonomy and independence and value emotions in relation to the subjective experience, Asian mothers promote the importance of shared goals and the evaluation of emotions in relation to others (Fivush, 2007; Halberstadt & Lozada, 2011).

Previous evidence indicates that parenting styles among Latin American caregivers promote the development of a hybrid self. This self combines aspects traditionally characterized as independent (e.g., autonomy) and aspects traditionally characterized as interdependent (e.g., relatedness) (Keller, 2013; Schröder et al., 2013). However, evidence about the way this hybrid pattern is reflected in the socialization of emotions of boys and girls is still scarce. Nolivos and Leyva (2013) analyzed the emotional content and the themes discussed during past event conversations between low-income, Chilean mothers and their children. They found dyads frequently referred to emotional terms, but rarely mentioned the causes and consequences of such emotions (see Carmiol & Schröder, 2019, for similar results). In other words, they focused on labeling the emotions but they provided few explanations about them. They also observed dyads talked a great deal about topics related to joint activities and social interactions (i.e., parties and family gatherings) where children's relatives and friends were involved. According to the authors, this showed the group was more highly valued than the individual. Likewise, dyads in this sample gave importance to topics about discipline and moral standards, where caregivers sought to have more control and showed more concern about transmitting a moral lesson to their children than about discussing the nature of the children's thoughts and feelings.

Carmiol and Schröder (2019) compared emotion talk in Costa Rican and German middle-class mother-child dyads during reminiscing and book sharing. They found that the complexity of their emotion talk did not differ between the groups, but Costa Rican dyads talked overall more about emotions than German dyads. Moreover, Costa Rican dyads showed a preference for referring to others as the agents of the emotions, but both cultural groups talked about the child as the agent of the emotion to a similar extent. According to the authors, this pattern shows the hybrid nature of the self-guiding of the parenting practices among Costa Rican caregivers, who value an autonomous self as much as German mothers do, but at the same time they value teaching about relatedness and the emotions of others.

Although cultural orientations about the self provide information regarding the phenomenon under discussion, it is essential to consider differences within a cultural group, and the way in which such differences are reflected in parenting and children's emotion socialization. Harwood, Schoelmerich, Ventura-Cook, Schulze, and Wilson (1996) documented differences in the socialization goals of low- and middle-income mothers in Puerto Rico and United States. American mothers gave more importance to socialization goals that promoted the self-maximization of their children (i.e., self-confidence, independence, and development of one's talents) than Puerto Rican mothers. Within each cultural group, middle-class mothers emphasized such goals to a greater extent than their lower class counterparts. On the other hand, Puerto Rican mothers granted more importance than

American mothers to socialization goals that promoted proper demeanor (i.e., respectfulness, acceptance by the larger community, and appropriate performance of role obligations). By the same token, in both groups, low-income mothers emphasized proper demeanor to a greater extent than middle-income mothers.

These findings suggest that sociodemographic characteristics such as educational level and income become important when explaining intracultural variability in parenting practices and socialization goals. For such reason, another goal of the present study was to explore differences in the amount, type, and complexity of emotion talk that takes place in conversations about personal events between children and their mothers with low levels of education and children and their mothers with high levels of education. We expected the frequency and complexity of emotion talk to be higher in dyads including mothers with high levels of education than in dyads including mothers with low levels of education.

The Present Study

The present study resolved to explore differences in the frequency, type, and complexity of emotion talk during reminiscing in Costa Rican dyads. We had three goals: a) to compare the frequency, type, and complexity of emotion talk during conversations about positive and negative events; b) to compare the frequency, type, and complexity of emotion talk produced by dyads including mothers with high educational levels and dyads including mothers with low educational levels; and c) to contrast the frequency, type, and complexity of emotion talk produced by mother-son and mother-daughter dyads. Due to the diversity in which emotion talk has been analyzed and classified in previous studies, it is not possible to provide hypotheses for frequency, type, and complexity of emotion talk for each of our goals. However, we expected to find the following results on the basis of the previous evidence available:

a) Differences in emotion talk as a function of the emotional valence of the events: We expected differences in complexity of emotion talk. Specifically, we expected dyads would refer more often to the causes, consequences, and resolutions of emotions when discussing negative emotion events than when discussing positive emotion events.

b) Differences in emotion talk as a function of maternal educational level: We expected differences in the complexity of emotion talk. Specifically, we expected dyads including mothers with high levels of education to talk more about emotions and in a more complex way, referring to the causes, consequences, and resolutions of emotions more often than dyads including mothers with low levels of education.
c) Differences in emotion talk in mother-son and mother-daughter dyads: Due to the conflicting evidence on this topic, it was not possible to provide hypotheses about variability in emotion talk as a function of children's sex.

Method

Participants

The sample included 64 Costa Rican 4-year-old children and their mothers. Dyads were contacted through day-care centers and preschools located in a large metropolitan area of Costa Rica. The researchers contacted the principals of the preschools and the day-care centers to explain the project. Upon gaining approval, invitations were sent to all of the families. Those families interested in participating were then contacted to coordinate a visit. Data collection took place either in the preschool or in the family house.

All dyads were monolingual Spanish speakers. None of the children had a diagnosis of language, hearing, or any developmental delays. Half of the sample included mothers with high levels of education. The other half of the sample included mothers with low levels of education. For the highly educated group, mothers had to meet the inclusion criterion of holding more than 12 years of education. For the low-educated group, mothers could report between one and 11 years of education. Sociodemographic information of both groups is shown in Table 7.1.

Criteria for maternal education were defined according to the household educational climate index (Comisión Económica Para América Latina y el Caribe, 2000), a commonly used measure in studies about academic development in Costa Rica (e.g., Programa Estado de la Nación, 2013). This index defines three household educational climate levels: low, when adults in a household have completed, on average, fewer than six years of education; medium, when adults in a household have completed, on average, between six and 12 years of education; and high, when adults have completed, on average, more than 12 years of education.

Table 7.1 Descriptive statistics of the sociodemographic variables according to maternal educational level (n = 64)

Variables	Highly educated group (n = 32) M (SD)	Range	Low-educated group (n = 32) M (SD)	Range
Maternal education (in years)	16.2 (1.30)	13–19	7.63 (2.12)	3–11
Child's age (in months)	52.4 (3.28)	48–59	54.9 (3.28)	48–59
Raw vocabulary scores	23.6 (2.19)	18–29	19.5 (3.34)	13–26
Percentage of girls (%, freq.)	53% (17)		50% (16)	

According to census data, 41.2% of Costa Rican children (0 to 6 years) live in households with a low educational climate, 42.3% live in households with a medium educational climate, and only 15.6% live in households with a high educational climate (INEC, 2012). Our sample selection attempted to explore possible differences in emotion talk between dyads from households with low and medium levels of educational climate (the most common levels in the country) and dyads from households with a high educational climate, whose characteristics correspond to those of the samples commonly studied in the international reminiscing literature.

Procedure and Materials

Data were collected between 2009 and 2011 by the second and third authors. All dyads met with a researcher. Dyads decided to complete the session either in their homes or in the child's preschool. After reading and signing the consent form with the researcher, mother and child completed a series of different tasks. Given the scope of this chapter, we only focused on the mother-child conversations about past personal events. During the session, all children also completed a measure of their general expressive language ability. Mothers completed a sociodemographic form.

General Expressive Language Ability
Children took the Woodcock-Muñoz "Subprueba de Vocabulario basado en Dibujos" (2005). Children's raw scores were used.

Mother-Child Conversations

Mothers were asked to nominate recent past events that were unique and salient in the child's life. A list was created that included: 1) a shared event (one that the parent and child had experienced together); 2) an unshared event (one in which the child had recently participated without the parent); 3) a child's misbehavior event; and 4) a child's good behavior event. This study only considered the two behavior-related conversations because they represented conversations with a positive and negative emotional valence, and therefore their exploration is what allowed us to address our research questions. All mothers were told to interact with their child as they would normally while engaging in conversation. Dyads were left alone in the room to complete the task. Conversations were audiotaped for transcription and coding.

Coding

We formulated a coding system based on systems previously used in the reminiscing literature (Fivush et al., 2003; Goodvin & Romdall, 2013; Lagattuta & Wellman, 2002), as well as evidence from Latino samples (Leyva et al., 2014; Melzi & Fernández, 2004; Nolivos & Leyva, 2013). This coding system was used to classify the participation of mothers and children in the conversations. The units of analysis consisted of propositions that included a noun and a verb. The coding system included the three levels described as follows. Categories within each level were exclusive and exhaustive.

Proposition Types

Propositions were initially classified as referring to: 1) off-topic talk, such as talk about the present (e.g., "Something was moving under here"); 2) talk about facts (e.g., "What did you take from my friend's fridge?"); 3) emotion talk (e.g., "Did you cry all the way back?"); or 4) mental states talk (e.g., "Do you know what a slog is?").

Emotional Terms

Emotional terms in each proposition previously classified as emotion talk were subsequently classified according to four different categories: 1) emotional states such as happy, sad, angry, scared, proud (e.g., "Why did you feel *embarrassed*?"); 2) emotional behaviors such as smiling, crying, hitting, kissing, hugging, or throwing a tantrum (e.g., "Even Alberto *cried*"); 3) evaluative-emotional references such as liking/disliking, enjoying, getting bored (e.g., "*Did you like* to share or *didn't you like* it?"); and 4) moral evaluations such as to behave well/bad (e.g., "I was happy for *how good you behaved*"). When a single proposition contained more than one emotional term, each emotional term was tallied. Typical expressions used in Costa Rica such as "hacer una malacrianza" and "portarse puros dieces" were considered.

Emotional Exchanges
This last and third level of coding aimed at classifying propositions previously classified as emotion talk according to the complexity of the exchange about the emotion. Propositions were then classified as: 1) attributions, when the emotion was only mentioned (e.g., "while you were *crying*"); 2) causes, when the reason of the emotion was explained (e.g., "Did you feel good *for helping others*?"); 3) consequences, when the consequence of the emotion was described (e.g., "You are right. I got very upset *so we went back home*"); and 4) resolutions, when the proposition attempted to solve the negative emotional experience coded (e.g., Child: "I missed my truck." Mother: "But you had more toys").

First and fourth authors independently coded 25% of randomly selected transcripts. Good levels of agreement were obtained for proposition types (Cohen's k = .85), emotional terms (Cohen's k = .94), and emotional exchanges (Cohen's k = .83). Disagreements were resolved and the remaining narratives were coded by the first author.

After completion of the coding, the number of propositions was explored for each event. Preliminary exploration indicated data were not normally distributed. Moreover, non-parametric Mann-Whitney tests for independent samples showed that mothers (U (32.32) = 203, p < .001, r = .52) and children (U (32.32) = 171, p < .001, r = .57) from the highly educated group produced significantly more propositions than mothers and children from the low-educated group. Wilcoxon tests for related samples indicated that mothers (z (60) = 2.28, p = .022, r = .40) and children (z (61) = 3.04, p = .002, r = .54) produced significantly more propositions when discussing positive rather than negative events. Given these differences, percentages of proposition types were used instead of raw frequencies to control for the total amount of talk produced by dyads.

Exploration also revealed very low percentages for the emotional terms coding level. A decision was then made to treat categories within this level as categorical (i.e., presence or absence). Percentages for emotional exchanges categories were extremely low as well, particularly for causes, consequences, and resolutions. Given that discussing the causes, consequences, and resolutions of emotions is far more complex than just attributing an emotion (Carmiol & Schröder, 2019; Dunn et al., 1991; Goodvin & Romdall, 2013), we decided to group the more complex exchanges (causes, consequences, and resolutions) into a single category called *explanatory emotion talk*. Therefore, categories for emotional exchanges were also treated as dichotomous (i.e., attributions or explanatory emotion talk).

Results

We examined three aspects of emotion talk during reminiscing conversations: the total proportion of emotion talk, the presence of different emotional terms (emotional states, emotional behaviors, evaluative-emotional references, and moral appraisals), and the presence of different emotional exchanges (attributions and explanatory emotion talk) in the conversations. In light of our research questions, statistical analyses aimed at identifying differences in these three aspects according to the following variables: emotional valence of the event, maternal education, and sex of the child. Table 7.2 presents a summary of the results.

Does Emotion Talk Vary as a Function of the Emotional Valence of the Event Under Discussion?

The first aim of this study was to determine whether there were differences in emotion talk when discussing past negative and past positive events. We expected dyads would refer more often to explanatory emotion talk (causes, consequences, and resolutions of emotions) when discussing negative emotion events than when discussing positive emotion events.

Proposition Types

Wilcoxon tests for related samples[2] indicated significant differences in the percentage of statements about emotions according to the emotional valence of the event. Mothers ($Z = 3.73$, $p < .001$, $r = .47$) and children ($Z = 3.82$, $p < .001$, $r = .48$) produced a significantly higher percentage of propositions

---

[2] Non-parametric tests were conducted to explore the percentage of propositions because data were not normally distributed.

Table 7.2 Summary of results

	Proposition type		Emotional terms		Emotional exchanges	
	Mothers	Children	Mothers	Children	Mothers	Children
Emotional valence						
Positive	–	–	*a	–	–	–
Negative	*	*	*b	*b	*c	*c
Maternal education						
Low-educated	†	–	–	–	–	–
Highly educated	–	–	*d	*a, d	–	–
Child's sex						
Boys	–	–	–	–	–	–
Girls	–	–	–	–	–	–

Notes: *Significant results; †Marginally significant results; ᵃ Emotional-evaluative references; ᵇ Emotional behaviors; ᶜ Explanatory discussions; ᵈ Emotional states

about emotions when discussing the negative event (mothers Mdn = 29.3%, children Mdn = 20.0%) than when discussing the positive event (mothers Mdn = 14.7%, children Mdn = 6.78%).

Emotional Terms

Results from the McNemar tests for related samples indicated significant differences in the use of emotional behaviors according to the emotional valence of the event. Emotional behaviors were present more often in negative events than in positive events, and this was the case for mothers ($\chi2$ (1, N = 64) = 24.3, p <.001) and children ($\chi2$ (1, N = 64) = 15.6, p <.001). Specifically, mothers mentioned emotional behaviors in 73.4% of the negative event conversations, but only in 25% of the positive event conversations. Children mentioned emotional behaviors in 51.6% of the negative event conversations, but only in 14.1% of the positive event conversations. Moreover, McNemar tests also indicated that mothers, but not children, made greater use of emotional-evaluative references when talking about positive events (p = .004). Specifically, mothers mentioned emotional-evaluative terms in 34.4% of the negative event conversations and only in 14.1% of the positive event conversations. No significant differences were observed for the remaining categories of emotional states and moral evaluations as a function of emotional valence of the event.

Emotional Exchanges

Differences in the presence of emotional exchanges were explored according to the emotional valence of the events. McNemar tests showed no significant differences in mothers' ($p = .38$) and children's ($\chi2$ (1, $N = 64$) = .6, $p = .44$) use of attributions according to the emotional valence of the event. For example, out of 64 positive event conversations, 84.4% (54 conversations) contained emotion attributions mentioned by mothers. Similarly, 90.6% (58 conversations) of negative event conversations contained emotion attributions mentioned by mothers. In contrast, significant differences were observed in the presence of explanatory emotion talk. Mothers ($\chi2$ (1, $N = 64$) = 8.3, $p = .004$) and children ($\chi2$ (1, $N = 64$) = 8.8, $p = .003$) produced explanatory emotion talk more when discussing negative events than when discussing positive events, therefore supporting our first hypothesis. Mothers produced explanatory emotion talk in 78.1% of the negative event conversations, but only in 51.6% of the positive event conversations. Children produced explanatory discussions in 54.7% of the negative event conversations, but only in 28.1% of the positive event conversations. That is, mothers and children talked about the causes, consequences, and resolutions of emotions more often during conversations about negative than during conversations about positive events.

Does Emotion Talk Vary as a Function of Maternal Education?

The second aim of this study was to determine whether there were differences in emotion talk between dyads including highly educated mothers and dyads including low-educated mothers. We expected dyads including mothers with high levels of education to talk more about emotions and in a more complex way, referring to the causes, consequences, and resolutions of emotions more often than dyads including mothers with low levels of education.

Proposition Types

Mann-Whitney test results indicated marginally significant differences in the percentage of emotion propositions produced by mothers ($U = 366$, $p = .050$, r = .25) according to their educational level. Low-educated mothers

(*Mdn* = 25.7%) produced a higher percentage of emotion propositions than highly educated mothers (*Mdn* = 17.8%), therefore providing evidence that contradicts our hypothesis about variability in the amount of emotion talk as a function of maternal education. No significant differences were found when analyzing the percentage of emotion propositions produced by children ($U = 439$, $p = .327$, $r = .12$) of highly educated (*Mdn* = 12.7%) and low-educated mothers (*Mdn* = 20%).

Emotional Terms

We explored the relationship between mothers' and children's use of emotional terms and maternal education. Results from Chi-square tests for independent samples indicated a significant relationship between the presence of emotional states and maternal education in mothers ($\chi2 (1, N = 64) = 6.67, p = .010$) and children ($\chi2 (1, N = 64) = 6.35, p = .012$). Mothers and children from the highly educated group referred more to emotional states than their counterparts in the low-educated group. Highly educated mothers mentioned emotional states in 16% of the conversations, while low-educated mothers mentioned emotional states only in 12% of the conversations. Children of highly educated mothers mentioned emotional states in 15% of the conversations, while children of low-educated mothers mentioned emotional states in only 7% conversations.

Significant differences were also observed in children's use of emotional-evaluative references ($\chi2 (1, N = 64) = 5.85, p = .016$). Children in the highly educated group produced emotional-evaluative references in 9% of the conversations while children in the low-educated group produced emotional-evaluative references in 2% of the conversations. No significant differences were found for the mothers ($\chi2 (1, N = 64) = 3.22, p = .073$), nor for any other emotional term.

Emotional Exchanges

Results from Chi-square tests for independent samples indicated no significant differences in the presence of any of the categories of emotional exchanges (i.e., attributions and explanatory discussions) as a function of maternal education. This was the case for mothers and children. This result therefore provides no evidence to support our hypothesis about variability of complexity of emotion talk as a function of maternal education.

Does Emotion Talk Vary as a Function of the Child's Sex?

The third aim of this study was to determine whether there were differences in emotion talk between dyads including boys and dyads including girls. Due to the conflicting evidence available on this topic, we did not provide hypotheses about variability in emotion talk as a function of children's sex.

Proposition Types
Results from Mann-Whitney tests showed no significant differences in the percentage of propositions about emotions produced by mothers ($U = 481$, $p = .682$, $r = .05$) or children ($U = 477$, $p = .638$, $r = .06$) during conversations including boys (mothers: $Mdn = 21.1\%$, boys: $Mdn = 16.7\%$) or girls (mothers: $Mdn = 19.5\%$, girls: $Mdn = 14.9\%$).

Emotional Terms
Chi-square tests for independent samples indicated no significant relationship in the use of any of the four categories of emotional terms (i.e., emotional states, emotional behaviors, emotional-evaluative references, and moral appraisals) and the sex of the child. This was the case for mothers' and children's participation.

Emotional Exchanges
Finally, we explored the relationship between emotional exchanges and sex of the child. Chi-square tests for independent samples indicated no significant relationship between the presence of emotional exchanges and the child's sex. This was the case for mothers' and children's participation.

Discussion

The present study examined the emotional content of the reminiscing conversations of Costa Rican dyads by focusing on the total proportion of statements about emotions, the presence of different types of emotional terms, and the presence of different levels of complexity when discussing emotions. The objectives of this study focused on identifying differences in the emotional content of these conversations according to: 1) the emotional valence of the event being discussed (positive or negative); 2) the maternal educational level; and 3) the sex of the child. Since research studies that have analyzed the emotional content of reminiscing in Latin American samples to the present are scarce (although, see Leyva et al., 2014; Melzi & Fernández, 2004; Nolivos & Leyva, 2013), the following results represent a pioneering effort to understand the socialization of emotions within the Costa Rican context, specifically, and of the region, in general.

Differences in the Emotional Content of Reminiscing According to the Emotional Valence of the Event Being Discussed

We hypothesized the complexity of emotion talk would vary between conversations about negative and positive emotions. Specifically, we expected dyads would refer more often to explanatory emotion talk (causes, consequences, and resolutions of emotions) when discussing negative events than when discussing positive events.

Our results revealed differences in the emotional content of past event conversations according to the emotional valence of the event under discussion. Mothers and children used a significantly higher percentage of statements about emotions when talking about negative events than when talking about positive events. Moreover, a higher number of conversations about negative events included explanatory discussions, and this confirmed our hypothesis. Dyads mentioned the causes, consequences, and resolutions of emotions to a greater extent when discussing negative events than when discussing positive events.

These findings are consistent with previous evidence that has shown how conversations about negative experiences or conflicts constitute scenarios where dyads discuss the emotions involved in the event on a more frequent basis (Goodvin & Romdall, 2013; Lagattuta & Wellman, 2002; Laible, 2010; Leyva et al., 2014; Melzi & Fernández, 2004; Nolivos & Leyva, 2013). This result could be explained by at least two reasons. First of all, by the interest of the mothers in helping their children regulate their negative experiences (Fivush et al., 2003; Laible, 2004). Second, because negative valence events tend to stand out predominantly in the memory of children (Burger & Miller, 1999), thus facilitating reference to the details of the event, including aspects of the narrative's landscape of consciousness (Bruner, 1990), such as it is the case of the emotions involved.

Results about the different types of emotional terms according to the emotional valence of events indicated that dyads used all types of emotional terms, in both negative and positive conversations. However, significant differences were only observed in the use of emotional behaviors (e.g., crying, smiling, kissing, hitting) and emotional-evaluative references (e.g., enjoying, (not) liking). A noticeable majority of negative conversations contained emotional behaviors, both in the mothers' and children's interventions. On the other hand, the use of emotional-evaluative references occurred to a greater extent in positive conversations. Such results suggest that dyads discuss more about emotional expressions when talking about negative emotional experiences, while the motivation to express likes or preferences lies primarily in talks about pleasant emotional events.

Appendix Table A1 shows two extracts from conversations that exemplify such results (see Appendix Table A4 for the Spanish version of the extracts). The first extract is from a positive emotional valence conversation where the dyad talks about how the child contributes to household chores, while the second is a negative emotional valence conversation where the dyad discusses a peer conflict. The comparison between both conversations shows the way in which emotions are discussed in more detail in the case of the negative event, where there is also a greater emphasis on emotional behaviors.

Differences in the Emotional Content of Reminiscing According to Maternal Educational Level

We expected dyads including mothers with high levels of education to talk more about emotions and in a more complex way, referring to the causes, consequences, and resolutions of emotions (explanatory emotion talk) more often than dyads including mothers with low levels of education. Our results partially contradicted our hypothesis. They indicated a significantly higher percentage of statements about emotions in dyads with mothers of low educational level than in dyads with mothers of high educational level. The same tendency was observed among children, although it did not reach statistical significance. Nevertheless, when analyzing emotional exchanges, no significant differences related to maternal education were found. That is, although dyads with mothers of low educational level made reference to emotions to a larger extent, the complexity of such discussions did not vary between both groups.

Differences were also observed in the types of emotional terms used according to the maternal educational level. Although all the types of emotional terms were used in both groups, dyads with mothers of high educational level used emotional states in a larger number of conversations, both the mothers and the children. Also, a larger number of conversations were observed where children of mothers of high educational level made emotional-evaluative references.

These differences could be explained by intracultural variations linked to orientations of the self and reflected in parenting styles and emotion talk. Specifically, the conversations of dyads with mothers of high educational level in our sample focused on the analysis of emotions in an inner-directed approach. That is, a preference to refer to emotions in terms of emotional states, as opposed to emotional behaviors, and a motivation for the children to express their tastes and preferences through the emotional-evaluative references. Such a pattern corresponds to a parenting vision that is more focused on emotional connection and that conceives children as autonomous beings, with their own subjective and personal experience. This is similar to the *cognitive* or *explaining* approach of emotion talk previous studies have identified in the United States, where caregivers value the development of an independent self (Wang, 2001; Wang & Fivush, 2005). In contrast, dyads with mothers of low educational levels in our sample focused on the behaviors related to the emotions, showing a preference for what has been previously characterized in the literature as a *behavioral* or *emotion-criticizing* style of emotion talk. This latter style has been observed to be more common among East Asian caregivers, whose parenting has been observed to reflect preferences for the development of an interdependent self.

Our results also indicated the absence of significant differences in the use of moral evaluations (e.g., "he/she behaved well," "he/she misbehaved"). These evaluations were used by most mothers of the low educational level group (24 out of 32 mothers) and by most mothers of high educational level (27 out of 32 mothers). Therefore, both groups displayed a strong interest in transmitting social rules during conversations. As such, these findings agree with the previously discussed evidence regarding the importance given by Latin American caregivers from different socioeconomic groups to good demeanor as a socialization goal (Harwood et al., 2000).

Appendix Table A2 shows two conversations that exemplify the differences in the emotional content of reminiscing according to the educational level of the mother (see Appendix Table A5 for the Spanish version of the extracts). The conversation in which the low educational level mother is involved stands out for displaying a larger number of propositions about emotions, while the conversation of the dyad with a high educational level mother stands out due to its interest in discussing emotional states (i.e., anger, fear).

Differences in the Emotional Content of Reminiscing According to Child's Sex

Due to the conflicting evidence on this topic, it was not possible for us to provide hypotheses about variability in emotion talk as a function of children's sex. Our results did not indicate any significant differences in the emotional content of the conversations according to the sex of the child. Mother-son and mother-daughter conversations showed percentages of statements about emotions that did not differ between them. Furthermore, no significant differences were observed in the use of attributions and explanatory emotion talk between both groups.

Previous studies indicated differences in conversations about emotions according to the sex of the child. Within the Latin American context, such evidence suggests that mothers make greater use of emotional terms when talking to their sons about positive emotional valence events and discussing them more deeply than when mothers talk to their daughters (Melzi & Fernández, 2004). In contrast, findings from Anglo dyads indicated that mothers talked more about emotions with their daughters, and that such conversations were more detailed, especially when dealing with negative emotional valence events (e.g., Fivush et al., 2003). A third group of studies addressing this question did not show any differences between the sexes in contexts such as the United States (e.g., Goodvin & Romdall, 2013), New Zealand, and Australia (Van Bergen & Salmon, 2010). This variation of the pattern could be explained by several reasons. The first reason refers to methodological differences, particularly to the use of different systems for categorizing the information from the conversations in the different studies. A second reason might be the sociocultural context and the difference in gender roles in each of the samples studied. In our case, a possible reason for not observing any differences could be the methodological strategy used. While other studies took into account the sex of the child and the context of the conversation simultaneously for predicting the amount and characteristics of emotional talk, both variables were impossible to consider at the same time in our study, given the limited number of analyzed events. While in our case it was possible to have one event for each type, Melzi and Fernández (2004) analyzed a total of six conversations per dyad. It is important for future studies to analyze the possible differences in the styles of conversation during reminiscing according to the sex of the child, taking into account the context of the conversation.

Also, it should be kept in mind that gender roles may vary internally in the cultural groups as these are affected by sociodemographic variables such as education and income. This might be one of the factors influencing the sample used in the present study, since such a sample brings together dyads from households with different educational climates. Gender roles from the low educational level mothers could be different from the gender roles of the high educational level mothers, and this could be reflected in the conversations with boys and girls. That is, the results do not show significant differences because there is not a homogeneous pattern in the sample concerning the expectations for handling emotions according to the child's sex. Once again, the exploration of such hypothesis by means of a study that includes a larger number of dyads and a greater amount of positive and negative events remains pending.

Although the variations according to the child's sex were not statistically significant, the trends observed are similar to the previous evidence presented by Melzi and Fernández (2004) in Peruvian dyads. We observed a larger number of mother-son conversations where emotional behaviors (e.g., crying, smiling, kissing, hitting) and emotional-evaluative references (e.g., enjoying, disliking) were mentioned. In contrast, a larger number of reminiscing conversations including emotional states (e.g., happy, angry) and moral evaluations (e.g., good/bad behavior) prevailed in mother-daughter interactions.

These variations might correspond to the expectations of the masculine gender role that are usually transmitted by this type of interaction. In the case of boys, emotions might be being treated externally. That is, emotions are discussed in terms of the behavior being expressed, and not in terms of mental states. In addition, the discussion of emotional-evaluative references is higher in conversations including boys, which could reflect their motivation to express their tastes and preferences, in agreement with the pattern pointed out by Melzi and Fernández (2004). On the other hand, the use of emotional states and moral evaluations in conversations with girls could be reflecting a more introspective handling of their emotions and the expectation for girls to show a behavior more in tune with social norms. As an example of these trends, Appendix Table A3 shows two excerpts of the conversations (see Appendix Table A6, for Spanish version of the extracts).

In conclusion, the results of the present study indicated that Costa Rican families with different educational climates refer naturally about emotions with their sons and daughters during conversations about past personal events. They also have a wide repertoire of emotional terms that they use daily in this type of conversation. Such results are particularly relevant for understanding the socialization of emotions within the Costa Rican context, specifically, and the Latin American context, in general. By the same token, they become relevant when planning and implementing training geared towards promoting a better way of handling violence in family and educational contexts. Furthermore, given that mothers already refer to emotions when reminiscing with their children, it becomes important to consider this conversational context as an ecologically valid tool for carrying out interventions. Future efforts could focus on helping mothers to increase the level of explanation and detail with which emotions are discussed, inasmuch as that has been identified as an element of significance in promoting the socioemotional development of preschool children (Valentino et al., 2013; Van Bergen & Salmon, 2010; Van Bergen et al., 2009).

Appendix

Table A1: Conversations as a function of emotional valence of the event

Positive emotional valence conversation	Negative emotional valence conversation
M: How did you manage to make your bed?	M: Uh-huh, and that you didn't fight with your class mates because?*
C: in everything!	C: because I am a Strawberry Shortcake girl and I am a Princess and I am a kitten.*
M: and what else?	M: because it is not okay to fight with children, right? You don't do that.*
C: tuck it in?	M: what else did I tell you?
M: tuck it in.	C: to bring the photograph, too, and also that.
M: where did you tuck the blanket?	M: that is not what I told you that day.
M: was the blanket tucked?	M: we were talking about the day when you were fighting with the children.
C: I put some soap on it.	C: oh, okay, they told me: "You see? A troublemaker, again" because I was fighting.*
C: I put soap on it! I washed it!	M: and what did I tell you? That I did not want them to make me what?
M: did you wash the blanket today?	C: Angry.
M: Marco, tell the truth.	M: more complaints.
C: I washed it. I laid it out and look, another thing.	C: more complaints.
M: so, you washed the blanket, you laid out the blanket.	M: you see, because otherwise, what would happen if they told me that you kept on fighting?*
M: and what else did you do?	M: what will happen if you kept fighting?*
C: I got up and made it.	C: you would call me a troublemaker.*
M: you made the blanket?	M: and what else?

Continued

Table A1: *Continued*

Positive emotional valence conversation	Negative emotional valence conversation
M: yes?	C: <u>they tell me, hm, hm, that I am a troublemaker.</u>
M: I made the blanket?	M: <u>and that if you kept fighting mommy would have to …</u>*
M: no, Marco did.	M: <u>punish me.</u>*
C: I made the drawing.	
M: oh, okay.	
M: and how was the bed, Marco?	
C: very pretty!	
M: and what did mommy say when she saw the bed so pretty?	
C: <u>that you liked it?</u>	
M: <u>oh, I loved that bed so well made, so clean!</u>	

Notes: <u>Underlined</u> text belongs to statements about emotions. Text in *italics* corresponds to emotional terms. Text followed by an asterisk (*) corresponds to explanatory discussions. "M" introduces maternal statements. "C" introduces statements produced by children.

Table A2: Conversations as a function of maternal education level

Low-educated mother	Highly educated mother
M: tell me something, <u>who hit Rosa yesterday?</u>	M: <u>why did mommy *got angry* today, in the morning?</u>
C: what?	C: because her little girl did not want to shower.
M: <u>who hit Rosa yesterday in the armchair# there?</u>	M: right.
C: Gerardo did.	M: and why did the student girl did not want to take a shower?
M: Gerardo? Gerardo is not here.	C: because, uh.
C: <u>because when we were at the kindergarten Gerald was *hitting* my little sister.</u>	C: <u>because she was afraid that soap would get in her eyes.</u>
M: no, but, <u>who *hit* your little sister # here in the house yesterday?</u>	M: because of that?

APPENDIX 149

Low-educated mother	Highly educated mother
C: Jonathan.	N: uh-huh.
M: uh-huh. <u>And why did Jonathan *hit* your sister?</u>*	M: how smart!
M: <u>why did he *hit* her?</u>*	M: <u>but you do know that your shampoo is special l. (*)</u>
C: No.	N: uh-huh.
M: you don't know? Mmhm.	M: so?
M: <u>but you *love* your little sister, right?</u>	N: but she doesn't have any.
M: <u>do you *love* her a lot?</u>	M: and what were you watching?
M: <u>and good kids don't *fight*, don't they?</u>	M: why didn't you want to go?
C: no.	M: I think you didn't want to go because you were doing something else.
M: so then, what happened?	N: yes, I was watching the movie.
C: (hitting sounds).	M: which movie?
M: okay, that's the end of that ...	C: Alvin's, madam student.

Notes: The <u>underlined</u> text corresponds to statements about emotions. Text in *italics* corresponds to emotional terms. Text with an asterisk (*) corresponds to explanatory discussions. "M" introduces statements made by the mother. "C" introduces statements made by the children.

Table A3: Conversations as a function of the sex of the child

Mother-son dyad	Mother-daughter dyad
M: <u>okay, why did you *misbehaved so badly* in the morning?</u>	M: and what do you all do then?
C: <u>I don't know.</u>	M: they hide.
M: <u>you cried all day, all morning, and you didn't like the card that mom and dad made you.</u>	M: from whom?
M: <u>why didn't you like it?</u>	N: to mommy!
C: <u>I wanted to be made a child, not a superhero.</u>	M: from mommy.
M: <u>ah, and we made you a superhero and you wanted one as a boy?</u>	N: and from Tilma.
C: <u>yes.</u>	M: and from Tilma.
M: <u>and why didn't you like that one?</u>	M: and you start to do what?

Continued

Table A3: *Continued*

Mother-son dyad	Mother-daughter dyad
C: because I didn't.	N: to run and we fall.
M: hmm, and what else?	M: to run about in the store.
M: why were you also so quarrelsome that day in the morning?	M: and how does mama get?
C: I don't know.	M: happy or sad?
	N: sad.
	M: sad or angry?
	N: angry.
	M: angry, right?
	M: and what does mama do?
	N: scold them.
	M: hmm.
	M: how should children behave when they go out running errands with their mom?
	N: well.
	M: well.

Notes: The underlined text corresponds to statements about emotions. Text in *italics* corresponds to emotional terms. Text with an asterisk (*) corresponds to explanatory discussions. "M" introduces statements made by the mother. "C" introduces statements made by the children.

Table A4: Conversations as function of emotional valence of the event, Spanish version

Positive emotional valence conversation	Negative emotional valence conversation
M: ¿cómo hizo usted para tender la cama?	M: ujum y que no se peleaba con los compañeritos ¿por qué?*
C: ¡en toda!	C: porque yo soy una chica Fresita y yo soy una princesa y yo soy una gatita y una.*
M: ¿y qué más?	M: porque no está bien pelear con los chiquitos, ¿verdad? Eso no se hace.*
C: ¿prensarla?	M: ¿qué más te dije?
M: prensarla.	C: que también trajera la foto y también que.
M: ¿dónde prensó la cobija?	M: eso no fue lo que te dije ese día.

APPENDIX 151

Positive emotional valence conversation	Negative emotional valence conversation
M: ¿la cobija prensó?	M: estamos hablando del día que usted estaba de peleona con los chiquitos.
C: le puse jabón sí.	C: ah bueno, me dijeron: "Ve, otra vez peliona" porque yo pelié.*
C: ¡le puse jabón la lavé!	M: ¿Y qué te dije? ¿Que no quería que me pusieran qué?
M: ¿usted lavó la cobija hoy?	C: brava.
M: Marco diga la verdad.	M: Más quejas.
C: la lave, la tendí y mira otra cosa.	C: Más quejas.
M: o sea usted lavó la cobija, tendió la cobija.	M: Ves, porque sino ¿qué iba a pasar si me decían que usted seguía peleando?*
M: ¿y qué más hizo?	M: ¿Qué iba a pasar si usted seguía peleando?*
C: la levante y la hice.	N: Me dice peliona.*
M: ¿hizo la cobija?	M: ¿Y qué más?
M: ¿sí?	N: Me dicen, este este, que que yo soy peliona.
M: ¿hice la cobija?	M: Y que si seguía peliando mamita la iba a tener que ...*
M: no Marco.	M: Castigar.*
C: yo hice el dibujo.	
M: ah bueno.	
M: ¿y cómo quedó la cama Marco?	
C: ¡muy linda!	
M: ¿y qué le dijo mamá cuando vio la cama tan linda?	
C: ¿que te gustó?	
M: ¡uy me encantó esa cama toda tendida, toda limpia!	

Notes: Underlined text belongs to statements about emotions. Text in *italics* corresponds to emotional terms. Text followed by an asterisk (*) corresponds to explanatory discussions. "M" introduces maternal statements. "C" introduces statements produced by children.

Table A5: Conversations as a function of maternal education level, Spanish version

Low-educated mother	Highly educated mother
M: contame una cosa ¿quién le _pegó_ ayer a Rosa?	
C: ¿ah?	M: ¿por qué se _enojó_ hoy mamita en la mañana?
M: ¿quién le _pegó_ ayer a Rosa en el sillón # ahí?	C: porque su niña no quería bañarse.
C: Gerardo.	M: ajá.
M: ¿Gerardo? Gerardo no está aquí.	M: ¿y por qué no se quiso bañar niña estudiante?
C: porque cuando estamos en el kínder Gerald le _pegaba_ a mi hermanita.	C: porque ah.
M: no pero ¿quién le _pegó_ ayer aquí a su hermanita # aquí en la casa?	C: porque le daba _miedo_ que el jabón se le cayera en los ojos.
N: Jonathan.	M: ¿por eso?
M: ajá. ¿Y por qué Jonathan le _pegó_ a su hermanita?*	N: uhhum.
M: ¿Por qué le _pegó_?*	M: ¡qué bandida!
N: No.	M: pero si vos sabés que el champú tuyo es especial. (*)
M: ¿no sabés? Mmm.	N: uhhum.
M: pero, tu _quieres_ a tu hermanita ¿verdad?	M: ¿entonces?
M: ¿tú la _quieres_ mucho?	N: pero ella no tiene ninguno.
M: y los niños buenos no _pelean_ ¿verdad que no?	M: ¿y qué estabas viendo?
N: no.	M: ¿por qué no querías ir?
M: y entonces ¿qué pasó?	M: yo creo que no querías ir porque estabas haciendo otra cosa.
N: (sonidos de golpe).	N: sí estaba viendo la película.
M: bueno, colorín colorado…	M: ¿cuál película?
	C: la de Alvin, señora estudiantil.

Notes: The underlined text corresponds to statements about emotions. Text in _italics_ corresponds to emotional terms. Text with an asterisk (*) corresponds to explanatory discussions. "M" introduces statements made by the mother. "C" introduces statements made by the children.

Table A6: Conversations as a function of the sex of the child, Spanish version

Mother-son dyad	Mother-daughter dyad
M: okay ¿por qué te *portaste tan mal* en la mañana? C: no sé. M: que lloraste todo el día, toda la mañana y no te gustó la tarjeta que mamá y papá te hicimos. M: ¿por qué no te gustó? C: yo quería que me hicieran niño, no superhéroe. M: ah ¿te hicimos un superhéroe y vos querías una del niño? C: sí. M: y ¿por qué no te gustó esa? N: porque no. M: hmm y ¿qué más? M: ¿por qué ese día también estabas peleón en la mañana? N: no sé.	M: ¿y qué se ponen a hacer ustedes? M: se esconden. M: ¿de quién? C: ¡a mami! M: de mami. C: y de Tilma. M: y de Tilma. M: ¿y se ponen a qué? C: a correr y nos caemos. M: a correr por la tienda. M: ¿y cómo se pone mamá? M: ¿contenta o triste? C: tiste (triste). M: ¿triste o enojada? C: enojada. M: enojada ¿verdad? M: ¿y qué hace mamá? C: regañarlas. M: hmm. M: ¿cómo deben portarse los niños cuando salen a hacer mandados con la mamá? C: bien. M: bien.

Notes: The underlined text corresponds to statements about emotions. Text in *italics* corresponds to emotional terms. Text with an asterisk (*) corresponds to explanatory discussions. "M" introduces statements made by the mother. "C" introduces statements made by the children.

Conclusions and Future Orientations

Mariano Rosabal-Coto and Javier Tapia-Balladares

First of all, we would like to note that undeniably a common thread links the scientific concerns of the contributors of this book and with those the editors also share.

This could be summarized as an interest in seeing developmental psychology as a means to fully understand how detrimental conditions diminish the potential for individuals to achieve; further, how the study of the family as the first socialization milieu is unavoidable, as are its ecological determinants, when psychology deals with such a question. In the same token, developmental psychology must bring to bear the keys to successfully enhance such potentials to the point that disadvantage can be reversed, at least insofar as ensuring that children have access to a wide range of resources from their early development that will guarantee the promotion of a generational breakthrough. Comprehension of specific social and cultural traits that underpin how development is viewed represents but the first step in connecting scientific knowledge and the psychological needs of people. In this sense, family is considered a network of relationships that configure the port of departure to broader socialization processes in contrasting settings and with diverse partners facing differential challenges.

The various contributions in this volume deserve to be highlighted as relevant in the discussion of family – in its particular form in Latin American milleus- as a context for development.

We have to acknowledge that the sum of the contributions in this volume does not represent the vastness of the existing facets of our subcontinent. However, relevant issues and concerns have been raised in different regards.

Important theoretical and methodological discussions have been elicited. As mentioned in the Introduction, these chapters represent a relevant axis, in our consideration, to theorize about the notion of family in Latin American contexts.

Theoretical Considerations

The main theoretical issues derived from the preceding contributions may be summarized as follows:

- Far more than mainstream developmental approaches, contextual approaches lead to a much better comprehension of the specificities of Latin American developmental paths.
- The chapters presented offer different perspectives much nearer to an ecological, cultural, and social perspective, and this echoes the need for a culturally sensitive approach, that will depict local particularities far from ethnocentrically mainstream tendencies.
- Both, geographical vastness and intracultural variability of Latin America demands sensitive theories that might assess the intracultural variability, not only between Latin American countries, but also within each country itself.
- Mainstream developmental psychology may overlook cultural and contextual particularities, therefore ecocultural approaches could lead to encompassing and assessing different development domains, such as intensive and vulnerable contexts, multigenerational cohabitation contexts, and contexts that have an influence even from the very beginning of life.
- Viewing the family as a development context acknowledges a culturally specific trait for more than 600 million inhabitants of this subcontinent, and more than 60 million with Latin American heritage in the USA.

Methodological Considerations

Along with the theoretical challenges, issues arise with regard to how future studies and assessments should be driven, specific methodologically.

Due to the fact that the Latino population in the USA hardly represents the standard profile of this culture should make us reconsider formulating psychological theory based upon a non-representative population (Salazar et al., Chapter 5 in this volume).

A vast reality demands diversity in methodologies that will reflect the multiplicity and richness of developmental scenarios. Therefore a crossover in innovation is needed regarding methodological approaches like community-based participatory research (CBTR) strategies, maximizing mixed-methods designs (specially based on narratives, looking at agents acting in these psychological processes), exposing different realities through qualitative approaches, and setting new and innovative scenarios involving, for example, multigenerational cohabitation and perinatal psychology.

Due to specific cultural traits, methods should also be sifted according to the extent of their validity. The CBTR approach seems to be a suitable tool in Latin American contexts, particularly with regard to vulnerable contexts that require prompt responses (Larissa Seibel et al., Chapter 2 in this volume).

Early interventions involving perinatal psychology can strengthen mother-child early bonds to mitigate contextual adversities, and prevent risks to a child's development (Oiberman et al., Chapter 3 in this volume).

As mentioned in the Introduction, these contributions thread through some axes, namely, the specificity and sensibility of familial functioning; levels of context of variable complexity; and Latin American core values such as familism, kinship bonds, authority, and in-group hierarchy.

With regard to the specificity and sensibility of the familial functioning, it could be stressed that:

- Family could be understood as a subsystem playing a role as an interface between culture and the individual.
- Unlike many approaches that define the family as a lens through which external inputs pass through, in Carillo and Ripoll's chapter (Chapter 1, in this book), families in adverse contexts can work as a protective factor to buffer and implement resilient response conditions in children with regard to socioemotional development, within hostile or disadvantageous contexts.
- Typical Latino family cohesion is presented from a vast perspective of protective factors when facing adversity—not only as a support network, but as providing an interactive world that teaches and drives ways to overcome adversity.
- This form of cohesion leads to different dimensions, mostly identified with the issue of "familismo" or familism. Different levels have been identified or tend to support it: as a social value, as attitudes or shared concerns, and as a way of structuring relations. Near to this concept we may cite Keller's (2018) "hierarchical relatedness" orientation, representative of proximal cultural contexts (see Jaramillo et al., Chapter 4 in this volume).

As a second axis, levels of context of variable complexity were mentioned. In this respect, we may assert that:

- For example, in adverse living conditions, Latino culture supports family-particular protective roles (Carrillo and Ripoll-Núñez, Chapter 1 in this volume).
- Despite the shift seen in most groups exposed to globalization and modernization, typical Latino values remain and still underlie parenting goals and practices. A change ascribed to acculturation is linked to a higher educational level among some specific groups (Jaramillo et al., Chapter 4 in this volume). Urban and more educated mothers foster independence-oriented socialization goals. Reasoning and negotiating as rearing strategies enhanced by the mother not only reflect the notion of the child as an independent agent but also a shift in parenting practices in the way mothers behave and rear children (Sáenz et al., Chapter 7 in this volume).

And finally, as a third axis are the Latin American core values: *familismo*, kinship bonds, authority, and in-group hierarchy.

- Despite the impact of acculturation reflected in parental goals and strategies, core values regarding interdependence and *familismo* tend to remain.
- Family is seen as providing networks, reference point, symbolic context, and a receptacle of culture. Here, Konner's (2007) description of "cultural-acquisition devices" matches with the family roles described: reactive processes in the cultural surroundings lead to social learning, support and guide emotional/affective learning processes, and embody symbolic processes.

Final Conclusions and Core Ideas

We dare to summarize the final core ideas:

- This is a family-oriented culture, where families work as subsystems mediating between culture and individual.
- The family manages with the discontinuity (or ecological transitions according to Bronfenbrenner 1979) between individual and culture.

It is about a historical mediation, leading to adaptation strategies, sometimes less successful than hoped and not always with the best timing, but with a relevant actor behind the development.
- Family can either protect or expose its members in adverse situations.
- Unlike many approaches that define the family as a lens through which external inputs can pass through, in this book family in adverse contexts is viewed, working as a protective factor which buffers and implements resilient response conditions in its children when facing hostile or disadvantageous contexts.
- Family behaves as an active domain (as proximal factor; Barcelata in Chapter 6) supplying adaptive and resilient mechanisms to cope with immediate contexts.
- Typical Latino family cohesion is presented from a vast perspective of protective factors when facing adversity. Not only as a support network, but as an interactive world that teaches and drives ways to overcome adversity.
- We understand family as a developmental context meant to widen the perspective that encompasses different domains.
- Within families there are vast domains that can function both as content and foster, and which play a relevant role in development across ages with regard to normative and non-normative situations, values, networks, dynamics, intergenerational support system, aging support, emotional support, and emotional attunement around common interests, strengthening strategies for adaptation to the context.
- We subscribe a to a life cycle cultural perspective which broadens previous and dominant approaches. A contextually sensitive approach is required, so that it can reflect such a variety of multicultural contexts.

We have to acknowledge that these contributions do not comprise a complete picture of the vast expanse which encompasses these multiple cultures. However, besides the relevant topics that have been explored, a wide and heterogeneous panorama still remains, a challenge to critical and historical and research issues. Consequently with the contextualized perspective held in this book, developmental psychological science owes a significant debt to local theory and research regarding indigenous and aboriginal populations, issues regarding gender, ethnicity, cultural and other kinds of diversity, and, finally, families in the context of the Global South.

References

Aaron, L., & Dallaire, D. H. (2010). Parental incarceration and multiple risk experiences: Effects on family dynamics and children's delinquency. *Journal of Youth and Adolescence*, *39*(12), 1471–1484.

Abels, H., & König, A. (2016). *Sozialisation Über die Vermittlung von Gesellschaft und Individuum und die Bedingungen von Identität*. 2. Überarbeitete und erweiterte Auflage. Springer: Germany.

Acuña Gurrola, M., & González Celis, A. L. (2010). Autoeficacia y red de apoyo social en adultos mayores. *Journal of Behavior, Health and Social Issues*, *2*(2), 71–81.

Aguilera, R., Salgado, N., Romero, M., & Medina-Mora, M. (2004). Paternal absence and international migration: Stressors and compensators associated with mental health of Mexican teenagers of rural origin. *Adolescence*, *39*(156), 711–723.

Aguirre, E. (2000). Cambios sociales y prácticas de crianza en la familia colombiana. In E. Aguirre & J. Yáñez (Eds.). *Diálogos. Discusiones en la psicología contemporánea*. No. 1 (pp. 211–223). Bogotá: Facultad de Ciencias Humanas, Universidad Nacional de Colombia. https://www.researchgate.net/publication/232415928_Cambios_Sociales_y_Practicas_de_Crianza_en_la_Familia_Colom-biana

Aguirre, E. (2000). Socialización y prácticas de crianza. In E. Aguirre & E. Durán (Eds.), *Socialización. Prácticas de crianza y cuidado de la salud* (pp. 211–223). Bogotá: CES-Universidad Nacional de Colombia.

Aguirre, E., & Durán, E. (1998). *Caracterización de prácticas de crianza y cuidado de la salud en padres y niños de transición en veinte escuelas públicas de Santafé de Bogotá. Informe final de investigación*. Santafé de Bogotá: CES-Universidad Nacional de Colombia.

Allen, J. G., & Fonagy, P. (2014). Mentalizing in psychotherapy. In R. E. Hales, S. C. Yudofsky, & L. W. Roberts (Eds.), *The American psychiatric publishing textbook of psychiatry* (pp. 1095–1118). Arlington, VA: American Psychiatric Publishing, Inc.

Als, H. (1978). Assessing an assessment: Conceptual considerations, methodological issues, and a perspective on the future of the Neonatal Behavioral Assessment Scale. *Monographs of the Society for Research in Child Development*, *43*(5/6), 14–28.

Als, H. (1986). Framework for the assessment of neurobehavioral development in the premature infant and for support of infants and parents in the neonatal intensive care environment. *Physical & Occupational Therapy in Pediatrics*, *6*(3), 3–53.

Alvarenga, P., & Frizzo, G. B. (2017). Stressful life events and women's mental health during pregnancy and postpartum period. *Paidéia (Ribeirão Preto)*, *27*(66), 51–59.

Amar, J. A. (2000). Niños invulnerables. Factores cotidianos de protección que favorecen el desarrollo de los niños que viven en contextos de pobreza. *Psicología desde el Caribe*, (5), 96–126.

Amarís, M., Amar, J., & Jiménez, M. (2007). Dinámica de las familias de menores con problemas psicosociales: el caso del menor infractor y la menor explotada sexualmente. *Revista Latinoamericana de Ciencias Sociales, Niñez y Juventud, 3*(2), 141-174

Amarís, M., Madariaga, C., Valle, M., & Zambrano, J. (2013). Estrategias de afrontamiento individual y familiar frente a situaciones de estrés psicológico. *Psicología Desde el Caribe, 30*(1), 123-145.

Amarís, M., Paternina, A., & Vargas, K. (2004). Relaciones familiares en familias desplazadas por la violencia ubicadas en "La Cangrejera." *Psicología Desde el Caribe, 14*, 91-124.

Anderson, S. A., & Sabatelli, R. M. (2011). *Family interaction: A multigenerational developmental perspective* (5th ed.). Boston, MA: Allyn & Bacon.

Anderson, S. A., Sabatelli, R. M., & Kosutic, I. (2013). Systemic and ecological qualities of families. In G. Peterson & K. Bush (Eds.), *Handbook of marriage and the family* (pp. 121-138). Boston, MA: Springer.

Andrade, P., Betancourt, D., Vallejo A., Ochoa, C., Segura, B., & Rojas, R. M. (2012). Prácticas parentales y sintomatología depresiva en adolescentes. *Salud Mental, 35*(1), 29-36.

Arenas, P., Durán, C., & Heredia, M. C. (2008). Psychological support and stress of adolescents and their parents. In K. Moore & P. Buchwald (Eds.), *Stress and anxiety: Application to adolescence, job stress and personality* (pp. 19-28). Berlín: Logos Verlag.

Ares, M. S., & Bertella, M. A. (2015). Límites implementados por padres en la crianza de niños de 3 a 6 años. *Avances en Psicología Latinoamericana, 23*(2), 203-221. http://revistas.unife.edu.pe/index.php/avancesenpsicologia/article/view/163/151

Ayon, C., Marsiglia, F. F., & Bermudez-Parsai, M. (2010). Latino family mental health: Exploring the role of discrimination and familismo. *Journal of Community Psychology, 38*(6), 742-768. doi: 10.1002/jcop.20392

Baca Zinn, M., & Wells, B. (2000). Diversity within Latino families: New lessons for family social science. In D. H. Demo, K. R. Allen, & M. A. Fine (Eds.), *Handbook of family diversity* (pp. 252-273). Oxford University Press.

Baltes, P. (1987). Theoretical propositions of life-span developmental psychology: On the dynamics between growth and decline. *Developmental Psychology, 23*(5), 611.

Baltes, P., & Schaie, K. W. (1973). *Life-span developmental psychology: Personality and socialization.* Nueva York: Academic Press.

Barcelata, B., Durán, C., & Lucio, E. (2012a). Coping strategies as predictors of resilience in adolescents with economic hardship. In P. Buchwald, T. Ringeisen, & K. Kaniasty (Eds.), *Stress and anxiety: Application to economic hardship, occupational demands and developmental challenges* (pp. 7-18). Berlin: Logos-Verlag.

Barcelata, B., Durán, C., & Lucio, E. (2012b). Valoración subjetiva de los sucesos estresantes en dos grupos de adolescentes de zonas marginadas, *Salud Mental, 36*(6), 513-520.

Barcelata, B., Farías, S., & Rodríguez, R. (2014). Embarazo adolescente: una mirada al funcionamiento familiar en un contexto urbano-marginal. *Revista de Psicología Eureka, 11*(2), 169–186.

Barcelata B., Granados A., & Ramirez, A. (2013). Correlatos entre funcionamiento familiar y apoyo social percibido en escolares en riesgo psicosocial. *Revista Mexicana de Orientación, 10*(24), 65–79.

Barcelata, B., & Lucio, E. (2012). Fuentes de estrés y su influencia en la adaptación psicológica en jóvenes con adversidad económica. *En-Claves del Pensamiento, 6*(2), 31–48.

Barceló, R. (2007). Displacement, health and poverty: Obstacles in the development of vulnerable adolescents in marginal settlements of Barranquilla (Colombia). *Revista Salud Uninorte, 23*(2), 302–316.

Barreto, J., & Puyana, Y. (1996). *Sentí que se me desprendía el alma. Análisis de procesos y prácticas de socialización.* Bogotá: Santafé de Bogotá, Instituto de Estudios para el Desarrollo y la Paz (INDEPAZ).

Baumeister, R. F., & Vohs, K. D. (2007). Self-regulation, ego depletion, and motivation. *Social and Personality Psychology Compass, 1*, 115–128. https://doi.org/10.1111/j.1751-9004.2007.00001.x

Beltran, A., & Cooper, C. R. (2018). Promising practices and policies to support grandfamilies that include immigrants. *Child Welfare, 96*(5), 103–125. https://search-proquest-com.ezproxy.sibdi.ucr.ac.cr/docview/2264892791?accountid=28692

Beltrán, A. J., & Rivas-Gómez, A. (2013). Intergeneracionalidad y multigeneralidad en el envejecimiento y la vejez. *Tabula Rasa, 18*, 277–294.

Beltrán, N. P. (2009). Consecuencias psicológicas iniciales del abuso sexual infantil. *Papeles del Psicólogo, 30*(2), 135–144.

Bengtson, V. L., Giarrusso, R, Mabry, B., & Silverstein, M. (2002). Solidarity, conflict, and ambivalence: Complimentary or competing perspectives on intergenerational relationships. *Journal of Marriage and Family, 64*, 568–576. DOI: 10.1111/j.1741-3737.2002.00568.x

Benjet, C., Borges, G., Medina-Mora, M. E., Zambrano, J., Cruz, C., & Méndez, E. (2009). Descriptive epidemiology of chronic childhood adversity in Mexican adolescents. *Journal of Adolescent Health, 45*(5), 483–489.

Bermejo, V. (1994). *Desarrollo cognitivo.* Madrid: Editorial Síntesis S.A.

Bernal, T, Jaramillo, J., Mendoza, L., Pérez, A., & Suárez, A. M. (2009). Significados que construyen niños, padres de familia y docentes vinculados a varias instituciones escolares de la ciudad de Bogotá sobre infancia, familia y escuela en el marco de la globalización. *Diversitas. Perspectivas en Psicología, 5*(2), 283–306. https://doi.org/10.15332/s1794-9998.2009.0002.06

Bernal, R., Martínez, M. A., & Quintero, C. (2015). *The state of Colombian children under five years of age, between 2010 and 2013.* Bogotá: Universidad de los Andes, CEDE.

Berry, J. W. (1979). A cultural ecology of social behavior. In L. Berkowitz (Ed.), *Advances in experimental social psychology* (Vol. 12, pp. 177–206). Academic Press.

Betancourt, D., & Andrade, P. (2011). Control parental y problemas emocionales y de conducta en adolescentes. *Revista Colombiana de Psicología, 20*(1), 27–41.

Bischoff, R. J., Springer, P. R., & Taylor, N. (2016). Global mental health in action: Reducing disparities on community at a time. *Journal of Marital and Family Therapy, 43*(2), 276-290. doi: 10.1111/jmft.12202

Blair, C., & Raver, C. (2015). School readiness and self-regulation: A developmental psychobiological approach. *Annual Review of Psychology, 66*(1), 711-731. https://doi.org/10.1146/annurev-psych-010814-015221

Blair, C., & Raver, C. C. (2012). Child development in the context of adversity: Experiential canalization of brain and behavior. *American Psychologist, 67*(4), 309-318. doi:10.1037/a0027493

Bock, J. (2010). An evolutionary perspective on learning in social, cultural and ecological context. In D. F. Lancy, J. Bock, & S. Gaskins (Eds.), *The anthropology of learning in childhood.* (pp. 11-34). Lanham, MD: Altamira Press.

Bogenschneider, K. (2006). *Family policy matters: How policymaking affect families and what professionals can do.* Mahwah, NJ: LEA.

Bogenschneider, K., & Corbett, T. J. (2010). *Evidenced-based policymaking: Insights from policy-minded researchers and research-minded policymakers.* New York: Routledge.

Bokszczanin, A., & Makowsky, S. (2007). Family economic hardship, parental support and social anxiety in adolescents. In P. Roussi, E. Vassilaki, K. Kaniasty, & J. Baker (Eds.), *Stress and psychosocial resources: Coping with life changes, occupational, demands, educational challenge, and threats to physical and emotional wellbeing* (pp. 57-69). Berlin: Logos Verlagh.

Bol, T., & Kalmijm, M. (2016). Grandparents' resources and grandchildren's schooling: Does grandparental involvement moderate the grandparent effect? *Social Science Research, 55,* 155-170. http://dx.doi.org/10.1016/j.ssresearch.2015.09.011

Boltvinik, J. (2013). Multidimensional measurement of poverty: Latin America from pioneer to laggard. *Revista Sociedad y Equidad, 5,* 4-49.

Boltvinik, J., & Damián, A. (2016). Growing poverty and increasingly unequal social structures in Mexico: A critical and integrated perspective. *Acta Sociológica, 70,* 271-296.

Bowlby, J. (1989). The role of attachment in personality development and psychopathology. In S. I. Greenspan & G. H. Pollock (Eds.), *The Course of life,* (Vol. *1,* pp. 229-270). International Universities Press, Inc. (Reprinted from *American Journal of Psychiatry,* 1987, Vol. 144 and *American Journal of Orthopsychiatry,* 1982, Vol. 52)

Bowlby, J. (1998). *El apego.* Barcelona: Paidós.

Boyden, J., & Bourdillon, M. (Eds.) (2012). *Childhood poverty: Multidisciplinary approaches.* London: Palgrave Macmillan.

Bradbury, H., & Reason, P. (2008). Issues and choice points for improving the quality of action research. *Community-Based Participatory Research for Health: From Process to Outcomes, 225-242.*

Brazelton, T., & Cramer, B. (1991). *The earliest relationship: Parents, infants and the drama of early attachment.* London: Karnac.

Brazelton, T. B. (2002). Strengths and stresses in today's families: Looking toward the future. In J. Gomes-Pedro (Ed.), *The infant and family in the twenty-first century* (pp. 23-30). Routledge: New York.

Brenes Camacho, G. (2009). El ritmo de la convergencia del envejecimiento poblacional en América Latina: Oportunidades y retos. *Revista Latinoamericana de Población*, 3(4–5), 9–26. Recuperado de http://www.redalyc.org/pdf/3238/323827368002.pdf

Bronfenbrenner, I. (2002). Preparing a world for the infant in the twenty-first century: The research challenge. In J. Gomes-Pedro (Ed.), *The infant and family in the twenty-first century* (pp. 45–52). Routledge: New York.

Bronfenbrenner, U. (1976). The experimental ecology of education. *Teachers College Record*, 78(2), 1–37.

Bronfebrenner, U. (1994). Ecological models of human development. In P. Peterson, E. Baker, & B. McGaw (Eds.), *International encyclopedia of education* (Vol. 3(2), pp. 37–43). Oxford: Elsevier.

Bronfenbrenner, U. (1977). Toward an experimental ecology of human development. *American Psychologist*, 32(7), 513–531.

Bronfenbrenner, U. (1979). *The ecology of human development: Experiments by nature and design.* Cambridge, MA: Harvard University Press.

Bronfenbrenner, U. (1996). *A ecologia do desenvolvimento humano. Experimentos naturais e planejados.* Porto Alegre: Artes Médicas (original publication in 1979).

Bruner, J. S. (1990). *Acts of meaning.* Cambridge, MA: Harvard University Press.

Bugental, D. B., & Grusec, J. E. (2006). Socialization theory. In N. Eisenberg, W. Damon, & R. M. Lerner (Eds.), *Handbook of child psychology: Social, emotional, and personality development* (6th ed.) (pp. 389–462). Hoboken, NJ: John Wiley & Sons Inc.

Burger, L. K., & Miller, P. J. (1999). Early talk about the past re-visited: Affect in working-class and middle-class children's co-narrations. *Journal of Child Language*, 26, 133–162.

Bydlowski, M. (2004). Transparence psychique de la grossesse et dette de vie. In "Becoming father, becoming mother" Devenir pere, devenir mere. Compiled by Dugnat M. ERES Editions. Ramonville Saint-Agne: Dugnat M. ERES Editions.

Cadavid, G., & Amarís, M. (2007). *Estrategias de afrontamiento que utilizan las familias en proceso de separación con jóvenes de 12 a 20 años en Santa Marta D.T.C.H.* Tesis inédita de Licenciatura. Universidad del Norte, Barranquilla.

Cadima, J., Doumen, S., Verschueren, K., & Buyse, E. (2015). Child engagement in the transition to school: Contributions of self-regulation, teacher-child relationships and classroom climate. *Early Childhood Research Quarterly*, 32, 1–12. https://doi.org/10.1016/j.ecresq.2015.01.008

Calzada, E. J., Tamis-LeMonda, C. S., & Yoshikawa, H. (2012). Familismo in Mexican and Dominican families from low-income, urban communities. *Journal of Family Issues*, 34, 1696–1724. doi:10.1177/0192513X12460218

Carbonell, O. A. M., Plata, S. J., Bermúdez, M. E., Suárez, L. C., Peña, P. A., & Villanueva, C. (2015). Caracterización de prácticas de cuidado en familias colombianas con niños en primera infancia en situación de desplazamiento forzado [Characteristics of caregiving practices in Colombian families with children in early childhood in forcibly displaced situation]. *Universitas Psychologica*, 14 (1), 67–80. http://dx.doi.org/10.11144/Javeriana.upsy14-1.cpcf

Cardona-Oviedo, M., & Terán-Reales, V. (2017). Pautas, prácticas y creencias de crianza de las familias afrodescendientes cordobesas. *Revista Eleuthera, 17*, 13–30. https://doi.org/10.17151/eleu.2017.17.2

Carlo, G., Koller, S. H., Raffaelli, M., & De Guzman, M. R. (2007). Culture-related strengths among Latin American families: A case study of Brazil. *Marriage & Family Review, 41*(3–4), 335–360. doi: 10.1300/J002v41n03_06

Carlson, V., & Harwood, R. (2003). Attachment, culture and the caregiving system: The cultural patterning of everyday experiences among Anglo and Puerto Rican mother-infant pairs. *Infant Mental Health Journal, 24*(1), 53–73. https://doi.org/10.1002/imhj.10043

Carmiol, A. M. (2015). *La educación preescolar en Costa Rica*. Ponencia preparada para el Quinto Informe Estado de la Educación. San José: Programa Estado de la Nación. http://estadonacion.or.cr/files/biblioteca_virtual/educacion/005/Ana_Maria_Carmiol_La_educacion_Preescolar_en_Costa_Rica.pdf

Carmiol, A. M., & Schröder, L. (2019). Emotion talk during mother-child reminiscing and book sharing and children's socioemotional competence: Evidence from Costa Rica and Germany. *Culture and Brain*, 1–22. doi: 10.1007/s40167-019-00078-x

Carrillo, S., & Ripoll-Núñez, K. (2014). Family policies in Colombia: A focus on policies for vulnerable families. In M. Robila (Ed.), *Handbook of family policies across the globe* (pp.445–458). New York: Springer.

Carrillo, S., Ripoll-Núñez, K., & Schvaneveldt, P. (2012). Family policy initiatives in Latin America: The case of Colombia and Ecuador. *Journal of Child and Family Studies, 21*, 75–87. doi: 10.1007/s10826-011-9539-z

Carstensen, L. L. (1995). Evidence for a lifespan theory of socioemotional selectivity. *Current Directions in Psychological Science, 4*, 151–156.

Carter, B. L., & McGoldrick, M. (2005). Overview: The expanded family life cycle. Individual, family, and social perspectives. In B. Carter & M. McGoldrick (Eds.), *The expanded family life cycle: Individual, family, and social perspectives* (pp. 1–26). New York: Allyn and Bacon.

Castellano Fuentes, C. L. (2014). La influencia del apoyo social en el estado emocional y las actitudes hacia la vejez y el envejecimiento en una muestra de ancianos. *International Journal of Psychology and Psychological Therapy, 14*(3), 265–377.

Casullo, M. M. (1998). *Adolescentes en riesgo. Orientación e identificación*. Buenos Aires: Editorial Paidós.

Chavajay, P., & Rogoff, B. (1999). Cultural variation in management of attention by children and their caregivers. *Developmental Psychology, 35*(4), 1079.

Cicchetti, D. (2010). Resilience under conditions of extreme stress: A multilevel perspectives. *World Psychiatry, 9*(3), 145–154.

Cicchetti, D. (2013). Annual research review: Resilient functioning in maltreated children past, present, and future perspectives. *Journal of Child Psychology and Psychiatry, 54*(4), 402–422.

Cienfuegos, J. (2014). Tendencias familiares en América Latina. Diferencias y entrelazamientos. *Notas de Población, 41*(99), 11–36. https://doi.org/10.18356/55932b57-es

Citlak, B., Leyendecker, B., Schoelmerich, A., Driessen, R., & Harwood, R. (2008). Socialization goals among first- and second-generation migrant Turkish and German mothers. *International Journal of Behavioral Development, 32*(1), 56–65. https://doi.org/10.1177%2F0165025407084052

Cohn, J., & Tronick, E. (1989). Specificity of infant's response to mother's affective behaviour. *Journal of the American Academy of Child Psychiatry, 28*(2), 242–248.

Colombian Institute for the Welfare of Families (2017). Technical and administrative guidelines for the families with welfare modality. https://www.icbf.gov.co/portafolio-de-servicios-icbf/modalidad-de-familias-con-bienestar

Colombian Institute for the Welfare of Families & The Observatory for Peace (2009). Anexo técnico. "Familias con Bienestar." http//www.icbf.gov.co

Comisión Económica Para América Latina y el Caribe (CEPAL) (2000). *Juventud, población y desarrollo en América Latina y el Caribe. Problemas, oportunidades y desafíos*. Santiago: CEPAL/FNUAP.

Comisión Económica para América Latina y el Caribe (CEPAL) (2014). *América Latina a 25 años de la aprobación de la Convención sobre los derechos del niño*. Santiago de Chile: Organización de las Naciones Unidas (ONU). https://www.unicef.org/ecuador/C1420868_WEB.pdf

Conger, R., & Conger, K. (2002). Reilience in midwestern families: Selected findings from the first decade of a prospective, longitudinal study. *Journal of Marriage and Family, 64*, 361–373.

Conger, R. D., Conger, K. J., & Martin, M. J. (2010). Socioeconomic status, family processes, and individual development. *Journal of Marriage and the Family, 72*(3), 685–704. doi: 10.1111/j.1741-3737.2010.00725.x

Conger, R. D., & Donnellan, M. B. (2007). An interactionist perspective on the socioeconomic context of human development. *Annual Review of Psychology, 58*, 175–199. doi: 10.1146/annurev.psych.58.110405.085551

CONAPO [Consejo Nacional de Población]. (2020). La situación demográfica de México. Secretaría General del Consejo Nacional de Población. Año 2, núm. 2.https://www.gob.mx/conapo/documentos/la-situacion-demografica-de-mexico-2020

Coohey, C. (2001). The relationship between familism and child maltreatment in Latino and Anglo families. *Child Maltreatment, 6*(2), 130–142. doi: 10.1177/1077559501006002005

Corredor, C. (2010). *La política social en clave de derechos*. Bogotá: Facultad de Ciencias Económicas.

Crespo, C., Kielpikowski, M., Pryor, J., & Jose, P. E. (2011). Family rituals in New Zealand families: Links to family cohesion and adolescents' well-being. *Journal of Family Psychology, 25*(2), 184.

Creswell, J. W. (2013). *Research design: Qualitative, quantitative, and mixed methods approaches*. London: Sage Publications.

Darling, M., Cumsille, P., & Mártinez, M. L. (2008). Individual differences in adolescents' beliefs about the legitimacy of parental authority and their own obligation to obey: A longitudinal investigation. *Child Development*, 79(4), 1103–1118. https://doi.org/10.1111/j.1467-8624.2008.01178.x

DATASUS (2017). Óbitos por causas externas 1996 a 2010. http://tabnet.datasus.gov.br/cgi/tabcgi.exe?sim/cnv/ext10uf.def (accessed May 25, 2017).

Davis, P., & Cummings, M. (2006). Interparental discord, family process and developmental psychopathology. In D. Cicchetti & D. Cohen (Eds.), *Developmental psychopatology*, Vol. 3: *Risk, disorder, and adaptation* (2nd ed.) (pp. 129–201). New York: John Willey & Sons, Inc.

Dayan, J. (2015). *Psychopatologie de la perinatalité et de la parentalité*. Paris: Elsevier Masson SAS, Francia.

Del Boca, D., & Mancini, A. L. (2013). Child poverty and child well-being in Italy in a comparative framework. In A. Moreno Minguez (Ed.), *Family well-being*. Social indicators research series, Vol. 49 (pp.55–72). Dordrecht: Springer. https://doi.org/10.1007/978-94-007-4354-0_4

Deleire, T., & Kalil, A. (2001). Good Things Come in Threes: Single-Parent Multigenerational Family Structure and Adolescent Adjustment. *JCPR Working Paper*.

Deleire, T., & Kalil, A. (2002). Good things come in threes: Single-parent multigenerational family structure and adolescent adjustment. *Demography*, 39(2), 393–413.

Delgado, S., Strawn, E., & Pedapati, E. (2015). *Contemporary psycodynamic psychotherapy for children and adolescents: Integrating intersubjetivity and neuroscience*. Dordrecht: Springer.

DeVore, E. R., & Ginsburg, K. R. (2005). The protective effects of good parenting on adolescents. *Current Opinion in Pediatrics*, 17(4), 460–465.

Dias, C., Azambuja, R., Rabinovich, E., & Bastos, A. C. (2017). Grandparents in Brazil: The contexts of care and economic support for grandchildren. In D. Schwalb & Z. Hossain (Eds.), *Grandparents in cultural context* (pp. 60–79). New York: Routledge.

Dias, R., Santos, R., Barroso, M., Lima, M., Torres, L., Belfort, B. & Nascimiento, M. (2015). Resilience of caregivers of people with dementia: a systematic review of biological and psychosocial determinants. *Trends Psychiatry Psychother*, 37(1), 13–19. doi: 10.1590/2237-6089-2014-0032

Díaz, A., & Eisenberg, N. (2015). The process of emotion regulation is different from individual differences in emotion regulation: Conceptual arguments and a focus on individual differences. *Psychological Inquiry*, 26, 37–47. https://doi.org/10.1080/1047840X.2015.959094

Diener, E. (2012). New findings and future directions for subjective well-being research. *American Psychologist*, 67(8), 590–597. http://dx.doi.org/10.1037/a0029541

Dinisman, T., Andresen, S., Monserrat, C., Strózik, D., & Strózik, T. (2017). Family structure and family relationship from the child well-being perspective: Findings from comparative analysis. *Children and Youth Services Review*, 80, 105–115.

Doherty, W. J., Kouneski, E. F., & Erickson, M. F. (1998). Responsible fathering: An overview and conceptual framework. *Journal of Marriage and the Family*, 60, 277–292. doi: 10.2307/353848

Dolbin-MacNab, M., Roberto, K., & Finney, J. (2013). Formal social support: Promoting resilience among grandparents raising grandchildren. In B. Hayslip & G. C. Smith (Eds.), *Resilient grandparent caregivers: A strengths-based perspective* (pp. 134–151). New York: Routledge.

Doménech, E., & Gómez de Terreros, M. (2003). In F. Silva Moreno (Ed.), *Evaluación psicológica en niños y adolescentes* (pp. 173–219). Madrid: Editorial Síntesis SA.

Domínguez Guedea, M. T., Mandujano Jaquez, M. F., Georgina Quintero, M., Sotelo Quiñónez, T. L., Gaxiola Romero, J. C., & Valencia Maldonado, J. E. (2013). Escala de Apoyo Social para cuidadores familiares de adultos mayores mexicanos. *Universitas Psychologica*, 12(2), 391–402. doi:10.11144/Javeriana.UPSY12-2.easc

Doyle, M., & Timonen, V. (2009). The different faces of care work: Understanding the experiences of the multi-cultural care workforce. *Ageing and Society*, 29, 337–350.

Dunifon, R., & Bajracharya, A. (2012). The role of parents in the lives of youth. *Journal of Family Issues*, 33(9), 1168–1194.

Dunifon, R. (2012). The influence of grandparents on the lives of children and adolescents. *Child Development Perspectives*, 7(1), 55–60.

Dunn, J., Brown, J., & Beardsalt, L. (1991). Family talk about feelings states and children's later understanding of other's emotions. *Developmental Psychology*, 27(3), 448–455. doi: 10.1037/0012-1649.27.3.448

Eisenberg, N., Spinrad, T. L., & Valiente, C. (2016). Emotion-related self-regulation, and children's social, psychological, and academic functioning. In C. Balter & C. S. Tamis-LeMonda (Eds.), *Child psychology: A handbook of contemporary issues* (3rd ed.) (pp. 219–244). New York: Routledge

Engle, P. (2012). Poverty and developmental potential. In J. Boyden & M. Bourdillon (Eds.), *Childhood poverty: Multidisciplinary approaches* (pp. 129–147). London: Palgrave Macmillan.

Estévez, R., Oliva, A., & Parra, Á. (2012). Acontecimientos vitales estresantes, estilo de afrontamiento y ajuste adolescente. Un análisis longitudinal de los efectos de moderación. *Revista Latinoamericana de Psicología*, 44(2), 39–53.

Everall, R., Altrows, J., & Paulson, B. (2006). Creating a future: A study of resilience in suicidal female adolescents. *Journal of Counseling & Development*, 84, 461–470.

Falceto, O. G., Giugliani, E. R. J., & Fernandes, C. L. C. (2004). Influence of parental mental health on early termination of breastfeeding: A case-control study. *Journal of American Board of Family Practice*, 17(3), 173–183. doi: 10.3122/jabfm.17.3.173

Falicov, C. (2002). Ambiguous loss: Risk and resilience in Latino immigrant families. In M. Suárez & M. Páez (Eds.), *Latinos: Remaking America* (pp. 183–217). Berkeley, CA: University of California Press.

Felner, R. D., & DeVries, M. L. (2013). Poverty in childhood and adolescence: A transactional-ecological approach to understanding and enhancing resilience in contexts of disadvantage and developmental risk. In S. Goldstein & R. B. Brooks (Eds.), *Handbook of resilience in children* (pp. 105–126). New York: Springer. DOI 10.1007/978-1-4614-3661-4_7

Felner, R. D., Felner, T. Y., & Silverman, M. M. (2000). Prevention in mental health and social intervention: Conceptual and methodological issues in the evolution of the science and practice of prevention. In J. Rappaport & E. Seidman (Eds.), *Handbook of community psychology* (pp. 9–42). New York: Kluwer Academic/Plenum.

Fernández, M., & Herrera, M. (2016). Distrés en hijas adultas que brindan apoyo a sus padres mayores. *PSYKHE, 25*(1), 1–14. doi:10.7764/psykhe.25.1.710

Figley, Ch. (1982). Catastrophes: An overview of reactions. In Ch. Figley & H. McCubbin (Eds.), *Stress and family*, Vol. II: *Coping with catastrophe* (pp. 3–20). Levittown, PA: Brunner/Mazel.

Finegood, E., & Blair, C. (2017). Poverty, parent stress, and emerging executive functions in young children. In K. Deater-Deckard & R. Panneton (Eds.), *Parental stress and early child development* (pp.181–207). New York: Springer.

Fiszelew, R. M., & Oiberman, A. J. (1995). Fuimos y seremos: una aproximación a la psicología de la primera infancia. In *Fuimos y seremos: una aproximación a la psicología de la primera infancia* (pp. 159–159).

Fitzpatrick, M. A. (2004). Family communication patterns theory: Observations on its development and application. *Journal of Family Communication, 4*(3-4), 167–179.

Fivush, R. (2007). Maternal reminiscing style and children's developing understanding of self and emotion. *Clinical Social Work Journal, 35*, 37–46. doi: 10.1007/s10615-006-0065-1

Fivush, R. (2011). The development of autobiographical memory. *Annual Review of Pychology, 62*, 559–582. doi: 10.1146/annurev.psych.121208.131702

Fivush, R., Berlin, L., McDermott, J., Mennuti-Washburn, J., & Cassidy, J. (2003). Functions of parent-child reminiscing about emotionally negative events. *Memory, 11*(2), 179–192. doi: 10.1080/09658210244000351

Fivush, R., Haden, C., & Reese, E. (2006). Elaborating on elaborations: Role of maternal reminiscing style in cognitive and socioemotional development. *Child Development, 77*(6), 1568–1588. doi: 10.1111/j.1467-8624.2006.00960.x

Fivush, R., & Vasudeva, A. (2002). Remembering to relate: Socioemotional correlates of mother-child reminiscing. *Journal of Cognition and Development, 3*(1), 73–90. doi: 10.1207/S15327647JCD0301_5

Fivush, R., & Wang, Q. (2005). Emotion talk in mother-child conversations of the shared past: The effects of culture, gender, and event valance. *Journal of Cognition and Development, 6* (4), 489–506. doi: 10.1207/s15327647jcd0604_3

Flórez-Alarcón, L. (2006). TIPICA. Una metodología de promoción de la salud escolar que incorpora la dimensión psicológica al aprendizaje de las competencias sociales. *TIPICA, Boletín Electrónico de Salud Escolar, 2*(2), 1–8.

Flórez-Alarcón, L., & Hewitt, N. H. (2013). Acciones de reforzamiento de la competencia social (ARCOS). Un programa de salud escolar fundamentado en conceptos de autodeterminación humana. *Psychologia. Avances de la Disciplina, 7*(2), 117–122.

Forbes (2016). Brazil is murder capital of the world, but Rio is safer than Compton, Detroit, St. Louis. https://www.forbes.com/sites/kenrapoza/2016/01/29/months-before-rio-olympics-murder-rate-rises-in-brazil/#63eaee072790 (accessed June 1, 2017).

Freisthler, B., Merritt, D. H., & LaScala, E. A. (2006). Understanding the ecology of child maltreatment: A review of the literature and directions for future research. *Child Maltreatment, 11*(3), 263–280.

Furstenberg, F. F. Jr. (1993). How families manage risk and opportunity in dangerous neighborhoods. In W. J. Wilson (Ed.), *Sociology and the public agenda* (pp. 231–258). Newbury Park, CA: Sage.

Fuster, D. T. (2011). Being bien educado in the United States: Mexican mother's childrearing beliefs and practices in the context of immigration (Dissertation). Tempe, AZ: Arizona State University.

Gallimore, R., Weisner, T., Kaufman, S., & Bernheimer, L. (1989). The social construction of ecological niches: Family accommodation of developmentally delayed children. *American Journal of Mental Retardation, 94*, 216–230.

García, M., Rivera, S., Reyes, I., & Díaz-Loving, R. (2015). *Continuidad y cambio en la familia: Factores intervinientes*. Bogotá: Manual Moderno

Garmezy, N. (1991). Resiliency and vulnerability to adverse developmental outcomes associated with poverty. *American Behavioral Scientist, 34*, 416–430.

Garmezy, N., Masten, A. S., & Tellegen, A. (1984). The study of stress and competence in children: A building block for developmental psychopathology. *Child Development, 55*, 97–111.

Gaskins, S., & Paradise, R. (2010). Learning through observation in daily life. *The Anthropology of Learning in Childhood*, 85–117.

Georgas, J., Berry, J. W., Van de Vijver, F. J., Kagitçibasi, Ç., & Poortinga, Y. H. (Eds.). (2006). *Families across cultures: A 30-nation psychological study*. Cambridge: Cambridge University Press.

Gershoff, E. T., Aber, J. L., Raver, C. C., & Lennon, M. C. (2007). Income is not enough: Incorporating material hardship into models of income associations with parenting and child development. *Child Development, 78*(1), 70–95. doi: 10.1111/j.1467-8624.2007.00986.x

Gibbons, J., & Fanjul de Marsicovetere, R. (2017). Grandparenting in Mexico and Central America: "Time and Attention." In D. Schwalb & Z. Hossain (Eds.), *Grandparents in cultural context* (pp. 17–40). New York: Routledge.

Gil, A. G., Wagner, E. F., & Vega, W. A. (2000). Acculturation, familism, and alcohol use among Latino adolescent males: Longitudinal relations. *Journal of Community Psychology, 28*, 443–458. doi: 10.1002/1520-6629(200007)28:4<443::AID-JCOP6>3.0.CO;2-A

Giles-Sims, J., & Lockhart, C. (2007). Culturally shaped patterns of disciplining children. *Journal of Family Issues, 26*, 196–218. doi: 10.1177/0192513X04270414

Glangeaud-Freudenthal, M. C. (1994). Psychological stress factors related to prenatal hospitalization. *Journal de Gynecologie, Obstetrique et Biologie de la Reproduction, 23*(3), 289–293.

Gómez, E., & Kotliarenco, M. A. (2010). Resiliencia familiar. Un enfoque de investigación e intervención con familias multiproblemáticas. *Revista de Psicología, 19*(2), 103–132.

González, C., Guevara, Y., Jiménez, D., & Alcázar, R. (2017). Relación entre prácticas parentales y el nivel de asertividad, agresividad y rendimiento académico en adolescentes. *European Scientific Journal, 13*(20), 37–54.

González-Bernal, J., González-Santos, J., Ortíz-Oria, V., & González-Bernal, E. (2010). La relación abuelos-nietos desde una perspectiva intercultural. *International Journal of Developmental and Educational Psychology, 2*(1), 669–676.

González-Rey, F. (2010). El pensamiento de Vygotski: Contexto, contradicciones y desarrollo. In S. Aburto & C. Meza (Eds.), *Tutoría para el desarrollo humano. Enfoques* (pp. 7–17). Nuevo León: Universidad Autónoma de Nuevo León.

Goodman, C., & Silverstein, M. (2005). Latina grandmothers raising grandchildren: Acculturation and psychological well-being. *The International Journal of Aging and Human Development, 60*(4), 305–316. https://doi.org/10.2190/NQ2P-4ABR-3U1F-W6G0

Goodvin, R., & Romdall, L. (2013). Associations of mother-child reminiscing about negative past events, coping, and self-concept in early childhood. *Infant and Child Development, 22,* 383–400. doi: 10.1002/icd.1797

Grantham-McGregor, S. (2007). Early child development in developing countries. *The Lancet, 369*(9564), 824.

Grantham-McGregor, S., Cheung, Y. B., Cueto, S., Glewwe, P. W., Richter, L., Strupp, B., & the International Child Development Steering Group (2007). Developmental potential in the first 5 years for children in developing countries. *The Lancet, 369*(9555), 60–70.

Greenfield, P. (2009). Linking social change and developmental change: Shifting pathways of human development. *Developmental Psychology, 45*(2), 401–418. https://doi.org/10.1037/a0014726

Greenfield, P. M. (2014). Sociodemographic differences within countries produce variable cultural values. *Journal of Cross-Cultural Psychology, 45*(1), 37–41. https://doi.org/10.1177/0022022113513402

Grotberg, E. H. (2004, July). Children and caregivers: The role of resilience. Paper delivered at the 2013 International Convention of Psychology (ICP), Jinan.

Grundy, E., Albala, C., Allen, E., Dangour, A., Elbourne, D., & Uauy, R. (2012). Grandparenting and psychosocial health among older Chileans: A longitudinal analysis. *Aging & Mental Health, 16*(8), 1047–1057.

Grusec, J. (2011). Socialization processes in the family: Social and emotional development. *Annual Reviews, 62,* 243–269. https://doi.org/10.1146/annurev.psych.121208.131650

Grusec, J., & Davidov, M. (2010). Integrating different perspectives on socialization theory and research: A domain-specific approach. *Child Development, 81,* 687–709. https://doi.org/10.1111/j.1467-8624.2010.01426.x

Grusec, J. E., & Goodnow, J. J. (1994). Impact of parental discipline methods on the child's internalization of values: a reconceptualization of current points of view. *Developmental Psychology, 30,* 4–19. https://doi.org/10.1037//0012-1649.30.1.4

Gutman, L. M., McLoyd, V. C., & Tokoyawa, T. (2005). Financial strain, neighborhood stress, parenting behaviors, and adolescent adjustment in urban African American families. *Journal of Research on Adolescence, 15*(4), 425–449. http://dx.doi.org/10.1111/j.1532-7795.2005.00106.x

Habib, D., & Dohert, K. (2007). Beyond the garden: Impacts of a school garden program on 3rd and 4th graders. *Seeds of Solidarity,* 11, 2–14.

Halberstadt, A., & Lozada, F. (2011). Emotion development in infancy through the lens of culture. *Emotion Review, 3* (2), 158–168. doi: 10.1177/1754073910387946

Halgunseth, L. C., Ispa, J. M., & Rudy, D. (2006). Parental control in Latino families: An integrated review of the literature. *Child Development,* 77, 1282–1297. https://doi.org/10.1111/j.1467-8624.2006.00934.x

Hancock, T. U. (2005). Cultural competence in the assessment of poor Mexican families in the rural Southwest United States. *Child Welfare, 85*(5), 689–711.

Harwood, R., Miller, A., & Lucca-Irizarry, N. (1995). *Culture and attachment: Perceptions of the child in context.* New York: Guilford.

Harwood, R., Schoelmerich, A., & Schulze, P. (2000). Homogeneity and heterogeneity in cultural belief systems. *New Directions for Child and Adolescent Development,* 87, 41–57. https://doi.org/10.1002/cd.23220008705

Harwood, R. L., Schoelmerich, A., Ventura-Cook, E., Schulze, P. A., & Wilson, S. P. (1996). Culture and class influences on Anglo and Puerto Rican mothers' beliefs regarding long-term socialization goals and child behavior. *Child Development, 67*(5), 2446–2461. https://doi.org/10.2307/1131633

Harwood, R., Schoelmerich, A., Schulze, P., & González, Z. (1999). Cultural differences in maternal beliefs and behaviors: A study of middle class Anglo- and Puerto Rican infant-mother pairs in four everyday situations. *Child Development, 70*(4), 1005–1016. https://doi.org/10.1111/1467-8624.00073

Harwood, R., Yalcinkaya, A., Citlak, B., & Leyendecker, B. (2006). Exploring the concept of respect among Turkish and Puerto Rican migrant mothers. *New Directions for Child and Adolescent Development,* 14, 9–24. https://doi.org/10.1002/cd.172

Hayslip, B., & Champa, B. P. (2007). Cognitive and affective theories of adult development. In J. A. Blackburn & C. N. Dulmus (Eds.), *Handbook of gerontology: Evidence-based approaches to theory, practice, and policy* (pp. 57–86). Hoboken, NJ : John Wiley & Sons, Inc.

Hayslip, B., Fruhauf, C., & Dolbin-MacNab, M. (2019). Grandparents raising grandchildren: What have we learned over the past decade? *The Gerontologist, 59*(3), 152–163. https://doi.org/10.1093/geront/gnx106

Hayslip, B., & Kaminski, P. (2005). Grandparents raising their grandchildren: A review of the literature and suggestions for practice. *The Gerontologist, 45* (2), 262–269.

Heikamp, T., Trommsdorff, G., & Fäsche, A. (2013). Development of self-regulation in context. In G. Seebass & P. Gollwitzer (Eds.), *Acting intentionally and its limits: Individuals, groups, institutions. Interdisciplinary approaches* (pp. 193–222). Berlín: De Gruyter. https://dx.doi.org/10.1515/9783110284461.193

Henrich, J., Heine, S. J., & Norenzayan, A. (2010). Most people are not WEIRD. *Nature, 466*(7302), 29.

Hernández-Cordero, A. L. (2016). Cuidar se escribe en femenino: Redes de cuidado familiar en hogares de madres migrantes. *Psicoperspectivas, 15*(3), 46–55.

Higgins, E. T. (1998). Promotion and prevention: Regulatory focus as a motivational principle. In M. P. Zanna (Ed.), *Advances in experimental social psychology*, Vol. *30* (pp. 1–46). New York: Academic Press. https://doi.org/10.1016/S0065-2601(08)60381-0

Hollist, C. S., Falceto, O. G., Ferreira, L. M., Miller, R. B., & Springer, P. (2012). Portuguese translation and validation of the Revised Dyadic Adjustment Scale. *Journal of Marital and Family Therapy, 38*(1), 348–358. doi: 10.1111/j.1752-0606.2012.00296.x

Hollist, C. S., Miller, R. B., Falceto, O. G., &Fernandes, C. L. (2007). Marital satisfaction and depression: A replication of the Marital Discord Model in a Latino sample. *Family Process, 46*(4), 485–498. doi: http://dx.doi.org/10.1111/j.1545-5300.2007.00227.x

Hoyuelos Planillo, A. (2004). Abuelos, abuelas, nietos y nietas. El punto de vista infantil. *Indivisa. Boletín de Estudios e Investigación, 5*, 35–42.

Hrdy, S. B. (2009). *Mothers and others: The evolutionary origins of mutual understanding*. Cambridge, MA: The Belknap Press.

Hughes, C., White, N., & Ensor, R. (2014). How does talk about thoughts, desires, and feelings foster children's socio-cognitive development? Mediators, moderators and implications for intervention. In H. Lagattuta (Ed.), *Children and emotion: New insights into developmental affective sciences* (pp. 95–105). Basel: Karger.

Ierullo, M. (2015). La crianza de niños, niñas y adolescentes en contextos de pobreza urbana persistente. *Revista Latinoamericana de Ciencias Sociales, Niñez y Juventud, 13*(2), 671–683.

Instituto Nacional de Estadística y Censos (INEC) (2012). *X censo nacional de población y VI de vivienda 2011. Resultados generales*. San José: Instituto Nacional de Estadística y Censos.

Internal Displacement Monitoring Center (IDMC) (2017). On the GRID: Internal displacement in 2016. http://www.internal-displacement.org/global-report/grid2017/

Israel, B. A., Schulz, A. J., Parker, E. A., & Becker, A. B. (1998). Review of community based research: Assessing partnership approaches to improve public health. *Annual Review of Public Health, 19*, 173–102. doi: 10.1146/annurev.publhealth.19.1.173

Jaramillo, J., Bernal, T., Mendoza, L., Pérez, A., & Suárez, A. (2010). Significados de familia en el marco de la globalización. *Hallazgos-Revista de Investigaciones, 7*(14), 60–84. DOI: https://doi.org/10.15332/s1794-3841.2010.0014.03

Jaramillo, J., Pérez, L., & González, K. (2013). Metas de socialización maternas. Relación con edad, formación académica y zona habitacional. *Revista Latinoamericana de Ciencias Sociales, Niñez y Juventud, 11*(2), 719–739. http://revistaumanizales.cinde.org.co/rlcsnj/index.php/Revista-Latinoamericana/article/view/947

Jaramillo, J. M., Rendón, M. I., Muñoz, L., Weis, M., & Trommsdorff, G. (2017). Children's self-regulation in cultural contexts: The role of parental socialization theories, goals, and practices. *Frontiers in Psychology, 8*(923). http://dx.doi.org/10.3389/fpsyg.2017.00923

Jaramillo, J. M., & Ruiz, M. I. (2013). Metas y prácticas de socialización de madres del área rural cundiboyacense. *Psicología Desde el Caribe, 30*(2), 277–308. http://rcientificas.uninorte.edu.co/index.php/psicologia/article/view/4511

Jiménez-Torres, A. L., Malavé de León, E., & Rodríguez-Quiñones, J. (2017). La familia como eje del desarrollo humano. In C. García-Coll & N. M. Vélez-Agosto (Ed.), *Perspectivas en desarrollo humano. Prevención y promoción en niños y adolescentes*, Vol. 1, pp. 279–294. Bogotá: GAviota.

Johnson, L. A., & Olshansky, R. B. (2016). *After great disasters: How six countries managed community recovery*. Cambridge, MA: Lincoln Institute of Land Policy.

Kağitçibaşi, Ç. (1996). The autonomous-relational self: A new synthesis. *European Psychologist, 1*, 180–186. https://doi.org/10.1027/1016-9040.1.3.180

Kağitçibaşi, Ç. (2005). Autonomy and relatedness in cultural context: Implications for self and family. *Journal of Cross-Cultural Psychology, 36*(4), 403–422. https://doi.org/10.1177/0022022105275959

Kağitçibaşi, Ç. (2007). *Family, self, and human development across cultures: Theories and applications*. Lawrence Erlbaum Associates Publishers.

Kaplan, M., Sanchez, M., & Hoffman, J. (2017). *Intergenerational pathways to a sustainable society: Perspectives on sustainable growth*. Cham: Springer International Publishing. DOI 10.1007/978-3-319-47019-1_4

Karreman, A., Van Tuijl, C., Van Aken, M. A., & Dekovic, M. (2009). Predicting young children's externalizing problems: Interactions among effortful control, parenting, and child gender. *Merrill-Palmer Quarterly, 55*(2), 111–134.

Kazdin, A. E., & Whitley, M. K. (2003). Treatment of parental stress to enhance therapeutic change among children referred for aggressive and antisocial behavior. *Journal of Consulting and Clinical Psychology, 71*, 504–515. doi: 10.1037/0022-006X.71.3.504

Keller, H. (2002). Development as the interface between biology and culture: A conceptualisation of early ontogenetic experience. In I. Poortinga & A. Schölmerich (Eds.), *Culture and biology: Perspective on ontogenic development* (p. 215). New York: Cambridge University Press.

Keller, H. (2013). *Cultures of infancy*. London: Psychology Press.

Keller, H. (2018). Universality claim of attachment theory: Children's socioemotional development across cultures. *Proceedings of the National Academy of Sciences, 115*(45), 11414–11419.

Keller, H., Borke, J., & Yovsi, R. (2005). Cultural orientations and historical changes as predictors of parenting behaviour. *International Journal of Behavioral Development, 29*(3), 229–237. doi: 10.1080/01650250544000017

Keller, H., & Chaudhary, C. (2017). Is the mother essential for attachment? Models of care in different cultures. In H. Keller & K. Bard (Eds.), *The cultural nature of attachment: Contextualizing relationships and development,* (pp. 109–138). Cambridge, MA: MIT Press.

Keller, H., & Kärtner, J. (2013). Development: The cultural solution of universal developmental tasks. In M. Gelfand, Ch. Chiu, & Y. Hong (Eds.), *Advances in culture and psychology* (pp. 63–116). New York: Oxford University Press.

Keller, H., Kuensemueller, P., Abels, M., Voelker, S., Yovsi, R., Jensen, H., Papaligoura, Z., Lohaus, A., Rosabal-Coto, M., Kulks, D., & Mohite, P. (2005). *Parenting, culture, and development. A comparative study*. San José: Universidad de Costa Rica.

Kelley, W. M., Wagner, D. D., & Heatherton, T. F. (2015). In search of a human self-regulation system. *Annual Review of Neuroscience, 38*, 389–411. https://doi.org/10.1146/annurev-neuro-071013-014243

Kelly, K. R. (2015). Insecure attachment representations and child personal narrative structure: Implications for delayed discourse in preschool-age children. *Attachment & Human Development, 17*(5), 448–471. doi: 10.1080/14616734.2015.1076011

Klein, A. (2015). La necesidad de cuidar de aquellos que solían necesitar ser cuidados. Vejez y tendencias familiares-demográficas. *Cultura y Representaciones Sociales, 10*(19), 128–153.

Kliksberg, B. (2005). La familia en América Latina. Realidades, interrogantes y perspectivas. *Convergencia. Revista de Ciencias Sociales, 12*(38), 13–41.

Kliksberg, B. (2014). *¿Cómo enfrentar la pobreza y la desigualdad? Una perspectiva internacional.* San José: Editorial UCR.

Knibiehler, Y. (2001). *Historia de las madres y de la maternidad en Occidente.* Austin, TX: Nueva visión.

Knutson, J. F., Demargo, D., Koeppl, G., & Reid, J. B. (2005). Care neglect, supervisory neglect, and harsh parenting in the development of children's aggression: A replication and extension. *Child Maltreatment, 10*(2), 92–107. doi: 10.1177/1077559504273684

Konner, M. (2007). Evolutionary foundations of cultural psychology. *Handbook of cultural psychology*, 77–105.

Kornadt, H.-J., & Trommsdorff, G. (1990). Naive Erziehungstheorien japanischer Mütter. Deutsch-japanischer Kulturvergleich [Japanese mothers' naive childrearing theories: A cross-cultural comparison between Germany and Japan], *Zeitschrift für Sozialisationsforschung und Erziehungssoziologie, 10*, 357–376. http://kops.uni-konstanz.de/handle/123456789/10527

Lagattuta, K., & Wellman, H. (2002). Differences in early parent-child conversations about negative versus positive emotions: Implications for the development of psychological understanding. *Developmental Psychology, 38* (4), 564–580. doi: 10.1037//0012-1649.38.4.564

Laible, D. (2004). Mother-child discourse in two contexts: Links with child temperament, attachment security and socioemotional competence. *Developmental Psychology, 40*, 979–992. doi: 10.1037/0012-1649.40.6.979

Laible, D. (2010). Does it matter if preschool children and mothers discuss positive vs. negative events during reminiscing? Links with mother-reported attachment, family emotional climate, and socioemotional development. *Social Development, 20* (2), 394–411. doi: 10.1111/j.1467-9507.2010.00584.x

Lake, A. (2017). *Los 1.000 primeros días. Un abanico de oportunidades.* Buenos Aires: UNICEF. https://blogs.unicef.org

Lay, C., Fairlie, P., Jackson, S., Ricci, T., Eisenberg, J., Sato, T., Teeaar, A., & Melamud, A. (1998). Domain-specific allocentrism-idiocentrism: A measure of family connectedness. *Journal of Cross-Cultural Psychology, 29*, 434–460.

Lázaro-Ruiz, V., & Gil López, A. (2005). Transmisión de conocimientos de los abuelos a los nietos. *International Journal of Developmental and Educational Psychology*, 3(1), 307–316.

Leboyer, F. (1978). Birth without violence. *India International Centre Quarterly*, 5(3), 155–162.

León, A., Rodríguez, M., & Hernández, L. (2016). Un análisis del vínculo abuelos nietos-adolescentes reflexión sobre la transmisión generacional. *Florianópolis*, 19(2), 251–259.

Lerner, R. M. (2011). Structure and process in relational, developmental systems theories: A commentary on contemporary changes in the understanding of developmental change across the life span. *Human Development*, 54, 34–43

Leventhal, T., & Brooks-Gunn, J. (2000). The neighborhoods they live in: The effects of neighborhood residence on child and adolescent outcomes. *Psychological Bulletin*, 126(2), 309–337. DOI: 10.1037//0033-2909.126.2.309

Leyendecker, B., Lamb, M., Harwood, R., & Schoelmerich, A. (2002). Mothers' socialization goals and evaluation of desirable and undesirable everyday situations in two diverse cultural groups. *International Journal of Behavioral Development*, 26(3), 248–258. https://doi.org/10.1080/01650250143000030

Leyendecker, B., Lamb, M., Schoelmerich, A., & Fracasso, M. (1995). The social world of 8- and 12-months old infants: Early experiences in two subcultural contexts. *Social Development*, 4, 194–208. https://doi.org/10.1111/j.1467-9507.1995.tb00060.x

Leyva, D., Berrocal, M., & Nolivos, V. (2014). Spanish-speaking parent-child emotional narratives and children's social skills. *Journal of Cognition and Development*, 15(1), 22–42 doi:10.1080/15248372.2012.725188

Lozoff, B., Jimenez, E., & Smith, J. B. (2006). Double burden of iron deficiency in infancy and low socioeconomic status: A longitudinal analysis of cognitive test scores to age 19 years. *Archives of Pediatric and Adolescent Medicine*, 160, 1108–1113.

Lucio, E., León, I., Durán, C., Bravo, E., & Velasco, E. (2001). Los sucesos de vida en dos grupos de adolescentes de diferente nivel socioeconómico. *Salud Mental*, 24(5), 17–24.

Luna, M., Fridman, D., Sánchez, M., Pesenti, M., & Salgado, V. (2010). *Niños, niñas y adolescentes sin cuidados parentales en América Latina*. Buenos Aires: RELAF-UNICEF

Lupica, C. (2011). *Anuario de la maternidad: madres solas en la Argentina; dilemas y recursos para hacer frente al trabajo remunerado y al cuidado de los hijos*. Buenos Aires. Observatorio de la Maternidad.

Lüscher, K., Hoff, A., Lamura, G., Renzi, M., Sánchez, M., Viry, G., & Widmer, E. (2013). *Generations, intergenerational relationships, generational policy: A multilingual compendium*. Konstanz: GENERATIONES. http://www.generationen-compendium.de/downloads/Luescher-Kompendium_7sprachig-komplett_online_15-10-2015.pdf

Luthar, S. (2006). Resilience in development: A synthesis of research across five decades. In D. Cicchetti & Y. D. Cohen (Eds.), *Developmental psychopathology*, Vol. 3: *Risk, disorder and Aadaptation* (pp. 739–795). Hoboken, NJ: John Wiley & Sons, Inc.

Macarini, S. M., Martins, G. D. F., Sachetti, V. A. R., & Vieira, M. L. (2010). Etnoteorias parentais. Um estudo com mães residentes no interior e na capital de Santa Catarina. *Psicologia: Reflexão e Crítica*, 23(1), 37–45. http://dx.doi.org/10.1590/S0102-79722010000100006

Magnusson, D., & Stattin, H. (2006). The person in context: A holistic-interactionistic approach. In R. M. Lerner & W. Damon (Eds.), *Handbook of child psychology: Theoretical models of human development* (pp. 400–464). Hoboken, NJ: John Wiley & Sons Inc.

Mallol, E. P., & Riba, S. S. (1994). Desarrollo de la inteligencia. In V. Bermejo (Ed.), *Desarrollo cognitivo* (pp. 191–213). Madrid: Editorial Síntesis S.A.

Márquez, M. E. (2008). Family correlates, rearing and parental' involve, as predictors of academic achievement (Unpublished PhD thesis). Faculty of Psychology, UNAM, Mexico City.

Marsico, G., Chaudhary N., Valsiner, J., & Lyberth, M. (2015). Maintenance of family networks: Centrality of peripheral communication. *Psycholical Studies*, 60, 185–192. doi: 10.1007/s12646-015-0308-8

Martín, E., Fajardo, C., Gutiérrez, A., & Palma, D. (2007). Estrategias de afrontamiento de crisis causadas por desempleo en familias con hijos adolescentes en Bogotá. *Acta Colombiana de Psicología*, 10(2), 127–141.

Martins, C. L., & Branco, U. A. (2001). Desenvolvimento moral. Considerações teóricas a partir de uma abordagem sociocultural construtivista. *Psicologia. Teoria e Pesquisa*, 17(2), 1–14.

Masten, A. (2007). Resilience in developing systems: Progress and promise as the fourth wave rises. *Development and Psychopathology*, 19, 921–930. https://doi.org/10.1017/S0954579407000442.

Masten, A., & Shaffer, W. (2006). How families matter in child development. In A. Clarke-Stewart & J. Dunn (Eds.), *Families count: Effects on child and adolescent development* (pp. 5–25). New York: Cambridge University Press.

Masten, A. S. (2001). Ordinary magic: Resilience processes in development. *American Psychologist*, 56(3), 227–238.

Masten, A. S., & Cicchetti, D. (2010). Developmental cascades. *Development and Psychopathology*, 22(3), 491–495.

Masten, A. S., & Reed, M. G. J. (2002). Resilience in development. In C. R. Snyder & S. J. Lopez (Eds.), *Handbook of positive psychology* (pp. 74–88). Oxford: Oxford University Press.

McClelland, M. M., & Cameron, C. E. (2011). Self-regulation and academic achievement in elementary school children. *New Directions for Child and Adolescent Development*, 133, 29–44. https://doi.org/10.1002/cd.302

McClelland, M. M., Geldhof, G. J., Cameron, C. E., & Wanless, S. B. (2015). Development and self-regulation. In W. Overton & P. C. M. Molenaar (Eds.), *Handbook of child psychology and developmental science: Theoretical models of human development* (7th ed.) (pp. 1–43). Hoboken, NJ: Wiley. https://doi.org/10.1002/9781118963418.childpsy114

McClelland, M. M., Ponitz, C. C., Messersmith, E., & Tominey, S. (2010). Self-regulation: The integration of cognition and emotion. In R. Lerner & W. Overton (Eds.), *Handbook of life-span development*, Vol. 1: *Cognition, biology and methods* (pp. 509–553). Hoboken, NJ: Wiley & Sons. https://doi.org/10.1002/9780470880166.hlsd001015

McConnell, D., Breitkreuz, R., & Savage, A. (2011). From financial hardship to child difficulties: Main and moderating effects of perceived social support. *Child: Care, Health and Development*, 37, 679–691. doi:10.1111/j.1365-2214.2010.01185.x

McCubbin, H. I., & Patterson, J. (1982). Family adaptation to crisis. In H. McCubbin, A. Cauble, & J. Patterson (Eds.), *Family stress, coping and social support* (pp. 26–47). Springfield, IL: Charles Thomas Publisher

McDermott, J., & Peterson, C. (2003). Parental reminiscing about positive and negative events. *Journal of Cognition and Development*, 4 (2), 185–209. doi:10.1207/S15327647JCD0402_03

McLoyd, V. C. (1990).The impact of economic hardship on black families and children: Psychological distress, parenting and socioemotional development. *Child Development*, 61, 311–346.

Mechan Salazar, R., & Díaz Mondray, R. (2013). Rol fundamental del adulto mayor en la familia extensa. Crianza de los nietos. *ACC CIETNA*, 1(1), 37–44.

Melzi, G., & Fernández, C. (2004). Talking about past emotions: Conversations between Peruvian mothers and their preschool children. *Sex Roles*, 50, 641–657. doi: 10.1023/B:SERS.0000027567.55262.10

Méndez, M., Andrade, P., & Peñaloza, R. (2013). Prácticas parentales y capacidades y dificultades en preadolescente. *Revista Intercontinental de Psicología y Educación*, 15(1), 99–118

Mendoza, A. M., & González, J. I. (2010). El desplazamiento forzado en Colombia y la intervención del Estado. Una mirada desde el goce efectivo de derechos y los factores asociados a su realización. *Serie Documentos Cede*, 44, 1–51.

Meneses, L., Arenas, M., & Pino, S. (2012). Pobreza y abandono parental. Macropoyecto Sujetos y Diversidad: Una mirada desde el Desarrollo Humano.

Meneses, L. A., Arenas, M. E., & Pino, S. L. (2013). Pobreza y abandono parental (Master's thesis). Universidad de Manizales, Caldas. http://ridum.umanizales.edu.co:8080/xmlui/handle/6789/954

Merrill, N., & Fivush, R. (2016). Intergenerational narratives and identity across development. *Developmental Review*, 40, 72–92. http://dx.doi.org/10.1016/j.dr.2016.03.001

Micolta León, A., & Escobar Serrano, M. (2010). Si las abuelas se disponen a cuidar, madres y padres pueden emigrar. *Revista Venezolana de Estudios de la Mujer*, 15(35), 91–115.

Miller, A., & Harwood, R. (2001). Long-term socialisation goals and the construction of social infants' social networks among middle class Anglo and Puerto Rican mothers. *International Journal of Behavioral Development*, 25(5), 450–457. http://journals.sagepub.com/doi/abs/10.1080/016502501316934888

Miller, I. W., Ryan, C. E., Keitner, G. I., Bishop, D. S., & Epstein, N. B. (2000). The McMaster approach to families: Theory, assessment, treatment and research. *Journal of Family Therapy*, 22, 168–190.

Ministry of Health and Social Protection (2012). Challenges of the public sector to provide integral services to victims of the armed conflict in Colombia. https://www.minsalud.gov.co/proteccionsocial/Paginas/Victimas_Inicio.aspx

Ministry of Health and Social Protection (2016). *Analysis of health conditions Colombia*. Bogotá: Office of Epidemiology and Demographics. http://www.minsalud.gov.co/sites/rid/Lists/BibliotecaDigital/RIDE/VS/ED/PSP/asis-colombia-2016.pdf

Minkler, M., Blackwell, A. G, Thompson, M., & Tamir, H. (2003). Community based participatory research: Implications for public health funding. *American Journal of Public Health*, 93, 1210–1213. doi: 10.2105/AJPH.93.8.1210

Minuchin, S., & Fishman, J. (1981). *Family therapy techniques*. Boston, MA: Harvard University Press.

Mistry, R. S., Vandewater, E. A., Huston, A. C., & McLoyd, V. C. (2002). Economic well-being and children's social adjustment: The role of family process in an ethnically diverse low-income sample. *Child Development*, 73(3), 935–951. doi: 10.1111/1467-8624.00448

Mistry, R. S., & Wadsworth, M. E. (2011). Family functioning and child development in the context of poverty. *The Prevention Researcher*, 18(4), 11–16.

Moffit, T., Poulton, R., & Caspi, A. (2013). Lifelong impact of early self-control. *American Scientists*, 101(5), 352–359. http://doi.org/10.1511/2013.104.352

Molénat, F. (1992). *Mères vulnérables*. Paris: Stock-Laurence Pernoud.

Molénat, F. (2001). *Naissances. Pour une éthique de la prévention*. Paris: Erès

Montero, X., Jurado, S., Valencia, A., Méndez, J., & Mora, I. (2014). Escala de carga del cuidador de Zarit. Evidencia de validez en México. *Psicooncología*, 11(1), 71–85. https://revistas.ucm.es/index.php/PSIC/article/viewFile/44918/42834

Montroy, J. J., Bowles, R. P., Skibbe, L. E., McClelland, M. M., & Morrison, F. J. (2016). The development of self-regulation across early childhood. *Developmental Psychology*, 52(11), 1744–1762. http://dx.doi.org/10.1037/dev0000159

Morlett, A., Perrin, P., Peralta, S., Stolfi, M., Morelli, E., & Arango-Lasprilla, J. (2015). Structural equation model linking dementia cognitive functioning, caregiver mental health, burden, and quality of informal care in Argentina. *Dementia*, 16(6), 766–779. doi: 10.1177/1471301215617080

Morris, A. S., Silk, J. S., Steinberg, L., Myers, S. S., & Robinson, L. R. (2007). The role of the family context in the development of emotion regulation. *Social Development*, 16, 362–388. doi:10.1111/j.1467-9507.2007.00389.x

Morris, A. S., Robinson, L. R., Hays-Grudo, J., Claussen, A. H., Hartwig, S. A., & Treat, A. E. (2017). Targeting parenting in early childhood: A public health approach to improve outcomes for children living in poverty. *Child Development*, 88(2), 388–397.

Moser, C. O. (1998). The asset vulnerability framework: reassessing urban poverty reduction strategies. *World Development*, 26(1), 1–19.

National Administrative Department of Statistics (NADS) (2017a). Boletín técnico pobreza monetaria y multidimensional 2017. DANE. http://www.dane.gov.co/files/investigaciones/condiciones_vida/pobreza/bol_pobreza_17.pdf

National Administrative Department of Statistics (NADS) (2017b). Gran encuesta de Hogares. http://www.dane.gov.co/files/investigaciones/condiciones_vida/pobreza/bol_pobreza_17.pdf

National Council of Population (CONAPO) (2020). World children's day. https://www.gob.mx/conapo/es/articulos/dia-mundial-de-la-ninez?idiom=es#:~:text=En%202021%2C%20en%20el%20pa%C3%ADs,932%20personas%20en%20esas%20edades.

National Department of Planning (2010). National plan: "Prosperity for all" 2010–2014. https://www.dnp.gov.co/Plan-Nacional-de-Desarrollo/PND-2010-2014/Paginas/Plan-Nacional-De-2010-2014.aspx

National Department of Planning (2014). Basis for the national development plan 2014–2018: "All for a new country." https://www.minagricultura.gov.co/planeacion-control-National

National Information Network (RNI) (2016). Registro único de víctimas. http://rni.unidadvictimas.gov.co/

National Institute of Health (2018). Boletín epidemiológico semanal BES. Ministerio de Salud, Bogotá. https://www.ins.gov.co/buscador-eventos/Paginas/Vista-Boletin-Epidemilogico.aspx

National Institute of Statistics and Geography (INEGI) (2014). Statistics on international youth day. http://www.inegi.org.mx/sistemas/biblioteca/ficha.aspx?upc=702825056636

National Institute of Statistics and Geography (INEGI) (2020). 2020 population and housing census: Population. https://en.www.inegi.org.mx/

National Population Council (2015). The demographic situation of Mexico 2015. https://www.gob.mx/conapo/documentos/la-situacion-demografica-de-mexico-2015

National Scientific Council on the Developing Child (2007). *The science of early child development: Closing the gap between what we know and what we do*. Cambridge, MA: National Scientific Council on the Developing Child. https://www.minagricultura.gov.co/planeacion-control-gestion/Gestin/Plan%20de%20Acci%C3%B3n/PLAN%20NACIONAL%20DE%20DESARROLLO%202014%20-%202018%20TODOS%20POR%20UN%20NUEVO%20PAIS.pdf

Navarro, H. (2005). *Manual for projects' and programs' impact evaluation in the war against poverty*. Santiago de Chile: Latin American and the Caribbean Institute of Economic and Social Planning (ILPES), CEPAL, United Nations.

Nichols, C. W. (2012). Roads to understanding family resilience: 1920s to the twenty-first century. In D. Becvar (Ed.), *Handbook of family resilience* (pp. 1–16). New York: Springer.

Mahrer, N. E., Holly, L. E., Luecken, L. J., Wolchik, S. A., & Fabricius, W. (2019). Parenting style, familism, and youth adjustment in Mexican American and European American families. *Journal of Cross-Cultural Psychology*, 50(5), 659–675.

Nikolaev, A. P. (1957). *El Parto sin dolor. Teoría y práctica sobre el método psicoprofiláctico y otros métodos de anestesia*. Buenos Aires: Cártago.

Nolivos, V., & Leyva, D. (2013). Fun and frustrations: Low-income Chilean parents reminiscing with their children about past emotional experiences. *Actualidades en Psicología, 27*(115), 15–32. doi: 10.15517/ap.v27i115.9278

O'Dougherty, M., Masten, A., & Narayan, A. (2013). Resilience processes in development: Four waves of research on positive adaptation in the context of adversity. In S. Goldstein, & R. B. Brooks (Eds.), *Handbook of resilience in children* (2nd ed.) (pp. 15–37). New York: Springer US. https://doi.org/10.1007/978-1-4614-3661-4_2

O'Fallon, L. R., & Dearry, A. (2002). Community-based participatory research as a tool to advance environmental health sciences. *Environmental Health Perspectives, 110*(2), 155–159. doi: 10.1289/ehp.02110s2155

Observatório da Cidade de Porto Alegre (ObservaPOA). (2010). Atlas do desenvolvimento humano. www.observapoa.com.br (accessed March 5, 2017).

Observatório da Cidade de Porto Alegre (ObservaPOA). (2014). Atlas do desenvolvimento humano. www.observapoa.com.br (accessed March 5, 2017).

Oiberman, A. (2000). El lugar de la palabra en las maternidades: Aproximación de una psicología perinatal. Psicodebate. *Revista de la Universidad de Palermo, 1,* 88–91.

Oiberman, A. (2005). Historia de las madres en occidente: repensar la maternidad. *Psicodebate, 5,* 115–130.

Oiberman, A. (Compilator). (2005). *Nacer y después. Aportes a la psicología perinatal.* Buenos Aires: JCE Ediciones.

Oiberman, A. (2013). *Nacer y acompañar. Abordajes clínicos de la psicología perinatal.* Lugar Editorial, 2013.

Oiberman, A., Fiszelew, R., Galíndez, E., & Mercado, A. (1998). Un modelo de entrevista psicológica en situaciones críticas de nacimiento. *Revista Interdisciplinaria, 15*(1–2), 39–48.

Oiberman, A., & Galíndez, E. (2005). Psicología perinatal. Aplicaciones de un modelo de entrevista psicológica perinatal en el posparto inmediato. *Revista del Hospital Materno Infantil Ramón Sardá, 24*(3), 100–109.

Oiberman A., Misic, M., & Santos, S. (2011). *Dispositivos de intervención perinatalidades (DIP). Instrumentos en salud mental perinatal.* Buenos Aires: Facultad de Psicología. Universidad de Buenos Aires.

Oiberman, A., & Santos, S. (2015). 25 años acompañando el nacer y sus después: la psicología perinatal. In Facultad de Psicología UBA (Ed.), *Premio Facultad de Psicología,* (pp. 11–35). Buenos Aires: Facultad de Psicología de la Universidad de Buenos Aires.

Oiberman, A., Schoham, C., Galíndez, E., Di Biasi, S., & Vega, E. (2000). Un nuevo instrumento diagnóstico en situaciones perinatales. La entrevista psicológica de diseño óptico. *Rev Investig Psicol,* 77–89.

Oliveira, N., Nestor, E., Bruna, M., Inouye, K., & Pavarini, S. (2017). Stress and optimism of elderlies who are caregivers for elderlies and live with children. *Revista Brasileira de Enfermagem, 70*(4), 697–703. https://dx.doi.org/10.1590/0034-7167-2017-0088

Olshansky, E., & Zender, R. (2016). The use of community-based participatory research to understand and work with vulnerable populations. In M. Chenay & B. A. Anderson

(Eds.), *Caring for the vulnerable: Perspectives in nursing theory, practice and research* (4th ed.) (pp. 243–250). New York: Jones & Bartlett Learning.

Olshen, E., McVeigh, K. H., Wunsch-Hitzig, R. A., & Rickert, V. I. (2007). Dating violence, sexual assault, and suicide attempts among urban teenagers. *Archives of Pediatrics & Adolescent Medicine, 161*(6), 539–545.

Olson, D. H. (2000). Circumplex model of marital and family systems. *Journal of Family Therapy, 22*, 144–166.

Organisation for Economic Co-operation and Development (OECD) (1999). Classifying educational programmes: Manual for ISCED-97 implementation in OECD countries. http://www.oecd.org/dataoecd/7/2/1962350.pdf

Ornaghi, V., Grazzani, I., Cherubin, E., Conte, E., & Piralli, F. (2015). "Let's talk about emotions!" The effect of conversational training on preschoolers' emotion comprehension and prosocial orientation. *Social Development, 24*(1), 166–183. doi: 10.1111/sode.12091

Orozco-Hormaza, M., Sánchez-Ríos, H., & Cerchiaro-Ceballos, E. (2012). Relación entre desarrollo cognitivo y contextos de interacción familiar de niños que viven en sectores urbanos pobres [Relationship between cognitive development and family interaction contexts of children living in poor urban areas]. *Universitas Psychologica, 11*(2), 427–440.

Ortiz Cochivague, K. (2012). Las madres de la Plaza de Mayo y su legado por la defensa de los derechos humanos. *Trabajo Social, 14*, 165–177.

Pachón, X. (2005). La familia en Colombia a lo largo del siglo XX. In M. H. Ramírez & Y. Puyana (Eds.), *Familias, cambios y estrategias* (pp. 145–159). Bogotá: Universidad Nacional de Colombia. Facultad de Ciencias Humanas, Alcaldía Mayor de Bogotá. Secretaría Distrital de Integración Social.

Palacios, J., Marchesi Ullastres, A., & Coll Salvador, C. (compilators) (1990). *Psicología evolutiva* (Vol. 1, pp. 15–38). España: Editorial Alianza.

Partidas, R. (2004). Trabajadoras de la electrónica. Las abuelas como proveedoras de cuidado infantil. *El Cotidiano, 19*(125), 68–77.

Parveen, S., Morrison, V., & Robinson, C. (2014). Does coping mediate the relationship between familism and caregiver outcomes? *Aging & Mental Health, 18*(2), 255–259. https://doi.org/10.1080/13607863.2013.827626

Patterson, J. (2002). Integrating family resilience and family stress theory. *Journal of Marriage and Family, 64*(2), 349–360.

Patterson, J. M., & Garwick, A. W. (1994). Levels of meaning in family stress theory. *Family Process, 33*(3), 287–304.

Pearson, E., & Rao, N. (2003). Socialization goals, parenting practices, and peer competence in Chinese and English preschoolers. *Early Child Development and Care, 173*(1), 131–146. doi: 10.1080/0300443022000022486

Perosa, L. M., & Perosa, S. L. (2001). Adolescent perceptions of cohesion, adaptability, and communication: Revisiting the circumplex model. *The Family Journal, 9*(4), 407–419.

Phillipson, C. (2010). Globalisation, global ageing and intergenerational change. In M. Izuhara (Ed.), *Ageing and intergenerational relations: Family reciprocity from a global perspective* (pp. 13–28). Bristol: The Policy Press.

Pick, S., García, G., & Leenen, I. (2011). A model for health promotion in rural communities through the development of personal agency and intrinsic empowerment. *Universitas Psychologica*, *10*(2), 327–340.

Pinazo-Hernandis, S., & Lluna, J. (2011). Menores criados por sus abuelas. Mejora de las pautas de cuidado a menores en acogimiento familiar en familia extensa a través de un programa de intervención psicoeducativo. *Revista Sobre la Infancia y la Adolescencia*, 1, 14–34. http://dx.doi.org/10.4995/reinad.2011.834

Pinderhughes, E. E, Dodge, K. A., Bates, J. E., Pettit, G. S., & Zelli, A. (2000). Discipline responses: Influences of parents' socioeconomic status, ethnicity, beliefs about parenting, stress, and cognitive-emotional process. *Journal of Family Psychology*, *14*, 380–400. doi: 10.1037/0893-3200.14.3.380

Pinderhughes, E. E., Nix, R., Foster, E. M., & Jones, D. (2007). Parenting in context: Impact of neighborhood poverty, residential stability, public services, social networks, and danger on parental behaviors. *Journal of Marriage and Family*, *63*(4), 941–953. doi: 10.1111/j.1741-3737.2001.00941.x

Porto, R. (2011). *Servicio de neonatología*. Nacer: Publicación del servicio de neonatología del HZGA Mi Pueblo.

Prato, A., Hernández, A., Techera, L., & Rivas, R. (2012). Abuelos y nietos ¿Una relación necesaria? *Biomedicina*, *7*(2), 22–36. ISSN 1510-9747

Presidencia de la República (2013). *Poverty and early childhood in Colombia*. Bogotá: Programa Cero a Siempre, Presidencia de la República.

Priest, S. R., Austin, M. P., Barnett, B. B., & Buist, A. (2008). A psychosocial risk assessment model (PRAM) for use with pregnant and postpartum women in primary care settings. *Archives of Women's Mental Health*, *11*(5–6), 307.

Prince-Embury, S. (2012). Translating resilience theory, 2: For assessment and application with children, adolescents, and adults: Conceptual issues. In S. Prince-Embury & D. H. Saklofske (Eds.), *Resilience in children, adolescents, and adults: Translating research into practice*, The Springer Series on Human Exceptionality (pp. 9–16). New York: Springer. DOI 10.1007/978-1-4614-4939-3_2

Prince-Embury, S., & Saklofske, D. H. (2013). Translating resilience theory for application: Introduction. In S. Prince-Embury & D. H. Saklofske (Eds.), *Resilience in children, adolescents, and adults: Translating research intro practice* (pp. 3–8). New York: Springer. DOI 10.1007/978-1-4614-4939-3_2

Profamilia, Ministry of Health (2015). *National demographics and health survey*. Bogotá: Profamilia, Ministry of Health.

Programa Estado de la Nación (2013). *Cuarto estado de la educación*. San José: PEN.

Quecha-Reyna, C. (2015). Migración femenina e incidencias en la crianza. El caso de una población afrodescendiente en México. *Alteridades*, *25*(49), 93–108.

Quiroz, N., Villatoro, J., Juárez, F., Gutiérrez, M. L., Amador, N., & Medina-Mora, M. E. (2007). Family and abuse as risk factors on antisical behaviour. *Mental Health*, *30*(4), 47–54.

Racamier, P. C. (1977). À propos des psychoses sur la maternalité. In M. Soulé (Ed.), *Mère mortifère, mère meurtrière, mère mortifiée*, Paper presented in 5e Journée scientifique du Centre de guidance infantile de l'Institut de puériculture de Paris. Paris: esf, 41–50.

Ramírez, M. H. (1998). Enfoques y perspectivas de los estudios sociales sobre la familia en Colombia. *Trabajo Social (Universidad Nacional de Colombia)*, (1), 11–24.

Ramírez, M., & Andrade, D. (2005). La familia y los factores de riesgo relacionados con el consumo de alcohol y tabaco en los niños y adolescentes (Guayaquil-Ecuador). *Revista Latino-Americana de Enfermagem*, 13(1), 813–818.

Reese, E., Leyva, D., Sparks, A., & Grolnick, W. (2010). Maternal elaborative reminiscing increases low-income children's narrative skills relative to dialogic reading. *Early Education & Development*, 21(3), 318–342. doi: 10.1080/10409289.2010.481552

Rentería-Pérez, E., Maldonado-Turra, C., & Lanza-Queiroz, B. (2007). Abuelos y nietos, ¿Una convivencia beneficiosa para los más jóvenes? El caso de Brasil y Perú. *Papeles de Población*, 13(52), 47–75.

Ribas, R. C., Jr., Seidl de Moura, M. L., & Bornstein, M. H. (2003). Socioeconomic status in Brazilian psychological research: II SES and parenting knowledge. *Estudos de Psicologia*, 8(3), 385–392. doi: 10.1590/S1413-294X2003000300005

Riegel, K. F. (1976). *Psychology of history and development*. New York: Plenum Press.

Riegel, K. F. (1979). *Foundations of dialectical psychology*. New York: Academic Press.

Ripoll-Núñez, K., & Carrillo Ávila, S. (2018). Integrative perspectives in the study of parent-child relationships. In G. Gutiérrez (Ed.), *Theories in psychology: Integration and the future of the discipline* (pp. 238–264). Bogotá: Manual Moderno.

Rivera, M. E., & Andrade, P. (2006). Recursos individuales y familiares que protegen al adolescente del intento suicida. *Revista Intercontinental de Psicología y Educación*, 8(2), 23–40.

Rivera, M. E., Martínez, L. G., & Obregón, N. (2013). Factores asociados con la sintomatología depresiva en adolescentes michoacanos. El papel de la migración familiar y los recursos individuales, familiares y sociales. *Salud Mental*, 36(2), 115–122.

Robeyns, I. (2005).The capability approach: A theoretical survey. *Journal of Human Development*, 6, 93–117.

Robeyns, I. (2006). The capability approach in practice. *Journal of Political Philosophy*, 14, 351–376. http://dx.doi.org/10.1111/j.1467-9760.2006.00263.x (accessed April 14, 2012).

Robinson, W. D., Carroll, J. S., & Watson, W. L. (2005). Shared experience building around the family crucible of cancer. *Families, Systems, & Health*, 23(2), 131.

Robinson, C. W., & Zajicek, J. M. (2005). Growing minds: The effect of a one-year school garden program on six constructs of life skills of elementary school children. *HortTechnology*, 15(3), 453–457.

Rodrigo, M. J., Byrne, S., & Rodríguez, B. (2014). Parenting styles and child well-being. In A. Ben-Arieh, F. Casas, I. Frones, & J. E. V.Korbin (Eds.), *Handbook of child wellbeing: Theories, methods, and policies in global perspectives* (pp. 2173–2195). New York: Springer.

Rodríguez, S. Pérez, V., & Córdova, A. (2007). Factores familiares y de pares asociados al consumo de drogas en estudiantes de educación media. *Revista Intercontinental de Psicología y Educación, 9*(1), 159-186.

Rogoff, B. (2003). *The cultural nature of human development*. Oxford: Oxford University Press.

Rosabal-Coto, M. (2012). Creencias y prácticas de crianza: el estudio del parentaje en el contexto costarricense. *Revista Costarricense de Psicología, 31*(1-2), 65-100. http://www.redalyc.org/articulo.oa?id=476748710006

Rueter, M. A., & Koerner, A. F. (2008). The effect of family communication patterns on adopted adolescent adjustment. *Journal of Marriage and Family, 70*(3), 715-727.

Ruggles, S., & Heggeness, M. (2008). Intergenerational coresidence in developing countries. *Population and Development Review, 34*(2), 253-281.

Russell, J., Douglas, A., Windle, R., & Ingram, C. (Eds.) (2001). *The maternal brain: Neurobiological and neuroendocrine adaptation and disorders in pregnancy and post partum*. Dordrecht: Elsevier.

Russo, F. (2016). The givers. *Scientific American Mind*, November/December, 29-37.

Rutter, M. (1987). Psychosocial resilience and protective mechanisms. *American Journal of Orthopsychiatry, 57*, 316-331. doi: 10.1111/j.1939-0025.1987.tb03541.x

Rutter, M. (2012). Resilience as a dynamic concept. *Development and Psychopathology, 24*, 335-344.

Ruvalcaba, N. A., Gallegos, J., Caballo, V., & Villegas, D. (2016). Prácticas parentales e indicadores de salud mental en adolescentes. *Psicología Desde el Caribe, 33*(3), 223-236.

Salazar-Villanea, M., Liebmann, E., Garnier-Villarreal, M., Montenegro-Montenegro, E., & Johnson, D. (2015). Depressive symptoms affect working memory in healthy older adult Hispanics. *Journal of Depress Anxiety, 4*(4), 204. DOI: 10.4172/2167-1044.1000204

Salvatierra Mateu, V. (1998). *Psicobiología del embarazo y sus trastornos*. Barcelona: Editorial Martinez Roca.

Sameroff, A. (2009). *The transactional model*. Washington, DC: American Psychological Association.

Sameroff, A., & Rosenblum, K. (2006). Psychosocial constraints on the development of resilience. *Annuary of New York Academy Science, 1094*(1), 116-124.

Sampson, R. J. (1992). Family management and child development: Insights from social disorganization theory. In J. McCord (Ed.), *Facts, frameworks and forecasts: Advances in criminological theory* (pp. 63-93). New Brunswick, NJ: Transaction Books.

Sánchez Molina, R. (2004). Cuando los hijos se quedan en El Salvador. Familias transnacionales y reunificación familiar de inmigrantes salvadoreños en Washington, D.C. *Revista de Dialectología y Tradiciones Populares, 59*(2), 257-276.

Santiago, C. D., Etter, E., Wadsworth, M., & Raviv, T. (2012). Predictors of responses to stress among families coping with poverty-related stress. *Anxiety, Stress and Coping, 25*(3), 239-258.

Santiago, C. D., Wadsworth, M. E., & Stump, J. (2011). Socioeconomic status, neighborhood disadvantage, and poverty-related stress: Prospective effects on psychological

syndromes among diverse low-income families. *Journal of Economic Psychology*, 32(2), 218–230.
Santos, M. S. (2010). *Psychoneonatology: Results of a new observation scale of bond mother-baby in incubator. Proceedings advances in perinatal medicine.* Granada: Monduzzi.
Santos, M. S. (2018). *Encontrarnos dentro de la incubadora.* Buenos Aires: Lugar Editorial.
Schröder, L., Keller, H., Kärtner, J., Kleis, A., Abels, M., Yovsi, R. D., ... & Papaligoura, Z. (2013). Early reminiscing in cultural contexts: Cultural models, maternal reminiscing styles, and children's memories. *Journal of Cognition and Development, 14*(1), 10–34. doi: 10.1080/15248372.2011.638690
Schwalb, D., & Hossain, Z. (Eds.) (2017). *Grandparents in cultural context.* New York: Routledge.
Seibel, B. L. (2016). A família com filhos e sua rede. Impacto da rede de apoio social nas relações familiares e na saúde mental dos cuidadores (Unpublished doctoral dissertation). Universidade Federal do Rio Grande do Sul, Porto Alegre, RS.
Seibel, B. L., Falceto, O. G., Hollist, C. S., Springer, P., Fernandes, C. L. C, & Koller, S. H. (2017). Rede de apoio social e funcionamento familiar. Estudo longitudinal sobre famílias em vulnerabilidade social. *Pensando Famílias, 21*(1), 120–136.
Seidl-de-Moura, M. L., Cruz de Carvalho, R. V., & Vieira, M. L. (2013). Brazilian mothers' cultural models: Socialization for autonomy and relatedness. In M. L. Seidl-de-Moura (Ed.), *Parenting in South American and African contexts* (pp. 1–15). Rijeka: IntechOpen. https://doi.org/10.5772/57083
Sen, A. (1999). La salud en el desarrollo. *Bull WHO, 77,* 619–623.
Sen, A. (2006). Conceptualizing and measuring poverty. In D. Grunsky & R. Kanbur (Eds.), *Poverty and inequality* (pp. 30–46). Stanford, CA: Stanford University Press.
Sharkey, P. (2010). The acute effect of local homicides on children's cognitive performance. *Proceedings of the National Academy of Sciences of the USA, 107,* 11733–11738. https://doi.org/10.1073/pnas.1000690107
Sharkey, P. (2012). An alternative approach to addressing selection into and out of social settings: Neighborhood change and African American children's economic outcomes. *Sociological Methods Research, 41,* 251–293 https://doi.org/10.1177/0049124112452391
Sharkey, P. T., Tirado-Strayer, N., Papachristos, A. V., & Raver, C. C. (2012). The effect of local violence on children's attention and impulse control. *American Journal of Public Health, 102*(12), 2287–2293.
Shelton, L. G. (2019). *The Bronfenbrenner primer: A guide to develecology.* New York: Routledge.
Sheridan, S., Sjuts, T. M., & Coutts, M. J. (2013). Understanding and promoting the development of resilience in families. In S. Goldstein & B. Brooks, R. (Eds.), *Handbook of resilience in children* (2nd ed.) (pp. 143–160). New York: Springer. DOI 10.1007/978-1-4614-3661-4
Shonkoff, J. P., & Phillips, D. A. (Eds.), (2000). *From neurons to neighborhoods: The science or early childhood development.* Washington, DC: National Academic Press.

Shor, R. (2000). Child maltreatment: Differences in perceptions between parents in low-income and middle income neighborhoods. *British Journal of Social Work*, *30*(2), 165–178. doi: 10.1093/bjsw/30.2.165

Shor, R. (2007). Differentiating the culturally-based help-seeking patterns of immigrant parents from the former Soviet Union by comparison with parents in Russia. *American Journal of Orthopsychiatry*, *77*(2), 216. doi: 10.1037/0002-9432.77.2.216

Silva-Ferreira, A. R., & Rodriguez-Wong, L. (2008). Perspectivas da oferta de cuidadores informais da populaçao idosa:. Uma análise comparativa entre Brasil e Mexico, 2000-2015. Sociedad Y Adulto Mayor En America Latina: Estuidos Sobre Envejecimiento En La Region, 183–203. Paper presented at the III Congress of the Latin American Population Association, ALAP, held in Córdoba - Argentina, from September 24 to 26, 2008. Rio de Janeiro: ALAP Editor.

Smith, G., & Palmieri, P. (2007). Risk of psychological difficulties among children raised by custodial grandparents. *Psychiatric Service*, *58*(10), 1303–1310.

Smith-Morris, C., Morales-Campos, D., Castañeda-Álvarez, E., & Turner, M. (2012). An anthropology of familismo: On narratives and description of Mexican immigrants. *Hispanic Journal of Behavioral Sciences*, *35*(1), 35–60. https://doi.org/10.1177/0739986312459508

Song, Q., & Wang, Q. (2013). Mother-child reminiscing about peer experiences and children's peer-related self-views and social competence. *Social Development*, *22*(2), 280–299. doi: 10.1111/sode.12013

Spitz, R. (1973). *El primer año de vida del niño*. Mexico City: Fondo de cultura económica.

Sroufe, A., Egeland, B., Carlson, E. A., & Collins, A. (2005). *The development of the person: The Minnesota study of risk and adaptation from birth to adulthood*. New York: The Guilford Press.

Steidel, A. G. L., & Contreras, J. M. (2003). A new familism scale for use with Latino populations. *Hispanic Journal of Behavioral Sciences*, *25*(3), 312–330.

Stuifbergen, M. C., & Van Delden, J. J. M. (2011). Filial obligations to elderly parents: A duty to care? *Medicine, Health Care and Philosophy*, *14*, 63–71. doi:10.1007/s11019-010-9290-z

Stutzman, S. V., Miller, R. B., Hollist, C. S., & Falceto, O. G. (2009). Effects of marital quality on children in Brazilian families. *Journal of Comparative Family Studies*, *40*(3), 475–492.

Super, C. M., & Harkness, S. (1986). The developmental niche: A conceptualization at the interface of child and culture. *International Journal of Behavioral Development*, *9*(4), 545–569.

Suitor, J. J., Sechrist, J., Gilligan, M., & Pillemer, K. (2011). Intergenerational relations in later-life families. In R. A. Settersten & J. L. Angel (Eds.), *Handbook of sociology of aging* (pp. 161–178). New York: Springer.

Sunkel, G. (2006). *El papel de la familia en la protección social en América Latina*. Santiago de Chile: Comisión Económica para América Latina y el Caribe (CEPAL). https://repositorio.cepal.org/bitstream/handle/11362/6121/1/S0600306_es.pdf

Sunkel, G. (2006). *The role of family in the social protection in Latin America.* Santiago de Chile: Naciones Unidad, CEPAL.

Tapia, J., Carmiol, A. M., & Rosabal, M. (2012). La psicología del desarrollo en Costa Rica. Alcances y perspectivas futuras. *Revista Costarricense de Psicología, 31*(1–2), 101–121.

Taumoepeau, M., & Reese, E. (2013). Maternal reminiscing, elaborative talk, and children's theory of mind: An intervention study. *First Language, 33*(4), 388–410. doi: 10.1177/0142723713493347

Thompson, R. (2018). Early attachment and later development: Refraiming the questions. In J. Cassidy & P. Shaver (Eds.), *Handbook of attachment: Theory, research and clinical applications* (3rd ed.) (pp. 330–348). New York: The Guilford Press.

Thrush, A., & Hayes, A. (2014). The neglected burden of caregiving in low- and middle-income countries. *Disability and Health Journal, 7,* 262–272. doi: 10.1016/j.dhjo.2014.01.003

Tobío Soler, C. (2011). Estado y familia en el cuido de las personas. Sustitución o complemento. *Cuadernos de Relaciones Laborales, 31*(1), 17–38. DOI: 10.5209/rev.CRLA.2013.v31.n1.41623

Tonyan, H. A. (2015). Everyday routines: A window into the cultural organization of family child care. *Journal of Early Childhood Research, 13,* 3.

Trepal, H. C., Wester, K. L., & MacDonald, C. A. (2006). Self-injury and postvention: Responding to the family in crisis. *The Family Journal, 14*(4), 342–348.

Triadó C., Celdrán, M., Conde, L., Montoro, J., Pinazo S., & Villar, F. (2008). *Envejecimiento productivo. La provisión de cuidados de los abuelos a los nietos, Implicaciones para su salud y bienestar.* Madrid: Instituto de Mayores y Servicios Sociales-IMSERSO. http://www.espaciomayores.imserso.es/InterPresent1/groups/imserso/documents/binario/envejproductivo.pdf

Triandis, H. C., Marín, G., Lisansky, J., & Betancourt, H. (1984). Simpatía as a cultural script of Hispanics. *Journal of Personality and Social Psychology, 47*(6), 1363–1375. http://dx.doi.org/10.1037/0022-3514.47.6.1363

Trommsdorff, G. (2009). Culture and development of self-regulation. *Social and Personality Psychology Compass, 3*(5), 687–701. https://doi.org/10.1111/j.1751-9004.2009.00209.x

Trommsdorff, G. (2012). Development of "agentic" regulation in cultural context: The role of self and world views. *Child Development Perspectives, 6,* 19–26. https://dx.doi.org/10.1111/j.1750-8606.2011.00224.x

Trommsdorff, G., Cole, P. M., & Heikamp, T. (2012). Cultural variations in mothers' intuitive theories: A preliminary report on interviewing mothers of five nations about their socialization of children's emotions. *Global Studies of Childhood, 2*(2), 158–169. http://dx.doi.org/10.2304/gsch.2012.2.2.158

Trommsdorff, G., & Kornadt, H.-J. (2003). Parent-child relations in cross-cultural perspective. In L. Kuczynski (Ed.), *Handbook of dynamics in parent-child relations* (pp. 271–306). London: Sage. http://dx.doi.org/10.4135/9781452229645.n14

Tronick, E. (1989). Emotions and emotional communication in infants. *American Psychologist 44,* 112–119. DOI: 10.1037//0003-066x.44.2.11

Tronick, E., Als, H., Adamson, L., Wise, S., & Brazelton, T. B. (1978). The infant's response to entrapment between contradictory messages in face-to-face interaction. *Journal of the American Academy of Child Psychiatry, 17*(1), 1–13.

Tuñón, I. (2015). Múltiples privaciones de derechos en la infancia [en línea]. En: Hernández Gómez, E., Ramírez Urquidy, M. A. (coords.) *Bienestar y pobreza en América Latina: una visión desde la frontera norte de México*. Mexicali, Baja California (México): Universidad Autónoma de Baja California: Ediciones Once Ríos. Disponible en: https://repositorio.uca.edu.ar/handle/123456789/14421

Umaña-Taylor, A. J., Updegraff, K. A., & Gonzales-Backen, M. A. (2011). Mexican-origin adolescent mothers' stressors and psychosocial functioning: Examining ethnic identity affirmation and familism as moderators. *Journal of Youth and Adolescence, 40*, 140–157.

UN Statistics Division (2006). Demographic yearbook system. https://unstats.un.org/unsd/databases.htm (accessed May 24, 2017).

UNICEF (January 2007). Teenage motherhood in Latin America and the Caribbean: Trends, problems and challenges. *Challenges, 4*, 1–12.

UNICEF-Colombia (2017). *Informe annual*. Bogotá: UNICEF. https://www.unicef.org.co/informes/informe-anual-unicef-colombia-2017-version-espanol

Unger, J. B., Gallaher, P., Shakib, S., Ritt-Olson, A., Palmer, P. H., & Johnson, C. A. (2002). The AHIMSA acculturation scale: A new measure of acculturation for adolescents in a multicultural society. *Journal of Early Adolescence, 22*, 225–251.

Unger, J. B., Baezconde-Garbanati, L., Shakib, S., Palmer, P. H., Nezami, E., & Mora, J. (2004). A cultural psychology approach to "drug abuse" prevention. *Subst Use Misuse, 39*, 1779–1820.

United Nations Children's Fund (UNICEF) (2011). *The state of the world's children 2011: Adolescence—an age of opportunity*. New York: UNICEF.

United Nations Children's Fund (UNICEF) (2021). The state of the world's children 2021: On My Mind: Promoting, protecting and caring for children's mental health. New York: UNICEF. https://www.unicef.org/reports/state-worlds-children-2021

Urrutia, A., Moisset de Espanés, G., Villar, F., Guzmán, E., & Dottori, V. (2016). May early intergenerational experiences be the seeds of a generative adulthood? A comparison between childhood narratives of highly generative and less generative older women, *Journal of Intergenerational Relationships, 14*(1), 1–16. DOI: 10.1080/15350770.2016.1125048

Valdivieso-Mora, E., Peet, C., Garnier-Villarreal, M., Salazar-Villanea, M., & Johnson, D. (2016). A systematic review of the relationship between familism and mental health outcomes in Latino population. *Frontiers in Psychology, 7*. DOI: 10.3389/fpsyg.2016.01632

Valentino, K., Comas, M., Nuttall, A., & Thomas, T. (2013). Training maltreating parents in elaborative and emotion-rich reminiscing with their preschool-aged children. *Child Abuse & Neglect, 37*(8), 585–595. doi: 0.1016/j.chiabu.2013.02.010

Van Bergen, P., & Salmon, K. (2010). The association between parent-child reminiscing and children's emotion knowledge. *New Zealand Journal of Psychology, 39* (1), 51–55.

Van Bergen, P., Salmon, K., Dadds, M., & Allen, J. (2009). The effects of mother training in emotion-rich, elaborative reminiscing on children's shared recall and emotion knowledge. *Journal of Cognition and Development*, *10*(3), 162–187.

Vega, E. Y. (2006). *El psicoterapeuta en neonatología: Rol y estilo personal*. Argentina: Editorial Lugar.

Velásquez Santa, J. M. (2017). *Análisis del concepto de intervención psicosocial desde Maritza Montero, en el desarrollo del programa generaciones con bienestar del 2013–2014*, del Instituto Colombiano de Bienestar Familiar de la Ciudad de Pereira.

Vélez-Agosto, N. M., Soto-Crespo, J. G., Vizcarrondo-Oppenheimer, M., Vega-Molina, S., & García Coll, C. (2017). Bronfenbrenner's bioecological theory revision: Moving culture. From the macro into the micro. *Perspectives on Psychological Science*, *12*, 5.

Victora, C. (2012). Los mil días de oportunidad para intervenciones nutricionales. De la concepción a los dos años de vida. *Archivos Argentinos de Pediatría*, *110*(4), 311–317.

Videla, M., & Grieco, A. (1993). *Parir y nacer en el hospital*. Austin, TX: Nueva Visión.

Villar, F., Celdrán, M., & Triadó, C. (2012). Grandmothers offering regular auxiliary care for their grandchildren: An expression of generativity in later life? *Journal of Women & Aging*, *24*(4), 292–312.

Vygotsky, L. (1978). *Mind in society. The development of higher psychological processes*. Cambridge, MA: Harvard University Press.

Wadsworth, M. E., Evans, G. W., Grant, K., Carter, J. S., & Duffy, S. (2016). Poverty and the development of psychopathology. *Developmental Psychopathology*, *4*, 1–44.

Wadsworth, M. E., & Santiago, C. D. (2008). Risk and resiliency processes in ethnically diverse families in poverty. *Journal of Family Psychology*, *22*(3), 399–410. doi.org/10.1037/0893-3200.22.3.399

Walker, S., Wachs, T. D., Meeks-Gardner, J., Lozoff, B., Wasserman, G., Pollitt, E., Carter, J., & the International Child Development Steering (2007). Child development: Risk factors for adverse outcomes in developing countries. *The Lancet*, *369*(9556), 145–157.

Walker, S. P., Wachs, T. D., Grantham-McGregor, S., Black, M. M., Nelson, C. A., Huffman, S. L., & Gardner, J. M. (2011). Inequality in early childhood: risk and protective factors for early child development. *The Lancet*, *378*(9799), 1325–1338.

Walsh, F. (2006). *Strengthening family resilience* (2nd ed.). New York: Guilford.

Walsh, F. (2012). *Normal family processes: Growing diversity and complexity* (4th ed.). New York: The Guilford Press.

Walsh, F. (2016). *Strengthening family resilience* (3rd ed.). New York: Guilford Press.

Wang, Q. (2001). Did you have fun? American and Chinese mother-child conversations about shared emotional experiences. *Cognitive Development*, *16*, 693–715. Doi: 10.1016/S0885-2014(01)00055-7

Weisbrot, M. A., & Giraudo, N. (2012). Conceptos y percepciones de las abuelas sobre el cuidado de sus nietos. Estudio cualitativo en una población del Hospital Italiano de Buenos Aires. *Archivos Argentinos de Pediatría*, *110*(2), 126–131. http://dx.doi.org/10.5546/aap.2012.126

Weisner, T. S. (2013). Why qualitative and ethnographic methods are essential for understanding family life. In W. M. McHale, P. Amato, & A. Booth (Eds.), *Emerging methods in family research* (pp. 163–178). Cham: Springer.

Weisner, T. S., McHale, S. M., Amato, P., & Booth, A. (Eds.) (2013). *Emerging methods in family research*, Vol. 4. New York: Springer Science & Business Media.

Werner, E. E. (1986). Resilient offspring of alcoholics: A longitudinal study from birth to age 18. *Journal of Studies on Alcohol, 47*(1), 34–40.

Whitebread, D., & Basilio, M. (2012). Emergencia y desarrollo temprano de la autorregulación en niños preescolares. *Profesorado, 16*(1). http://www.ugr.es/~recfpro/rev161ART2.pdf

Whiting, B. B., & Whiting, J. W. (1975). *Children of six cultures: A psycho-cultural analysis.* Harvard University Press.

Wilson, W. J. (1987). *The truly disadvantaged: The inner city, the underclass and public policy.* Chicago, IL: University of Chicago Press.

Wilson, W. J. (1991a). Public policy research and the truly disadvantaged. In C. Jencks, & P. E. Peterson (Eds.), *The urban underclass* (pp. 460–481). Washington, DC: Brookings Institution.

Wilson, W. J. (1991b). Studying inner-city social dislocations: The challenge of public agenda research. *American Sociological Review, 56*, 1–14. doi: 10.2307/2095669

Winnicott, D. (1958). *Escritos de pediatría y psicoanálisis.* Barcelona: Laia.

Winnicott, D. (1981). *La teoría de la relación paterno-filial. Capítulo III. El proceso de maduración en el niño.* Estudio para una teoría del desarrollo emocional. Barcelona: Editorial Barcelona.

Winnicott, D. (1987). *Los bebés y sus madres.* Buenos Aires: Paidós.

Woodcock-Muñoz (2005). *Batería R. Pruebas de habilidad cognitiva y pruebas de aprovechamiento.* Itaska, IL: Riverside Publishers.

World Bank (2021). World Bank country and lending groups: Country classification. https://datahelpdesk.worldbank.org/knowledgebase/articles/906519-world-bank-country-and-lending-groups

World Bank (2009). World development report 2009: Reshaping economic geography. https://openknowledge.worldbank.org/handle/10986/5991 (accessed May 24, 2017).

World Health Organization (2012). *Risks to mental health: An overview of vulnerabilities and risk factors.* Geneva: WHO. http://www.who.int/mental_health/mhgap/risks_to_mental_health_EN_27_08_12.pdf

World Health Organization (2014). *Social determinants of mental health factors.* https://apps.who.int/iris/bitstream/handle/10665/112828/9789241506809_eng.pdf

World Health Organization (2017). Adolescents: health risks and solutions. http://www.who.int/mediacentre/factsheets/fs345/es/

World Urban Forum (2010). Unhabitat for a better urban future. http://mirror.unhabitat.org/categories.asp?catid=584 (accessed May 24, 2017).

Worthman, C. M. (2010). The ecology of human development: evolving models for cultural psychology. *Journal of Cross-Cultural Psychology, 41*, 4.

Wyman, P. A. (2003). Emerging perspectives on context specificity of children's adaptation and resilience: Evidence from a decade of research with urban children in adversity. In S. S. Luthar (Ed.), *Resilience and vulnerability: Adaptation in the context of childhood adversities* (pp. 293–317). New York: Cambridge University Press.

Yunes, M. A. M. (2001). A questão triplamente controvertida da resiliência em famílias de baixa renda (Unpublished doctoral thesis). Pontifícia Universidade Católica de São Paulo, São Paulo.

Zamberlan, M. A., & Biasoli-Alves, Z. M. (1997). *Interações familiares. Teoria, pesquisa e subsídios à intervenção*. Londrina: Editora Universidade Estadual de Londrina (UEL).

Zapata Posada, J. J., Castro Rodelo, Y. Y., & Aguelo Bedoya, M. E. (2016). Abuelas antes de lo esperado. Cambios, participación en la crianza y relaciones intergeneracionales. *Prospectiva, 22*, 117–140

Zhang, S., Huang, X., & Tan, H. (2013). Prenatal anxiety and cesarean section with non-medical indication. *Zhong Nan da Xue Xue Bao. Yi Xue Ban [Journal of Central South University: Medical Sciences], 38*(10), 1070–1074.

Zimmerman, Sh. (2013). Conceptualizing family well-being. In A. Moreno Mínguez (Ed.), *Family well-being: European perspectives* (pp. 9–25). New York: Springer.

Index

For the benefit of digital users, indexed terms that span two pages (e.g., 52–53) may, on occasion, appear on only one of those pages.

abandonment research, 27
Abels, H., 4
absolute dependence, 61
action-oriented research, 55–56
active domains, 157
adaptability, 114–116, 118, 124–125
adolescence
    adolescent development, 111–116
    in developmental psychology, 58–59
    development in, 25
    families and, 112–113, 123–126
    Latin American contexts for, 105–106
    in Mexico, 16
    pregnancy in, 67
    research on, 19–20
    risk-protective factors in, 116–118
adults, 5, 59. *See also specific topics*
adversity, 26–31, 113–117, 123
affective bonds, 128
Alcázar, R., 122
alternative intervention models, 34–35
Amarís, M., 120
Andrade, P., 121
Anglo societies, 129
Argentina, vii, 57–58, 69–70, 99, 106. *See also* perinatal interventions
Asian mothers, 129
Asociación Civil Abuelas de Plaza de Mayo, 106
association analysis, 71–72, 71*t*, 72*t*
attachment theory, 62
Australia, 144–145

baby development, 59–61, 65
Barcelata, B., 119–120
Baumeister, R. F., 75
behavior control, 121, 143
beliefs, 76
Bengston, V. L., 102
Benjet, C., 119–120
Berry, J. W., 3

bias, for Western middle-class, vii
bioecological approaches, 31
biology, 2, 22–23, 47
Birch, Herbert, 118–119
Bogenschneider, K., 35
Bowlby, J., 62
Bradbury, H., 46
brain development, 22
Brazelton, T., 5
Brazil. *See also* Vila Jardim
    CBPR in, 36–38
    Colombia and, 7
    community in, 40–43
    Costa Rica and, 77–78
    familism in, vii
    Flourishing Through Education Program in, 37, 47–54
    Latin American contexts for, 38–40
    low-income neighborhoods in, 38–40
    Peru and, 103
    poverty in, 55–56
    research from, 78
    Venezuela and, 99
    Vila Jardim, 38–42
Bronfenbrenner, Igor
    on adolescent development, 113–114
    on childhood, 3–6
    on chronosystem, 97
    Ecological Theory by, 109
    on ecological transitions, 109–110, 157
    on psychology, 39–40
    on psychosocial environment, 98–99
Buenos Aires. *See* Argentina
Bydlowski, Monique, 61

Cameroon, vi, 77–78
Carbonell, O. A. M., 27–28, 30–31
caregiving
    cross-cultural approaches to, 129
    by grandparents, 106
    in Latin America, 129–130
    psychology of, 3, 109

socialization and, 108
socioeconomics and, 23–24
Caribbean region, 29–30
Carmiol, A. M., 130
CBPR. *See* community-based participatory research
Census of Population and Housing, 112–113
Central America, 76–77. *See also specific topics*
Chaudhary, C., 6–7
childhood. *See also* parent-child relationships
  activities in, 5–6
  affective bonds in, 128
  behavior in, 84–88
  bonds in, 4
  Bronfenbrenner on, 3–6
  child development, 58–60, 128
  child psychology, 58–60
  child-raising, 14
  child's sex, 144–146
  in Colombia, 27, 80–84
  conflictive experiences in, 128–129
  in Costa Rica, 132–133, 142, 147t, 150t
  day-care in, 105
  developmental gains in, 108–109
  in developmental psychology, 154
  in developmental science, 119
  drug trafficking in, 49–50
  early interventions in, 156
  exploration in, 135–136
  families and, 2–3, 107–110
  gender and, 129, 131, 136, 137t, 140
  grandparents in, 97–101, 103–107
  human development in, 5, 11
  in Latin America, 10
  Latin American contexts for, 6–7, 57–58, 78–79, 123–126
  long-term goals for, 88–92
  in Mann-Whitney tests, 133, 140
  maternal attributions and, 82–86, 85t
  memory development in, 141
  in migrant families, 105, 121–122
  in modernity, 3
  mother-child conversations, 134
  motherhood and, 4, 14, 16–17, 136–138, 144–146
  in "ought self" theory, 93–94
  perspectives in, 29–30
  positive contact in, 108
  poverty in, 18–20, 22–23, 26–31, 33–35
  problem-solving in, 86–88, 89t
  protective factors in, 28–31
  research on, 22–23, 82–84, 92–96
  resilience in, 21–22
  risk factors in, 27–28
  self-regulation in, 75–80
  social factors of, 24–25
  socialization in, 14–15
  UNICEF on, 18, 74
  in United States, 99, 115
  in vulnerable conditions, 31–33
  Weaving Links, Weaving Dreams, Weaving Life from Early Childhood program, 32–33
  in Woodcock-Muñoz "Subprueba de Vocabulario basado en Dibujos," 133
Chile, 99, 106, 120, 129–130
chronosystem, 97
clinical psychology, 62
cognitive approaches, 143
co-habitation, 99–101
Cohn, J., 63
co-learning, 46
collaboration, 47, 54, 55–56
collaboration, for CBPR, 45–46
collectivism, 15–16
Colombia. *See also* intuitive theories
  Brazil and, 7
  Caribbean and, 29–30
  childhood in, 27, 80–84
  Chile and, 120
  Colombian Institute for the Welfare of Families and the Observatory for Peace, 32–33
  Colombian Longitudinal Survey, 28
  culture of, 25–26
  families in, 28–31, 33
  familism in, vii
  field research from, 11–12
  government of, 32–33, 125
  grandparents in, 106
  integrative perspectives from, 21–25
  modernity in, 24–25
  motherhood in, 75–80
  poverty in, 20, 27–28
  poverty reduction in, 31
  programs and policies in, 31–33
  public politics programs in, 12
  research from, 29–30, 77–78, 80–84, 92–96
  social development in, 18–20, 33–35
  social policies in, 31–32
communication, 4–5, 114–115
community-based participatory research (CBPR)
  in Brazil, 36–38

community-based participatory research
    (CBPR) (*Continued*)
  co-learning from, 46
  collaboration for, 45–47
  community-based development from, vii
  data from, 46, 54
  on developmental scenarios, 155–156
  ecological perspectives in, 47
  failures in, 45
  as iterative process, 46–47
  Latin American contexts for, 156
  in low-income neighborhoods, 43–44
  methodology, 40–43, 55–56
  planning, 47–54
  with poverty, 38–40
  process of, 44–54
  scholarship with, 13
  social support networks in, 44
compensation model, of resilience, 122–123
conflictive experiences, 128–129
Conger, K. J., 115
Conger, R. D., 115
context-process model, 9
contraception, for women, 60
conversations. *See* emotion talk
Corbett, T. J., 35
co-residence data, 98
core-values, 156
Costa Rica. *See also* emotion talk
  Argentina and, 99
  Brazil and, 77–78
  childhood in, 132–133, 142, 147*t*, 150*t*
  Costa Rican dyads, 131, 133, 138, 140–142
  culture of, 15–16, 97–101, 107–110, 140–141
  educational backgrounds in, 127–131
  familism in, vii
  gender in, 131–146
  general expressive language ability in, 133
  Germany and, 130
  language in, 134–135
  Latin American contexts with, 15
  Mexico and, 7
  motherhood in, 77–78, 132–133, 133*t*, 136–138, 137*t*, 140–146
  multigenerational cohabitation contexts in, 101–107
  research from, 17, 134
  socialization in, 17, 146
  United States and, 102
culture
  biology and, 2

  of Chile, 129–130
  of Colombia, 25–26
  of Costa Rica, 15–16, 97–101, 107–110, 140–141
  cross-cultural approaches, 1–3, 129
  cultural diversity, 108
  culturally sensitive approach, vii, 2, 37, 130–131
  ecocultural approach, vii, 6–7, 155
  language and, 127, 132–133
  life cycle cultural perspective, 157
  moral evaluations in, 143
  self and, 16
  society and, vii, 154
custody arrangements, 97–98, 107

data
  analysis, 84
  from Argentina, 57–58
  from CBPR, 46, 54
  collection, 42, 46, 49
  co-residence, 98
  on ecological development, 16
  health care, 49
  on motherhood, 133–134
  from National Administrative Department on Statistics, 20
  from perinatal interventions, 70–71, 70*t*
  on self-regulation, 84–88
  from teachers, 50–51
Davidov, M., 26
day-care, 105, 108, 132
delayed satisfaction, 92–93
develecological perspectives, 7
developmental contexts, vi–vii, 6, 16, 154
developmental crises, 63
developmental gains, 108–109
developmental psychology, 58–59, 62, 65, 98–99, 154, 155
developmental psychopathology, 113–114
developmental scenarios, 155–156
DeVries, M. L., 26–27
displacement, 30–31
drug trafficking, 38, 49–50

early interventions, 156
early pregnancy, 120–121
ecology
  bioecological approaches, 31
  develecological perspectives, 7
  developmental, 16
  ecocultural approach, vii, 6–7, 155

ecological development, 16
ecological perspectives, 9, 36, 47, 111–112
ecological-systemic perspectives, 116
Ecological Theory, 109
ecological-transactional model, 125
ecological transitions, 109–110, 157
   psychology and, 2–3
   resilience in, 19–20, 26–31
   systemic ecological perspectives, 7–8
economically active population, 112–113
education. *See also specific topics*
   adaptability with, 125
   co-learning, 46
   Flourishing Through Education Program, 37, 42–43, 47–54
   general expressive language ability, 133
   household educational climate index, 132
   initiatives in, 54
   Latin American contexts for, 157
   in life planning workshops, 52–53
   in low-income neighborhoods, 41
   mixed-method analysis of, 48
   motherhood and, 80, 81*t*
   in poverty, 39–40
   priorities in, 47–54
   public, 37–38
   school interventions, 125–126
   socioeconomics of, 80, 81*t*, 84, 94
   stakeholders in, 45–46
   for teachers, 45
   of women, 58
educational backgrounds
   in Costa Rica, 127–131
   emotion talk and, 138–139, 142–144, 148*t*, 152*t*
   gender and, 137*t*
   in motherhood, 133*t*, 137*t*, 138–139, 142–144, 148*t*, 152*t*
   scholarship on, 132–133
emotional distance, 11
emotional support, 62–65, 104–105
emotion-criticizing, 143
emotion talk
   coding, 134–136
   educational backgrounds and, 138–139, 142–144, 148*t*, 152*t*
   emotional valence of, 136, 141–142, 137*t*, 147*t*, 150*t*
   exchanges in, 135–136, 138, 139–140
   gender and, 127–131, 140, 144–146, 149*t*, 153*t*
   general expressive language ability and, 133

McNemar tests for, 137–138
   in mother-child conversations, 134
   motherhood and, 136–138
   participants of, 132–133
   proposition types for, 134, 136–140
   researching, 131–134, 136, 140–146, 137*t*
   sociodemographics of, 133*t*
   terms of, 134–135, 137, 139–140
Engel, G. L., 21–22
Engle, P., 26
ethnicity, 108
ethnography, 2–3
Europe, 15
evidence-based interventions, 14
explaining approaches, 143
exploration, in childhood, 135–136
extreme poverty, 11–12, 67

familial functioning, 8–9, 156, 157
familism, 97–101, 107–110
familismo, 9–10, 157
family. *See specific topics*
family-based developmental intervention. *See* community-based participatory research
family development, 113–116
family dynamics, 7–9
family mechanisms, 111–112
family-particular protective roles, 157
Family Stress Model, 115
Fanjul de Marsicovetere, R., 99
fatherhood, 60
Felner, R. D., 26–27
Fernández, C., 129, 144–146
Flourishing Through Education Program, 37, 42–43, 47–54. *See also* community-based participatory research
Fonagy, Peter, 62
Fracasso, M., 76–77
Frizzo, G. B., 64

gender. *See also* emotion talk
   childhood and, 129, 131, 136, 137*t*, 140
   in Chile, 106
   in Costa Rica, 131–146
   educational backgrounds and, 137*t*
   Latin American contexts for, 108
   motherhood and, 133
   research, 127–131, 133*t*, 149*t*, 153*t*
   roles, 145
   socialization and, 33–34
general expressive language ability, 133
Georgas, J., 6–7

Germany, 77–78, 130
Gibbons, J., 99
girls, 145–146, 149t, 153t. See also childhood
globalization, of communication, 4–5
global science, vii
Global South, 158
González, C., 122
grandparents
  Asociación Civil Abuelas de Plaza de Mayo, 106
  caregiving by, 106
  in childhood, 97–101, 103–107
  in Colombia, 106
  with custody arrangements, 107
  in families, 101–103
  grandparenting, 103–104
  Latin American contexts for, 101–107
  multigenerational cohabitation contexts for, 107–110
Grieco, A., 64
Grupo Hospitalar Conceição, 41–42
Grusec, J., 26
Guevára, Y., 122
Gussow, Joan, 118–119

Harwood, R., 130–131
Hayes, A., 103
health care
  collaboration in, 54
  data, 49
  for families, 50–51
  with Grupo Hospitalar Conceição, 41–42
  mental health, 125–126
  Neonatal Intensive Care Units, 69, 72
  public health services, 40, 125–126
  "Safe and Family Centered Care in Maternity Hospitals" report on, 64–65
  services, 51–52
  vaccines, 123
  in Vila Jardim, 40–41
  World Health Organization, 64, 112
hierarchical relatedness, 156
Hill, Reuben, 115
household educational climate index, 132
Hoyuelos Planillo, A., 104
Hsu, H.-C., 3
human development
  in childhood, 5, 11
  developmental niches, 6
  ecological perspectives of, 9
  indexes, 118–119
  individual factors in, 22–23

  psychology of, 8, 13
  risk factors in, 27–28
  scholarship on, vi–vii, 1–2

Ibero-American contexts, 102
income disparity, 39
independence, 29–30, 76
individual factors, 22–23
individualism, 15–16
inequality, 38
infancy, 11, 62, 63, 65, 73–74
institutional situations, 67
integrative perspectives, 21–25
interdependent values, 76
intervention models, 34–35
intuitive theories
  interviews on, 84–92
  measures of, 82–84
  motherhood and, 84
  participants with, 80
  research on, 75–84, 92–96
Israel, B. A., 44–45

Jiménez, D., 122

Kağitçibaşi, Ç., 4, 6, 94, 100
Kärtner, J., 6–7, 76–77, 156
Keller, H., 6–7, 76–78, 156
Kliksberg, B., 112
König, A., 4
Konner, M., 157
Kornadt, H.-J., 82
Kuensemueller, P., 77–78

Lamb, M., 76–77
language
  in Costa Rica, 134–135
  culture and, 127, 132–133
  general expressive language ability, 133
  in research, 142–144, 147t, 148t, 150t, 152t
Latin America. See specific topics
Latin American contexts
  for adolescence, 105–106
  for Brazil, 38–40
  for CBPR, 156
  Central America with, 76–77
  for childhood, 6–7, 57–58, 78–79, 123–126
  for core-values, 156
  with Costa Rica, 15
  for day-care, 105
  for education, 157
  for familial functioning, 156–157

families in, 8, 14–15, 157–158
for familism, 97–101, 107–110
for familismo, 157
for gender, 108
in global science, vii
for Global South, 158
for grandparents, 101–107
international research on, 116–118
for multigenerational cohabitation contexts, 97–101
overview of, 112–113
for parent-child relationships, 79–80
psychology and, 1, 110
research on, 1, 12, 98, 112–113, 155
for risk, 118–123
scholarship with, 9–11
for socialization, 93–94
for solidarity family strategies, 108
theoretical frameworks for, 113–116
for United States, 155–157
Leboyer, F., 64
Leyendecker, B., 76–77
life cycle cultural perspective, 157
life debt, 62
life planning workshops, 52–53
long-term goals, 88–92
low-income neighborhoods
    in Brazil, 38–40
    CBPR in, 43–44
    education in, 41
    parent-child relationships in, 49–50
    poverty in, vii, 36–38
    public education in, 37–38
low-middle-income countries, 112–113

mainstream developmental psychology, 155
mainstream psychology, 1, 155
malnutrition, 20, 22–23
Mann-Whitney tests, 133, 140
Márquez, M. E., 122
maternal attributions, 82–86, 85t
maternal behaviors, 82–84, 86–88, 90f, 89t
maternal emotions, 82–84, 86, 87t
maternal socialization goals, 78, 82–84, 88–92, 91t
McMaster Family Functioning Model, 113–114
McNemar tests, 137
Mediterranean contexts, 102
Melzi, G., 129, 144–146
memory development, 127, 141
mental health, 125–126

Mexico
    adolescence in, 16
    Costa Rica and, 7
    families in, 118–123
    familism in, vii
    Latin America and, 113, 124–125
    National Institute of Statistics and Geography on, 112–113
    World Health Organization on, 112
midwives, 63
migrant families, 100–101, 105, 121–122
Mi Pueblo Hospital, 69–70
mixed-method analysis, 48–49
modernity, 3, 5, 24–25
Molénat, F., 64
Molitor, A., 3
moral evaluations, 143
motherhood. See also emotion talk; perinatal interventions; pregnancy
    age of, 33–34
    Asian mothers, 129
    as child development, 58–60
    childhood and, 4, 14, 16–17, 136–138, 144–146
    in Colombia, 75–80
    in Costa Rica, 77–78, 132–133, 133t, 136–138, 137t, 140–146
    in data analysis, 84
    data on, 133–134
    divisions in, 66–67
    early pregnancy, 120–121
    educational backgrounds in, 133t, 137t, 138–139, 142–144, 148t, 152t
    education and, 80, 81t
    gender and, 133
    for grandmothers, 104
    intuitive theories and, 84
    in Mann-Whitney tests, 133, 140
    maternal attributions, 82–86, 85t
    maternal behaviors, 82–84, 86–88, 89t, 90f
    maternal emotions, 82–84, 86, 87t
    maternal socialization goals, 78, 82–84, 88–92, 91t
    mother-child conversations, 134
    negative emotions in, 93
    with newborns, 69–70
    in poverty, 13–14, 57–58, 72–74
    pregnancy and, 63–65
    psychological interventions in, 13–14
    research on, 77–78, 80–84, 92–96, 127–140
    scholarship on, 60–63

motherhood. *See also* emotion talk; perinatal interventions; pregnancy (*Continued*)
  socialization by, 15
  socioeconomics of, 88, 92, 94–96
  in urbanism, 157
mourning, 67
multigenerational cohabitation contexts
  in Costa Rica, 101–107
  for grandparents, 107–110
  Latin American contexts for, 97–101
  paradigms of, 101–103
  research on, 15
  with solidarity family strategies, 103–104

National Administrative Department on Statistics (NADS), 20
National Information Network, 24–25
National Institute of Statistics and Geography, 112–113
Navarro, H., 31
negative emotions, 93
negative parent-child relationships, 121
negotiation, 78–79, 83, 86–88, 90f, 93–95
Neonatal Intensive Care Units, 69, 72
newborns. *See* perinatal interventions
New Zealand, 144–145
non-acceptance pregnancy, 71 72t
non-controlled pregnancy, 71–72, 72t
non-nesting, 67

Olson's Circumflex Family Model, 113–114
Orozco-Hormaza, M., 27–28
"ought self" theory, 93–94

parent-child relationships. *See also* emotion talk
  grandparenting and, 103–104
  interventions for, 55
  Latin American contexts for, 79–80
  in low-income neighborhoods, 49–50
  negative, 121
  parental neglect, 40
  parents in, 30–31
  personality and, 63
  positive, 29
  protective factors of, 29
  psychology of, 86–88
  research on, 19
  socioeconomics and, 76–77
  support for, 117
  traditional, 23
  transactional perspectives on, 25–26

Paternina, A., 120
perceived social support networks, 115–116
perinatal interventions
  association analysis after, 71t, 71–72, 72t
  data from, 70–71, 70t
  instruments for, 66–68
  interviews in, 66–67
  methodology of, 66
  at Mi Pueblo Hospital, 69–70
  objectives of, 66
  participants in, 69–70
  Perinatal Intervention Devices, 66
  Perinatal Psychological Interviews, 66–67, 69, 72
  procedure for, 68–69
  in psychology, 57–58, 66–74
  psychosocial-perinatal risk categories, 66–69, 70t, 70–71, 73
personality, 63
Peru, 103, 106
Porto Alegre (Brazil), 38–42
positive contact, 108
poverty
  adaptability in, 118
  in Brazil, 55–56
  CBPR with, 38–40
  in childhood, 18–20, 22–23, 26–31, 33–35
  chronic financial stress from, 112–113
  circle of, 118–119
  in Colombia, 20, 27–28
  ecological perspectives of, 111–112
  education in, 39–40
  extreme, 11–12, 67
  families in, 23–24, 27, 30–31
  inequality and, 38
  in low-income neighborhoods, vii, 36–38
  marginalization from, 117–118
  motherhood in, 13–14, 57–58, 72–74
  in Porto Alegre, 38–40
  psychology of, 21–25
  public health services in, 40
  reduction, 31
  research on, 28–31
  risk-factors of, 28
  social factors of, 24–25
  transactional perspectives of, 25–26
  violence and, 38–39
  vulnerable conditions of, 31–33
pregnancy
  in adolescence, 67
  denial of, 67
  early, 120–121

motherhood and, 63–65
  non-acceptance, 71 72t
  non-controlled, 71–72, 72t
  unintended, 71, 71t
Priest, S. R., 73
problem-solving, 31–32, 86–88, 94–95, 89t
protective factors, in childhood, 28–31
proximal risk, 123
psychic transparency, 62, 73
psychological characteristics, 11
psychological interventions, 12–14
psychological processes, 10–11
psychological risk, 57–58, 66–72
psychology
  baby development in, 61
  of beliefs, 76
  biology and, 47
  Bronfenbrenner on, 39–40
  of caregiving, 3, 109
  child, 58–60
  of child-raising, 14
  clinical, 62
  context-process model of, 9
  of delayed satisfaction, 92–93
  developmental, 58–59, 62, 65, 98–99, 154, 155
  developmental psychopathology, 113–114
  ecology and, 2–3
  of emotional support, 63–65
  of emotions, 86
  of families, 1, 3–4, 155
  of human development, 8, 13
  of infants, 63
  Latin American contexts and, 1, 110
  of long-term goals, 88–92
  mainstream, 1, 155
  mainstream developmental, 155
  mental health, 125–126
  of parent-child relationships, 86–88
  perinatal interventions in, 57–58, 66–74
  Perinatal Psychological Interviews, 66–69, 72
  of poverty, 21–25
  realities, vii
  of relationships, 6–7
  research in, 155–158
  of self-regulation, 14–15
  of social situations, 69–70
  of socioeconomics, 13, 108
  of students, 53
psychosocial environment, 98–99

psychosocial-perinatal risk categories, 66–71, 70t, 73
psychosocial problems, 118–119
psychosocial risk, 120–121
public education, 37–38
public health services, 40, 125–126
public policy, 34
public politics programs, 12
Puerto Rico, 130–131

questionnaires, 49

Racamier, P.C., 64
Reason, P., 46
relational atmosphere, 11
relief plans, 34
reminiscing. See emotion talk
research. See specific research
resilience
  adaptability and, 116
  in childhood, 21–22
  compensation model of, 122–123
  in ecology, 19–20, 26–31
  models, 30
  for problem-solving, 31–32
  research on, 122
revitalization projects, 53–54
risk
  adaptability and, 124–125
  Latin American contexts for, 118–123
  proximal, 123
  psychological, 57–58, 66–72
  psychosocial, 120–121
  psychosocial-perinatal risk categories, 66–69, 70t, 70–71, 73
  risk factors, 27–28
  risk-protective factors, 116–118
  social-familial, 67
  stress from, 123–124
Rogoff, B., 10
Rosenblum, K., 118
Rutter, M., 118–119

"Safe and Family Centered Care in Maternity Hospitals" report, 64–65
Sameroff, A., 118
Schoelmerich, A., 76–77, 130–131
school interventions, 125–126
Schröder, L., 130
Schulze, P. A., 130–131
self-regulation
  behavior and, 88–92

self-regulation (*Continued*)
  in childhood, 75–80
  data on, 84–88
  psychology of, 14–15
  research on, 80–84, 92–96
Sen, A., 34
Shelton, L. G., 5–6
social development, 18–20, 29–30, 33–35
social-familial risk, 67
social inequality, 46
socialization
  caregiving and, 108
  in childhood, 14–15
  in Costa Rica, 17, 146
  in families, 14
  gender and, 33–34
  goals, 131
  Latin American contexts for, 93–94
  maternal socialization goals, 78, 82–84, 88–92, 91*t*
  by motherhood, 15
  Socialization-Situation Test, 82–83
social perspectives, 155
social policies, 31–32
social situations, 69–70
society, vii, 154
socioeconomics
  caregiving and, 23–24
  of education, 80, 81*t*, 84, 94
  for families, 39–40
  in motherhood, 88, 92, 94–96
  parent-child relationships and, 76–77
  psychology of, 13, 108
  research on, 57, 90–92, 116–117
  socioeconomic burdens, 13
socioemotional development, 127
sociology, 2–4
sociopolitics, 101
solidarity family strategies, 102–104, 108
Spitz, Rene, 61
stakeholders, 13, 37, 44–46, 55
students, 51–54
sub-Saharan Africa, vi
support networks
  in CBPR, 44
  emotional support and, 62–65, 104–105
  families and, 101–102, 116
  parent-child relationships and, 117
  perceived social, 115–116
  scholarship on, 42, 44
  social, 44
  solidarity family strategies as, 102

teachers, 45, 50, 51–52
Thrush, A., 103
toddlerhood, 11
traditional parent-child relationships, 23
transactional perspectives, 25–26
Trommsdorff, G., 76, 82
Tronick, Edward, 62–63

unbalanced family care, 103
UNICEF, 18, 74
unintended pregnancy, 71, 71*t*
United States
  childhood in, 99, 115
  cognitive approaches in, 143
  Costa Rica and, 102
  Europe and, 15
  Latin American contexts for, 155–157
  Latino families in, 15–16, 98, 107–108
  migrant families in, 100–101
  New Zealand and, 144–145
  Peru and, 106
  Puerto Rico and, 130–131
Universidade Federal do Rio Grande do Sul, 40–43, 53
University of Buenos Aires, 64
University of Nebraska-Lincoln, 42–43
urbanism, 119–120, 157

vaccines, 123
Vargas, K., 120
variable complexity, 9
Venezuela, 99
Ventura-Cook, E., 130–131
Victora, C., 74
Videla, M., 64
Vila Jardim (Brazil), 38–42
violence, 38–39, 53, 106, 117, 119–120
Vohs, K. D., 75
vulnerable conditions, of poverty, 31–33

Wadsworth, M. E., 115
Walsh, F., 30
Weaving Links, Weaving Dreams, Weaving Life from Early Childhood program, 32–33
Weisner, T. S., 2–3, 6
Western middle-class, vi–vii
Whiting, B. B., 3
Whiting, J. W., 3
Wilcoxon tests, 135–137
Wilson, S. P., 130–131
Winnicott, D., 61
women. *See also* motherhood; pregnancy

Asian mothers, 129
contraception for, 60
early pregnancy, 120–121
education of, 58
in families, 61
in familism, 100–101
girls, 145–146, 149*t*, 153*t*

life debt for, 62
as single parents, 58
Woodcock-Muñoz "Subprueba de Vocabulario basado en Dibujos," 133
World Bank, 112–113
World Health Organization, 64, 112

Zhang, S., 64